published by
University of Hertfordshire Press

First published 1997 in
Great Britain by
University of Hertfordshire Press
University of Hertfordshire
College Lane
Hatfield
Hertfordshire AL10 9AD

ISBN 0 900458 76 3 (paperback)
ISBN 0 900458 81 X (hardback)

Designed by
Beverley Stirling

Cover design by
John Robertshaw

based on a photograph by
David Smith
of a Bill Wright replica bow-topped wagon
painted by Yorkie Greenwood circa 1990, and encamped
at Gilmorton, Leicestershire, September 1991

Page layout by
John Robertshaw

Printed by
Antony Rowe Limited

Contents

Introduction

Culture is not something fixed, inherited, unchallengeable, unchanging. On the contrary, it is constantly developing, enabling the self-expression of our self-realisation, re-inventing as well as representing and reproducing our ethnic identities. This is as true of Gypsies as of anyone else.

During 1993 and 1994 a small group of scholars, professionals and Gypsy activists met regularly at a series of seminars funded by the Economic and Social Research Council at the University of Greenwich. The idea was that Romani studies, instead of stagnating in a series of repetitive books (usually based on PhD theses) by isolated scholars, should develop into a cumulative and collaborative effort which would end the marginalisation of Romani studies in the world of knowledge. Our aim was both to challenge the easy assumptions of academic study in and of nation-states and to serve the teachers, community workers and activists seeking to remedy old injustices and bring to an end ancient quarrels.

The chapters of these books are not the papers as they were brought to those seminars. Rather they are the result of a collaborative effort, drawing in additional scholars, over the past three years to exemplify and illustrate the processes – and through the education system, the management – of cultural change.

A companion volume, *Gypsy Politics and Traveller Identity*, looks at the political interactions between Gypsy groups and host societies which shape patterns of discrimination and disadvantage. Politics, however, is a facilitator, not an end in itself. However desperate and passionate our struggles, the point of life is to enjoy, to glorify.

One result of the emergence of Romani culture into the public arena of literature and art is that it becomes more accessible to, more respected by those brought up in other cultures. The unsung hero of David Smith's first chapter is the wagon-painter Jimmy Berry. Virtually unknown in the wider world, he is nonetheless a cult figure to contemporary Romanichal painters like Yorkie Greenwood, whose work is pictured on the front cover of this book. A measure of the success of the enterprise to which this book seeks to contribute will be the time it takes for Jimmy Berry to be recognised as the marker of a moment in the general history of art.

Thomas Acton and Gary Mundy, Editors

Figure 1. *Motif forms*

1 *Tommy Gaskin*

6 *Tom Stephenson*

2 *Jimmy Berry*

3 *Tommy Gaskin*

5 *Jimmy Berry*

4 *Jimmy Berry*

3 *Tommy Gaskin*

Chapter 1 Gypsy aesthetics, identity and creativity: the painted wagon

David Smith, Researcher and Consultant, Traveller Research Projects, Leicester

In the eyes of many in mainstream society the Gypsy's painted wagon is one of the few acceptable symbols of Traveller society. Although uniquely associated with Gypsies the painted wagon represents an art form that paradoxically owes much to mainstream society, for the six motifs forming the basis of the decorative schemes of most painted wagons are derived from traditional art forms once widely employed within the host society.

The motif repertoire

The six motifs [see Figure 1 opposite and Plates 1 - 4] can be identified as:

1 *the running scroll*: the present scroll forms are derived from two sources: the engraved glass once commonly seen in public house windows and scroll forms used to decorate fairground rides. The precursor form is found in carved reliefs of classical antiquity.

2 *horses, horseshoes, horses' heads, buckled belts* and similar motifs commonly associated with horse culture.

3 *coach-lining*: a severe and reserved art form intended to enhance the subtle contouring of coachwork. In this context it becomes an over-enriched form developed far beyond its original purpose.

4 *fishtail lettering*: a brush-stroke form originally used by wheelwrights on farm carts and minor trade vehicles to show registered ownership and where sign-writing was not an important feature.

5 *ribbonwork*: a common means of 'showing' battle honours on military regalia such as drums and honours boards. Ribbonwork was adopted by fairground and commercial vehicle owners as part of their company livery. It is from these sources that ribbonwork became a feature on Gypsy carts.

6 *fruit, flowers and birds*: a recurrent motif in both carved and painted decoration.

Figure 2. *Adaptation of Mainstream motifs into Gypsy wagon decoration*

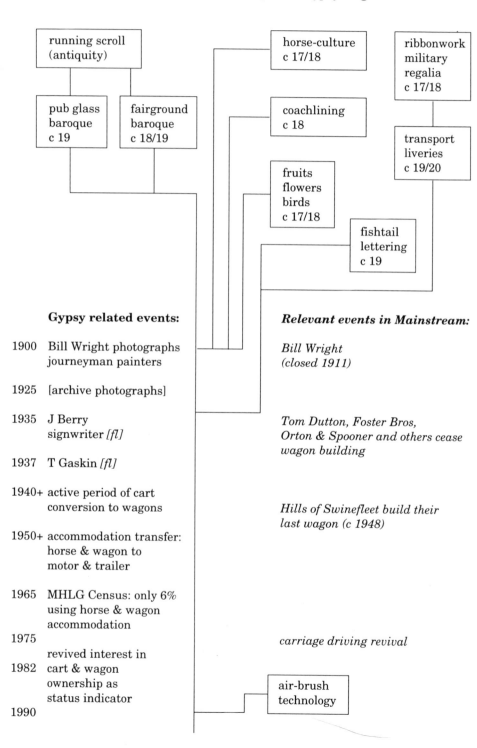

| running scroll (antiquity) | | horse-culture c 17/18 | ribbonwork military regalia c 17/18 |

pub glass baroque c 19 — fairground baroque c 18/19 — coachlining c 18 — transport liveries c 19/20

fruits flowers birds c 17/18

fishtail lettering c 19

Gypsy related events:

Relevant events in Mainstream:

1900   Bill Wright photographs journeyman painters

Bill Wright (closed 1911)

1925   [archive photographs]

1935   J Berry signwriter *[fl]*

Tom Dutton, Foster Bros, Orton & Spooner and others cease wagon building

1937   T Gaskin *[fl]*

1940+ active period of cart conversion to wagons

Hills of Swinefleet build their last wagon (c 1948)

1950+ accommodation transfer: horse & wagon to motor & trailer

1965   MHLG Census: only 6% using horse & wagon accommodation

1975

carriage driving revival

     revived interest in
1982   cart & wagon ownership as status indicator

air-brush technology

1990

Historical background

Examination of late nineteenth and early twentieth century photographs of groups of Gypsies indicates that decoration on Gypsy wagons, where it occurs, was chiefly carved, with painting used to highlight carved forms.

A series of photographs of 'ex-works' carts and wagons of the legendary Bill Wright of Rothwell Haigh, near Leeds, taken by his brother, an enthusiastic amateur photographer, can be found at the Castle Museum, York. Others are with descendants of the Wright brothers while two, labelled "photographer unknown" appear as Plates 5 and 6 in Huth (1944, 1973). These provide evidence suggesting the client's demand of the wagon builder in the early 1900s was the same as that reported by contemporary cart and wagon builders and painters. It is a demand which was recorded as a common feature of clients' demands to the specialist caravan manufacturers Vickers of Morecambe and, as with Bill Wright, contributed to their ultimate demise as a business.

Simply stated the client's demand is: "Make my wagon (or trailer) as good as the last one you made, and then make it better." Thus no two examples will ever be the same. In the case of the Bill Wright wagons, although key features such as a wagon door might carry his classic motif of a horse or a sunflower, the majority of the hand-carved decoration was custom-cut for the specific job. Inevitably, because such terms preclude mass-production of details for use in wagon decoration, the cost of carved work was always high. By the end of the Edwardian era, which had also seen the closure of Bill Wright's works (1911), the rising cost of hand-carved decoration for wagons meant that only the wealthiest of Gypsy families commissioned the making of such wagons and many Gypsy families sought the cheaper alternative of painted decoration. The few wheelwrights who owned businesses large enough to employ full-time painters would be prepared to undertake coach-lining on the wagons and also produce simple motifs such as horseshoes and horses' heads, but the majority of wheelwrights met their painting needs through the services of journeyman painters who moved from yard to yard lining out and putting small additional decorative details on vehicles made in the yard. The consequence is that the early painted decoration of wagons and carts may best be described as inconclusive.

The inter-war period, 1920-1938, was characterised by an increasing popularity in the use of motor vehicles in both private and commercial spheres. This presaged a general decline in the use of horse-drawn vehicles causing many wheelwrights to switch their main business activities into coachbuilding and abandon their traditional lines of building horse-drawn vehicles. This cycle of changes meant an increasing number of Gypsy families found it necessary to provide for their own accommodation forms.

Oral testimony from several Gypsy families indicates that during the late 1930s and throughout the 1940s Gypsy wagon builders possessing varying degrees of competence emerged in different parts of the country. Where examination of these individuals' work has been possible through family photographs it appears most of them might be more accurately described as cart converters, as they were individuals who built an accommodation onto an existing cart bed. It was this generation of wagons that provided the base on which the unique art form of the painted wagon was to develop. Coincident with the development of the Gypsy-made wagon was the emergence of two individuals who were to play important roles in the development of this new art form: Jimmy Berry and Tommy Gaskin.

The wagon painters

Contemporary photographic evidence from the northern counties of England and analysis of surviving examples of Jimmy Berry's early decorative painting (both c.1946) suggest he was largely responsible for synthesising the motif repertoire already described into the unique art form associated with the Gypsy's painted wagon. Photographs of Gypsy groups in the 1930s include carts where named ribbonwork occurs with the horse's head motif occasionally included as a central feature. The overall decoration of the backboard with a complex inter-relationship of motifs does not seem to have occurred until Jimmy Berry commenced painting.

In interviews between 1989 and 1992 with the late Bernard Shaw of Bawtry, a Gypsy sign-writer who was a contemporary of Jimmy Berry and worked and travelled on jobs with him in the 1930s, I heard described how the complex overlapping designs of Axminster and similar carpets intrigued Jimmy who would spend "hours" looking at displays of them in shop windows. Although carpet motifs cannot be identified in the motifs of painted wagons, the complex interlacing of scrolls and the covering of entire surface areas with decoration and the sonorous colour relationships they contain may reflect a more subtle influence in terms of design organisation [see Plate 1].

Many of the older generation of Gypsies claimed Tommy Gaskin copied Jimmy Berry's work. If one accepts the existence of a motif repertoire, such as that already outlined, the nature of the alleged 'copying' is difficult to identify. Both men were competent painters but came to their subject from distinctly different traditions. Jimmy Berry had received some formal training in sign-writing. (He claimed he was never as good as the man who taught him how to paint, allegedly Daniel Stamper of the Penrith-based haulage firm, Stampers.) Tommy Gaskin's training was by the informal process of observing and experimenting. It may be in this latter area of watching and then trying out the ideas observed that allegations of 'copying' have their origins.

The running scrolls in the earlier work of both men, i.e. the late 1930s to c.1960, are fluently executed in a single stroke where differential pressure applied to the brush on the surface being decorated influences the varying thickness of the line of the scroll. This 'one-stroke' painting technique ensured fluidity of form in the scroll being painted and was a valuable asset when painting wagons at roadside stops where the constant threat of being moved on was a major constraint on time available. The threat of being moved on also caused painters to use a 'quick drying' medium when painting. With many painters, including Jimmy Berry and Tommy Gaskin, this consisted of a mixture of varnish and petrol or lighter fuel. When, as happened on occasions, too much petrol was used the decoration would often peel off after a comparatively short period of time, only eighteen months or so.

By the end of the 1950s most Gypsy families had switched their main accommodation mode from horses and wagons to motors and trailers. For a brief period during the 1950s and 1960s the painted motifs of the wagons and carts were applied to the door panels, wings and bodywork of the

Plate 1. *(detail) from cart backboard painted by the late Jimmy Berry and showing the combined motifs of: running scroll; horse's head; ribbonwork; fishtail lettering; coachlining. Also containing his cherry motif.*
[photograph: Appleby Fair, 1993]

Plate 2. *(detail) Wagon side panel showing relief carved version of the zoomorphic horse-head scroll motif on wagon built by John Pickett.*
[photograph: Stow Fair, 1993]

Plate 3. *(detail) Pan-box of bow-topped wagon, running scrolls painted by the late Tommy Gaskin.* [photograph: Appleby, 1991]

Plate 4. *(detail) Backboard of four-wheel dray with carved and painted work by Tom Stephenson, showing interlaced running scrolls and his characteristic basket of fruit motif. The signature motif referred to in the text is the small bluebell shaped motif situated between the interlacing lines of the scrolls.* [photograph: Appleby, 1996]

'motors' used to tow the newly acquired trailer caravan. Unfortunately, when this unique form of decoration was applied to mass-produced vehicles it made them quite conspicuous and they were subjected to frequent police checks. As a consequence this form of vehicle embellishment ceased, creating an unusual situation in which a developing folk art form was abruptly halted through the activities of an external agency. The new trailer caravan accommodation was never considered a suitable base for decoration. This would appear to be chiefly because new and nearly new trailers were bought from and 'traded' through established dealers who worked on 'book' prices and would consider idiosyncratic decoration, such as the Gypsy motif series, a distinct detraction when it came to their re-sale.

With the abandonment of 'motor' decoration, the two-wheel spring cart or four-wheeled dray – vehicles used to undertake numerous everyday tasks in the horse-and-wagon era – and the few wagons remaining with the surviving wagon-dwelling families became the mainstay for sustaining the new decorative tradition.

The switch in preferred accommodation mode from horses and wagons to motors and trailers had preceded the major legislation (Caravan Sites Act 1968) which brought about the creation of permanent sites for Gypsy families and with it a major change in the nature of travelling. One of the consequences of legally imposed sedentarism was a revival of interest in the more traditional means of expressing a Gypsy identity. By the late 1970s interest in horse-drawn carts and wagons began to increase among sedentarised Gypsy families who saw ownership of such vehicles as an important symbol of their identity.

This renaissance of interest brought with it a competitive desire among new owners to have the best 'turnout' available for 'show' occasions such as Appleby Horse Fair, Epsom's Show Sunday and fairs at Stow-on-the-Wold. This, in turn, has led to an excess of decoration being applied to areas of carts and wagons that would have been impractical on vehicles in everyday use. Many of the new generation of painted carts and wagons are conspicuously decorated versions of their humbler forebears and the competitive drive for 'show' has led to the production of a number of 'prodigy' pieces. Chief among these have been the 'hippy' or Eden cart, a two-wheeled spring-cart made by Keith Payne from Norfolk. This cart has serpents intertwined on its bodywork and wheels as well as more than a hundred horses' heads carved into its bodywork and lurchers hunting up the shafts. 'The Challenge' is also a two-wheeled spring cart decorated with air-brush painted scenes of fighting stallions, lurchers running down a hare and fighting cocks, as well as conventionally painted motifs of scrolls and horses' heads. This over-enrichment culminates in a series of engraved mirror glass panels set on the inside faces of the backboard and cheeks and a sovereign set into its flatbed. Decorated by 'Big Roy' Morris, 'The Challenge' was intended to announce his arrival as "the best painter on Appleby Hill." It made its debut at Appleby in June 1990 where its alleged asking price was rumoured variously between £20-25,000 – a figure it failed to attract; it was sold for a figure in the low teens, some eighteen months later.

By the time this revival of interest in carts and wagons commenced Jimmy Berry and Tommy Gaskin were in their seventies and undertaking fewer painting commissions and a new generation of wagon painters had emerged who brought new interpretations to the same motif repertoire.

Chief amongst the new group of painters were 'Yorkie' Greenwood, 'Lol' Thompson (who is claimed to have been schooled by Jimmy Berry) and Tom Stephenson who acknowledges his debt to an extremely fine although lesser known wagon painter from Hartlepool, the late George Nixon. The last name in this new group is 'Big Roy' Morris. Without exception all these painters, like most of their predecessors, live in the northern counties of England.

When it comes to developing the decorative possibilities available within the limited motif repertoire outlined in figure 1, these four painters have all made unique contributions. Each brings individual interpretations to his subject: 'Lol' Thompson's naturalistic horses, 'Yorkie' Greenwood's fluid scroll forms, Tom Stephenson's basket of fruit motif gives new meaning to old forms [see Plate 4] and 'Big Roy' Morris's air-brush techniques bring ultra-realism to some of his forms. None, however, have developed any uniquely original forms. 'Big Roy' claimed a 'first' with his introduction of the form of a dolphin in his painting, but in fact Bill Wright had used a dolphin motif on the door panels of some of his wagons between around 1880 and 1910. (The present form of the running scroll is actually an abstraction of a zoomorphic scroll found in classical antiquity based on a dolphin form.)

Surviving vehicles from the horse-and-wagon era were a finite resource that was soon outstripped by the number of people seeking to own and drive them. This created a new market which saw the emergence of a new generation of wagon builders specialising in making new carts and wagons which replicated earlier designs similar to those originally built by Bill Wright and Tom Dunton. Chief amongst these new wagon builders who have come to prominence in the course of the past two decades are Phillip Jowitt and Roy Peters. These men, along with established restorers and builders such as Peter Ingram, John Pickett and John Pockett have ensured high standards of craftsmanship in the restoration and building of carts and wagons. Like their nineteenth and early twentieth century predecessors these men occupy permanent workshop locations and undertake other contracts as well. Nonetheless, a significant part of their reputation is derived from the work they have undertaken for Gypsies, one of the most fickle client groups anyone could wish to work for. As such their reputations are hard won and jealously guarded.

The wagon painters: Jimmy Berry and Tommy Gaskin

While Jimmy Berry and Tommy Gaskin are the two best-remembered names of the early generation of wagon painters there have been numerous others whose abilities have ranged from accomplished craftsmen sign-writers and painters to independent, self-taught painters who produced decorative schemes for their own vehicles but rarely worked beyond the needs of their immediate families. Although divided by craft skills most of these painters qualify as 'followers' as they all produced satisfactory decorative schemes using the standard series of motifs and rarely strayed beyond conventional arrangements of the motif series. Such a statement requires qualification. Because they work mainly to satisfy their own particular needs, self-taught painters have a greater opportunity for originality than craftsmen-painters responding to client demands. Present evidence suggests the horse-head scroll, (a zoomorphic scroll), [see Plate 2] was introduced by one of the self-taught painters and has subsequently been drawn up into the motif repertoire of the more sophisticated painters. The apparent absence of this motif from the work of Jimmy Berry and Tommy Gaskin may imply it is a relative latecomer in the motif series.

Figure 3.

The folklore of reputations

Long before their deaths, in 1988 and 1984 respectively, stories of the painting abilities of both Jimmy Berry and Tommy Gaskin had acquired legendary characteristics, some of which continue to circulate to the present time. Most of these stories possess an element of reality and get progressively more distorted as their raconteurs strive to convince the listener of the greater merits of their preferred painter. Both men are alleged to have manufactured lining brushes with hairs drawn from a horse's tail tied round a matchstick. (This particular source for lining brushes, and variations such as a goat's beard or a favourite daughter's long hair, has been recorded in relation to other wagon painters both in England and Ireland.)

While there is evidence that Jimmy Berry could paint scrolls fluently with either hand, the claim that he could paint bi-manually, i.e. simultaneously with a brush in either hand, requires physical movements of an impossible nature and the idea must be judged enhancement. Numerous informants have claimed that Jimmy Berry could line out using two lining brushes simultaneously and one informant claimed he once saw him paint using three brushes: no less a person than Jimmy Berry himself dismissed all these claims! Among Tommy Gaskin's alleged talents were the use of dock leaves as a palette on which to mix paints and roadside grasses tied together for brushes. Apart from the impractical nature of working with such instruments there is a far greater body of evidence, including surviving examples of their equipment, to indicate both men were extremely particular over the brushes they used and about keeping them clean and well oiled. The rich imagining behind the stories of these two men's talents are more valuable as indicators of the high status in which both were held in the world of wagon painting than realistic claims regarding their actual abilities.

Signature motifs

Working for a client group with few literacy skills, signed work had little relevance. As an alternative to formally signing his work Jimmy Berry introduced into much of his painted work what is described here as a 'signature motif'. In Jimmy Berry's case the 'signature motif' perpetuated the medieval tradition of the rebus: his chosen motif was 'borrowed' from a proprietary brand of shoe polish, Cherry Blossom, which, despite its name, used a bunch of ripe cherries for a trade mark. From Cherry to Berry was one simple step and Jimmy Berry introduced the motif as a sign for his painting [see Plate1].

A distinct advantage of using a motif, such as the cherries rather than a signature, was that it could be repeated extensively across the surfaces to be decorated. The cherry motif has been observed in several photographs c.1949 while the explanation given above was first recorded from a group of the Lees and Prices travelling in the Midlands during the autumn of 1956. Jimmy Berry used a variety of forms of this motif. These can be seen in early photographs as a multiple feature with five or six cherries bunched on several stalks. A 1949 example, repeated on a wagon painted by Jimmy in 1962, shows, like most later illustrations, the motif reduced to two cherries on stalks with two leaves – an abstraction similar to that which occurred to the trade mark itself.

Inevitably such a potent signature form did not stay unique for long and, by the early 1960s, it was recorded in the motif repertoire of Tommy Gaskin. By the late 1970s the cherry motif, although still used by Jimmy Berry had become an established motif within the repertoire used by cart and wagon painters. However, few painters ever achieved the subtle integration of the motif into the running scroll form that was so characteristic of Jimmy Berry's work and some of Tommy Gaskin's.

Tommy Gaskin had a fascination for Appaloosa horses and frequently used them as a motif in his later works. Their characteristic coat markings were achieved by a series of thumb prints.

Discussing 'signature motifs' with Tom Stephenson it seemed self-evident that his motif was the fruit basket. This suggestion was dismissed and Tom drew attention to a small floral-derived form that appears on the running scroll form he uses. This, it was pointed out, was the motif he always introduced to work he considered of merit. Unlike the fruit basket, whose unique asymmetric shape has already been copied by other painters, this detail was something small enough for his copyists to overlook [see Plate 4].

Amongst many of the earlier generations of Gypsy and Traveller families there was a widespread belief that "if the work was good enough it spoke for itself." The use of signature motifs as a covert means of signing painted works seems to have been acceptable but in more recent years that form of business communication has gradually been replaced by the introduction of signed pieces which have become an increasingly observable feature of painted carts and wagons since the mid-1980s. The chief location of the signature has remained the same since signature motifs were first recorded in the 1940s – the pan-box – while in several recent pieces the name of the wagon builder has also been featured.

The introduction of both the builder's and the painter's names reflects another business innovation. In recent years a number of carts and wagons have appeared at fairs and been offered for sale painted in grey or aluminium primer. These represent speculative sales and the deal, when it is made, includes the cost of painting the vehicle in a colour scheme of the purchaser's choosing. Trading arrangements of this type are increasingly being made between the various wagon builders and painters already mentioned. Such an arrangement has the advantage of removing the chance element of always guessing what the market will require, although the driving competitive concern always to have the best turnout can result in much frustration for the wagon painter who has to respond to the client's changing demands yet stay within a pre-determined budget imposed by the wagon builder's deal.

Conclusion

Today most horse-drawn vehicles used in Gypsy and Traveller society are seen as providing surface areas for displaying decorative painting which itself has assumed increasing significance by functioning as a social and cultural indicator. Prior to the motor-and-trailer era the wagon, irrespective of whether it was a showman, ledge, bow-top or open-lot, being the principal accommodation mode, was predominantly a functional form. The majority of today's wagons function as artefacts possessing more of a symbolic reference than providing an accommodation base which is often focused on the living trailer pulled alongside the wagon. Because an important function of many of today's wagons is as a 'show piece' rather than accommodation the tendency has been for them to become over-enriched with paintwork and ornament. This 'display' role is exemplified by the fact that many wagons and carts spend the greater part of their 'travelling' life being moved on a low-loader. One outcome of this change in function is that the modern Bill Wright or Tom Dunton repro-wagon can afford to carry substantially more carving because it is not in daily use.

For the wagon painters, change in the circumstances of the wagons has brought new challenges although the client's demand remains much the same, i.e., to paint it good and then paint it even better. The motif repertoire has not expanded and the dynamic of wagon decoration as an art form is to create original form from the same repertoire of motifs that were first introduced some sixty years ago. It is a testimony to the individual abilities of the new generation of decorators that they continue to respond with originality to that challenge.

Reference

HUTH F G 1940 "Gypsy Caravans" *Journal of the Gypsy Lore Society* Series III, Vol. XIX (3-4), reprinted 1973 *Journal of the Gypsy Lore Society* Series III, Vol. LII (1-2)

Chapter 2 The English folktale corpus and Gypsy oral tradition

Ginny Lapage, Teacher, Cornwall, and Researcher, University of Reading

The major contribution made by the Gypsies of nineteenthth and early twentieth century England to the 'corpus' of the folktale (that is, the total of the stories gathered by collectors) in the English language has been obscured by our lack of information about many of the story-teller informants. This paper focuses on the major collections of, and containing, Gypsy folktales, gathered at the turn of the century and the methodology which might be used to show Gypsy identity in the tales.

Calling these collections 'oral literature', as is usually done, is problematic. 'Oral literature' refers to the spoken form in a written context. The English language offers no satisfactory alternative (Ong 1982:10-15). There has always been a literate preference for the written over the oral word and this also causes difficulty. In order to study oral events and pass them on to other literate people the speech event must be written down. In the process what is essentially dynamic becomes static. In spoken form words are repeated and transformed everywhere they are used (Edwards and Sienkewicz 1990:1-3).

A fundamental problem with analysing, or even asserting the survival of orally transmitted tales, let alone seeking markers of Gypsy identity, is the appearance of variants, contrasting with the fixed nature of the tale transmitted in writing by collectors. While a narrative is being told it demands both telling and listening skills and is inseparable from its variants. It is made, or re-made, for the occasion for which it is told.

There are, therefore, great difficulties in seeking a method by which to consider narratives which were collected at a time before modern technology was readily available. Many different methods have been applied to the analysis of the folktale, such as classification according to their origins (Benfey 1859); to structure (Olrik 1909; Luthi 1970;

Propp 1984; Dundes 1962, 1964; Lévi-Strauss 1955); to motif and type classification (Aarne 1973); to archetypes (Thompson 1977) or to performance (Georges 1969); or a holistic approach may be attempted (Tedlock 1971; Hymes 1975). The Finnish school's historico-geographical method sought for the archetypical tale with its variants and motifs with the extensive tale-type index and the Russian school explored the laws operative behind the variants. Briggs (1970) has used these tale-type and motif indexes to categorise the tales in her collection. No single approach, however, goes far enough to help the researcher to identify a body of traits in the content of tales to identify specific tales or groups of tales that might be attributed to the Gypsies. This paper argues, however, that to leave the matter there disguises the extent to which 'national' bodies of written folktales have in fact appropriated Gypsy oral culture.

The collection of folk narratives
Historically, there has been a conflicting pattern of responses to the concept of 'oral tradition' in literate societies and the spoken word as a means of transmitting knowledge was seen as belonging only to the popular culture. During the Romantic movement of the eighteenth century scholars regarded folk narratives as cultural artefacts. They wanted to know the extent of storytelling; how similar stories had arisen and the significance of the story content. They accepted the universality of storytelling but a survivalist approach underlay their research and their method of recording was written. Since then hundreds of collectors worldwide have brought a new respectability to the oral or near-oral tradition. By the start of this century Andrew Lang (1886) and others had discredited the view that oral folklore was simply the left-over debris of a 'higher' literary mythology. By the mid-nineteenth century many middle-class collectors were at work and in 1878 the Folk Lore Society was formed. Folklorists and anthropologists shared the responsibility of recording stories in the field; the folklorists retaining an historical perspective, sorting texts into types and motifs while the anthropologists examined narratives from different societies, looking for relationships between the content and behaviouristic or structural aspects of individual cultures.

However, two major assumptions were being made: first, that popular culture was separate from the culture to which the collectors belonged and secondly, that the oral tradition was in decline. There was a fear that if the songs and stories were not collected they would be lost.

The oral tradition
What exactly is 'oral tradition'? This expression applies both to a process and to its products. The products are spoken 'messages' which have been passed down over at least one generation. The process is the transmission of such messages by word of mouth over time until the message disappears. As well as news, the interpretation of experience and oral history, it can include narratives and sayings. It is a dynamic process using memorised speech and specific formulae and it includes the folktale.

For at least three or four thousand years storytelling has been carried on in every rank of society. In this study, the term 'folktale' is used to mean the oral narrative in general. It need not have always been oral and can have passed in and out of the printed form several times. There are many forms of the folktale which are present in all cultural groups. The 'novella' is a story where marvels occur but in a recognisable time and place; the 'saga' is the story of a local legend or tradition; the explanatory tale, giving the origins of a place, for example; animal tales; the fable, an animal tale with a moral; and the humorous tale. The most frequent and popular form of the folktale, however, is the märchen. Märchen in traditional usage has the specialised meaning of a 'magical tale', 'wonder tale' or 'tale of enchantment'. It can also include comic or joke tales. It is basically a tale of some length involving a succession of motifs or episodes. Märchen are isolated from time and place and contain magic as wish fulfilment. They are also structurally different from other forms of narrative as they usually contain three tasks or trials which require elaborated narrative development. Märchen are aptly described by Linda Dégh (1972:62-5):

> "They tell about the ordinary human being's encounter with the superhuman world and his becoming endowed with qualities that enable him to perform supernatural acts. The märchen is, in fact, an adventure story with a single hero ... The hero or heroine's career starts as eveyone else's, in the dull miserable world of reality. Then, all of a sudden, the supernatural world involves him and challenges the mortal, who undertakes his long voyage to happiness. He enters the magic forest, guided by supernatural helpers, and defeats evil powers beyond the boundaries of man's universe. Crossing several borders of the beyond, performing impossible tasks, the hero is slandered, banished, tortured, trapped, betrayed. He suffers death by extreme cruelty but is always brought to life again. Suffering turns him into a real hero: as often as he is devoured, cut up, swallowed or turned into a beast, so does he become stronger and handsomer and more worthy of the prize he seeks. His ascent from rags to riches ends with the beautiful heroine's hand, a kingdom, and marriage. The final act of märchen brings the hero back to the human world: he metes out justice, punishes evil, rewards good."

Gypsies and their part in the transmission of folktales
The awareness of the existence of different groups of Travellers, some of whom identify themselves as Gypsies, had a specific effect on the area of study of the Gypsy folktale. There were several collections of Gypsy Folktales published in the late nineteenth century and many individual tales were published in the *Journal of the Gypsy Lore Society*. It was not, however, until the publication of Katharine Briggs' *The Dictionary of British Folktales* in 1970 that a large number of contributions from Gypsy sources were gathered together in one volume along with narratives from other sources. A notable feature of this collection is the high proportion of Gypsy and Traveller folktales contained in it, the greatest number being from the unpublished collection of T.W. Thompson.

It is clear that several groups of Travelling people are represented in the collection and their tales must be considered separately. The many narratives of the Romanichals (the English Gypsies) and the few from Welsh Gypsy sources may be thought to have a different character from those of the the Scottish Tinkers and reflect to a certain extent the culture of the people whom they lived amongst. However, it is also possible that each community operated as a closed group with its own collection of narratives; they may also have exchanged narratives with other groups that they met.

Sawyer (1962) in a rather stereotyped and impressionistic book had already suggested a link between the style of Gypsy stories and the Traveller lifestyle when she says that some of the best storytellers she knows live close to the heart of things – close to the elements, knowing silence and solitude. She also echoed the Gypsylorists in asserting that the Gypsies were amongst the main distributors of folktales as they wandered from the East. They were praised for their storytelling but she also claimed that they 'thieved' and 'made over' their literature. That is, they made the stories their own by adding Gypsy characters or setting them according to the Gypsy lifestyle. The originator of this view was perhaps F.H. Groome (1888 a,b), who suggested that it was Gypsy storytellers who had spread tales wherever they went.

In the earliest volumes of the Gypsy Lore Society Journals considerable debate arose over the transmission of folktales. Groome (1899: lxiii-lxvi) repeated his theory that the Gypsies, at some time before the eleventh century, carried with them Indian folktales which they disseminated among the peoples of the Balkan Peninsula. This was not easy to prove and the argument cannot be based simply on the existence of counterparts in Indian and Gypsy Folktales. John Sampson (1862-1931) took down stories in Wales as they were told to him and published Punjabi and Romani parallels in the *Journal of the Gypsy Lore Society*, later reprinted as a collection in English (Sampson, 1933). His main purpose was to explore the language of the Gypsies at that time and as most Gypsy tales have variants common to the whole Indian family, Sampson concluded that original Gypsy song and folktale did not exist. Where Groome had suggested that the ubiquity of the 'Gypsy race' allowed an excellent opportunity for transmission, Sampson warned that our romantic view might be that the original 'Luri' brought their own songs with them from India but it would be likely that words and tunes would have lost their original character in the tellings, taking on the colour of their last environment.

Ownership of narratives
A question common to the study of folktale is whether specific characteristics can ever be attributed to the tales of a particular national or cultural group? It seems that the only way to link specific folktales to the Gypsies is to look for internal evidence in the content, motifs or telling styles that would reflect Gypsy culture. The many contributors of folktales to the early editions of the *Journal of the Gypsy Lore Society* were collecting against a background of the resurgence of the Romantic movement and a desperate search for a special culture of the Gypsies. Mayall (1988:73) shows how these collectors encouraged the "vision of a small Gypsy elite of pure blood". They worked desperately to salvage the culture and identity of a group that they believed to be disappearing and maintained that the Gypsy people in Britain were a 'pure race'. They argued for separateness of a minority group based on a stereotype of appearance, dress, customs and so on. Mayall shows that the problem is not whether customs were followed

by most or some of the nineteenth century Travellers but in the attempt to attach practices to racial analysis. The Romanies were seen as respectable and represented the ideal of Rousseau's noble savage. However, Mayall (1988:24) deconstructs this image by questioning the likelihood that no marriages took place outside of Romany families, the cultural group remaining intact from the sixteenth to the nineteenth century when the folklorists began collecting. Acton (1979:44) suggests that as the genocidal persecution of the sixteenth century began to subside, the surviving Gypsies would have been "mixing culturally, linguistically and genetically with local host populations." Mayall (1988:84) also gives clear evidence in the eighteenth century records that intermarrying with the Gaujos took place including in the families of Wood, Boswell and Heron. This mixing is often thought to have led to the formation of the mixed Anglo-Romani contact language, the *pogadi jib*. Mayall concludes that the Gypsies are a separate people but that the identity of the group is based on cultural patterns rather than on 'racial' background.

Collectors of Gypsy folk narratives

Because so many stories which have parallels in both European and Indian culture were identified in the late nineteenth century, a whole generation of scholars concluded that India was the great homeland of European folktales. Most modern scholars acknowledge India as an important source of many stories but only one of several centres of invention and dissemination. Lang's (1886) theory of polygenesis, the theory that resemblances in stories are due to independent invention in many places because beliefs and customs, etc., are common to peoples at the same stage of culture, comes under criticism. It is based on the assumption that all cultures develop at the same rate everywhere and this is clearly not so.

Joseph Jacobs was editor of *Folklore*, the Journal of the Folklore Society, during its most brilliant period. He published his collections of tales between 1890 and 1894 (Jacobs, 1979). He championed the diffusionist theory to explain the scatter of folktales and disagreed with the survivalists. He claimed his collection of eighty-seven English tales represented the English Folktale nucleus at the time. He included thirty-eight märchen.

Until this time, the folklore movement had been primarily concerned with dating systems and other speculation at the writing desk and in libraries. No one had been collecting in the field. From the 1860s, however, field workers came into their own. While an oral tradition was being documented by the Folklore Society, interest grew in the stories told by Gypsies. In 1888 the first *Journal of the Gypsy Lore Society* appeared. The leading collectors of Gypsy folklore were John Sampson in Wales, F.H. Groome (both in the 1890s) and T.W. Thompson in the North of England and Midlands (from 1915). Dora Yates and earlier editors of the *Journal of the Gypsy Lore Society* published much of this work alongside East European Romani folktales sent by other scholars and collectors. Many of these tales have been reprinted by Katharine Briggs in her *Dictionary of British Folktales* (1970).

Groome also collected translations of Eastern European tales. His main interest was in the language of the Gypsies and he joined the ranks of the diffusionists attempting to trace the Gypsies back to India by way of their language. In 1880 he married Esmeralda Lock, the daughter of one of his major informants.

Groome posed a valid question: to what extent have Gypsies influenced European folk cultures? He merged the two trains of thought that were current at the time: the idea that India was the birth-place of the folktale and the belief that the Gypsies travelled into Europe from India. He concluded from this that; "It might be necessary to admit that Europe owes a portion of its folk-lore to the Gipsies" (1879:611-18).

According to a later study by Michael Owen Jones (1967:79-80) the majority of Groome's collection of tales do have variants to be found amongst the non-Gypsy collections. Groome, however, was unable to find variants for certain tales and this suggested to him that they might be Gypsy in origin. These are No. 29 "Pretty-Face" from Bukowina; No. 55 "An Old King and his Three Sons in England" from Wales; No. 61" The Dragon" from Wales; and No. 66 "Fairy Bride" from Wales in *Gypsy Folktales* (Groome, 1899). In other tales Groome found motifs that appeared to him to be uniquely Gypsy without parallels in the published collections to which he had access. Cautiously, however, he admitted the necessity of making comparisons with a wider distribution of tales.

During the early twentieth century T.W. Thompson meticulously recorded stories in his notebooks from the English Gypsy familes Gray, Smith and Boswell and his concern was with the formulation of the stories. He later presented these notebooks to Katharine Briggs who used them as a major source in gathering material for her *Dictionary of British Folk-Tales* although she was only permitted to publish most of them in summary as they were recorded in the notebooks. T.W. Thompson at first worked on the assumption that the lack of Gypsy tales in print at the turn of the century indicated that the English Gypsy repertoire was poor and what tales there were, were dying out.

T.W. Thompson
The work of T.W. Thompson (1888-1968) is particularly important to the study of English Gypsy folktales. He first became interested in Gypsy lore, language and genealogy whilst an undergraduate at Cambridge University and began collecting tales when he became a schoolmaster at Repton. His notes, until recently, have been largely unrecognised and remain unpublished in the Brotherton Library, University of Leeds, and the Bodleian Library, University of Oxford, apart from two brief essays (Thompson 1914, 1922-3). The second of these gives a clear and vivid description of the varying storytelling styles of Eva Gray ("Doctor Forster":166) and her brothers Reuben ("Wanted a Husband":197), Gus ("Sorrow and Love":80) and Shanny and Josh.

Thompson was particular about hearing stories more than once and enquired thoroughly into sources. He wanted to know which parts of the text were fixed and what parts subject to variation. He was open-minded enough to recognise that new stories might be invented.

> "My chance came when Eva declared one day that out of loneliness she had an evening or two earlier told herself a 'brand new tale'. 'I med it up myself from beginning to end,' she said; 'and it was a long'un! But I sat up till I'd finished it: I couldn't

give it up till I'd got everything to come right again.' What she had done, I discovered, was to invent a new plot, using incidents from märchen she already knew. 'I've med up many a new tale,' she said, 'when I hadn't nobody to talk to, and was feeling a bit down, but I never think nothing more about 'em, and if you was to ask me to tell you one I couldn't for the life o' me; they're all clean gone out'n my head. But the owld tales as I've know'd since I was no height, I can al'ays remember them." (1922-23:136)

Thompson faced considerable problems without the sound recording equipment which is available today. However, he made specific priorities, in particular:

"**1** To set down accurately and in their right order the main incidents of the tales.
2 To work in with these a good proportion of the wealth of detail with which the narrators embroidered their stories in most cases.
3 To reproduce verbatim all phrases that appeared to have been memorised, or to the wording of which the tale-tellers attached importance.
4 To report fully the drift of all monologues and dialogues put into the mouths of the characters, and as far as possible the actual words used whenever they seemed to be worth preserving.
5 To record the subject matter and, when it could be recalled, the actual wording, of all striking descriptive passages.
6 To indicate the nature of all repetitions and summaries.
7 To note all formal beginnings and endings, all places where the narrators identified themselves with their stories, and all modernisation and topical allusions." (1914-15:172)

Clinch (1982) asserts that Thompson felt he was inadequate as a folklorist and thought he was more of a Gypsiologist. He collected tales on forty-seven occasions during the period 1908-24 and gathered over 140 tales in all. The tales are narrated in English and Thompson considered that a large number were English folktales which had been preserved by certain Gypsies. His main interest was in the Gypsies of the Lake District. He sent tales collected from Noah Lock, Eva and Gus Gray, Ashton and Taimi Boswell to E.O. Windstedt, a Gypsylorist who worked at the Bodleian library, who was fluent in German and with an interest in Gypsies, for comments to be given and parallels to be found in the tales collected by the Grimm brothers and others.

Thompson's notebooks were meticulous: he noted occasions, places and names of informants and he prepared for publication on the basis that the tales were specifically Gypsy. He felt that the Gypsy flavour of the narratives was enhanced by the use of Romani words. Clinch suggests that the actual quality of the tale which was finally written up depended on the amount of time which elapsed between the original recording and the final copy. The tales of Noah Lock were written up most immediately after collection and so are the closest to the originals.

Clinch (1982:55) believes that Thompson's "essential achievement was that he collected the largest corpus of folktales in England single-handed.

Amongst them are numerous märchen, a genre of tale difficult and notably rare to be collected in England". The Thompson came to consider the tales, however, not to be Gypsy but English, perhaps because he could not identify any Gypsy day-to-day life or ethos directly permeating the tales he collected. He felt that the specific Gypsy aspect was tacked on rather than being an integral part of the tale. Although the collection was of great importance he left the tales unpublished for over thirty years. By the time he had finished collecting, he felt his work was more related to English folklore than to Gypsies although he had seen himself as a Gypsiologist rather than a folklorist. Despite this Neil Philip (1992:xviii) declares T.W. Thompson to be one of the "greatest of all folktale collectors" for his "efforts to record and set in context the oral narratives of English Gypsies".

Many of the tales collected at the turn of the century from Gypsies also appeared in several other printed collections but can be traced back to the same source. For example, the source of "De Little Fox " (Briggs, 1970), is given as F.J. Norton. His source, however, was Sampson (1892:204-8). The same tale is recorded by Groome (1899) again acknowledging Sampson as the source. The teller of this tale was Wasti Gray, wife of Johnny Gray. Variants of the tale, collected by Thompson, are: "The Little Squirrel" and "The Little Red Squirrel" which were told by Eva Gray in 1914 and by Taimi Boswell in 1915 (cf. Thompson 1914:Notebook 3; 1915 Notebook 8). The Grays and the Boswells would have been likely to have met regularly. These tales appear to be family versions of "The Wonder Child" (Aarne, 1973 No. 708).

Variants of the "Aladdin" group, such as "The Magic Ring" (Aarne 1973 No.560) could be found across a far wider area. John Roberts, a Welsh harper who was uniquely able to transcribe his own tales, and was the original source for "Jack and the Golden Snuff Box" to be found summarised in Briggs (1970:334-6) who took it from Yates (1948:173-82). Yates, in turn, took her version from the original in Groome (1899:209-220). This, however, is a tale type which is extremely widespread. Two other variants of the type such as "The Water of Life" in Grimm (1975:449-456) and "Sir Bumble and the Wonderful Ring" in Flora Annie Steele's *Wide Awake Tales* (1884:5-16) which were collected in India, show the extent of the spread of these tales across Europe and India. A detailed discussion of this is given in Groome (1899:lxxv-lxxxiii) and he concludes, from this evidence, that there is a common stock of Indo-European folktales. Incidents and characters may vary in detail from country to country but it is precisely by these variations that he could judge the authenticity of a traditional tale.

Clinch (1982), however, concludes that as there are insufficient collections of English folktales to make comparisons of individual tales in the Thompson collection: "To compare them to the Ur-forms or archetypes of tales in the Tale-type index is, apart from indexing and reference purposes, not a useful exercise since it cannot be established whether their variations at least had their origin in English tradition" (1982:61).

The argument over Gypsy specificity in other countries
English folklorist arguments over the orgins of tales have been paralleled in Europe. In Hungary, Josef Vekerdi (1968:150-53) questioned whether the Gypsies have any folk culture with ancient elements brought with them

from India. Vekerdi's strongly right-wing Hungarian nationalist perspective clearly coloured his view. He tries to model ethnographic analysis on the method of historical linguistics. When the Hungarian, Rumanian, South Slav, Greek and Persian loan-words are identified and removed from the Romani language, the Indian part remains. Could the same be done with folktales? This is much more difficult because there are no reliable complete collections and because many folktales are more or less identical over many countries. Vekerdi suggested that although the contents of the folktales were not necessarily brought from India the attitude, character and probably style of performance was. All the narratives told by the Hungarian Gypsies in his study repeat elements of the contents of Hungarian tales. He concludes that the difference between Hungarian and Gypsy folktales lies not in their content but in the way they are developed.

In a later article, Vekerdi (1976: 79-86) suggests that, when traditonal societies died out, a wide range of folk practices including folksong and folktales died with them. However, the inter-action between Travelling groups and the host villages made it possible for the Gypsies to have access to the folk-culture of the peasantry. He suggests tales told by the non-Gypsy community were assimilated into the repertoire of the Gypsy group as they continued to live as they always had and so the Gypsies became the conservators of non-Gypsy traditions that they, the Gypsies, had originally borrowed from the non-Gypsy community. After World War II traditional folktales practically disappeared amongst the settled community but, the Gypsies resisted change and continued in the traditional ways. Dobos (1981) is an example of a writer who simply presents the Gypsies in the role of guardians of country traditions. The original collectors had often not even identified whether the teller was Gypsy or not. With the coming of industrialisation, just as in Britain, the practice of storytelling died out amongst the host community and folklorists had turned to Gypsy tale-tellers who had kept the art alive. Vekerdi does, however, argue that Gypsy preservation of borrowed non-Gypsy material differs considerably from hereditary non-Gypsy transmission of oral culture. Gypsies alter their texts constantly both at the moment of borrowing and in the process of singing.

These Hungarian nationalists had to deal with a corpus of folktales comparable in size to the collections by English Gypsy folklorists at the turn of the century in Britain. Sandor Erdész (1968) collected from both Hungarian Gypsies and from the Hungarian peasantry. He recorded the highest number of tales (262) from one teller, a sixty-five year old illiterate Gypsy. He argued that Gypsy tales do have certain distinct properties such as the unhappy ending for the hero in the wonder tales, which sets them apart from the Hungarian tales. He also suggests the very realistic repres-entation of the difficulties of existence suggest that certain properties of the Gypsy tales could have been present in Hungarian tales in former times.

From the end of the 1950s several collections of texts in Romani made their appearance. Sandor Csenki (1974) published sixty-two tales in Hungarian translation from many of these collections. The debate over these, and the endeavour to assert, against Vekerdi, that a Gypsy cultural identity can be identified, can be traced in the volume edited by Görög-Karády (1990). In the 1980s Hungarian Gypsy studies began to analyse separately the tales told only in Romani, those told in Romani and Hungarian and those told in Romanian. Olga Nagy (1978), while researching the oral art of the Hungarian peasantry, had discovered bi-lingual and even tri-lingual Gypsy tale-tellers. Agnes Kovacs (1985), a specialist in Hungarian oral history, warned that only rigorous analysis of parallel texts of Gypsy and Hungarian tales would show the truth of the matter. Until this time all the tales have been treated as Hungarian without considering that there might be a distinction between Gypsy tales and Hungarian tales. Researchers found a significant difference between those groups who had lived for long period in Hungary and had lost their native language whilst retaining their oral narrative style and those Gypsies who retained their original language. The story content of the first group was linked more closely with Hungary and told in Hungarian. Other Gypsies told tales in two languages depending on the needs of their audience. Olga Nagy argued that it is impossible to speak of a Gypsy tale in general terms but the investigator must treat each text separately to establish the relationship between the teller and his audience, to discover degree of 'archaism' in the repertoire of the teller. She also comments that what might appear to be structurally cohesive and permanent in European tales could in fact be the result of their being taken down and rewritten, even corrected, which was the regular practice of of collectors before the advent of the tape-recorder.

As far as choice of genre goes, the specific preference of the Gypsy tellers, according to Veronika Görög-Karády (1990), is for telling the *paramiči* (the wonder tales or märchen). In such tales she notes how the protagonist is generally the killer of dragons – a poor Gypsy who will save the princess or the hero who is endowed with magic powers and succeeds in trials which the whole world has failed. The final sequences in the *paramiči* are often modified. It is not unusual to find a tragic ending for the hero: he does not always win the hand of the princess and the guilty are not regularly punished. Perhaps, she argues, this brings into question the reflection of Gypsy life, where a socially dominated group reflect their vision of the world or even reflect how they imagine their world to be. She continues that Gypsy tellers depict the weaknesses of their protagonists; their hesitation in the face of superhuman tasks, even if it tends to strengthen their courage and their impulsive moods, sentimental character and uncertainties. The Gypsies are the tools of their own fate rather than the masters. The Gypsy hero often learns in a dream of the nature of the enterprise to which he is called, a motif which is absent from the body of Hungarian stories. It is his associates or protectors who recognise him as the bearer of a project and who help him to make it come to a satisfactory end. In the repertoire of Berki the motif of predestination is recurrent. It appears in a stereotype formula when the adversary addresses to the hero. "I knew when you were still in your mother's womb that you would make trouble for me."

Quite separately from European researches, American Romani Studies also offer us data which may bear on the specifity of Romani oral culture. The pioneer Rena Cotten (now Gropper) (1954:261-6) made it clear that *paramiči* are not the only tale-type amongst the American Rom. Her research shows that storytelling amongst Kalderash Rom in New York is a 'private' event intended for the closed group. There are, in fact, four distinct types of story told in Gypsy communities but it is only the *paramiči*, the equivalent to the European märchen, which are shared with gaje who want to hear a story. The other three types are the *svarta*, the textbooks of the Gypsy culture, the *hira*, tales about known people, and the *kris* stories of court trials of the Vlach Rom.

Diane Tong (1989), like Görög-Karády, suggests there are specific themes prevalent in the Gypsy tale. These include the Gypsy being held in contempt, dislike of a work-centred life, high regard for hospitality, respect for the dead, and the fear of childlessness. These themes, she says, reflect the Gypsy way of life. Specific motifs which Tong highlights as original to Gypsy tales are: a somersault preceding a metamorphosis and throwing swords or shooting arrows into the air and waiting to see where they fall to determine one's fate. These themes could, however, also reflect the lifestyle of other groups.

A Gypsy identity within the English folktale corpus?

It was the wonder-tales, the märchen similar to *paramichi*, which were the first interest of English collectors at the turn of the century. Thompson's collection of Romanichal narratives, however reveals a wider repertoire which includes first person experience stories and tales of well-known characters in Gypsy culture that would appear, despite the well-known differences between Rom and Romanichal culture, to be similar to the *hira* of the Rom, as reported by Cotten. It is through the selection of specific tales by individual narrators for their personal repertoires that they reveal their 'world view'. The past does not exist as a place or a time until it has been narrated through a story. We continually re-invent ourselves through our personal storying and these narratives inevitably contain some invention however genuinely they are portrayed as the truth. Different genres have different ways of calling upon the listener for suspension of disbelief or credibility.

The storytelling events recorded by the collectors at the turn of the century, particularly those of T. W. Thompson, are fascinating in that they reflect many of the problems faced by both the narrators and the listeners. Steiner (1975:17) wrote that: "any thorough reading of a text out of the past of one's own language and literature is a manifold act of interpretation." Orally transmitted tales must be considered both from a temporal and a cultural viewpoint. Literate observers, however, may tend to judge the importance of various elements of performance from a literary perspective. If the structure or plot is highlighted over descriptive passages and other elements not essential to the storyline they create an impression of structural simplicity. It would then be possible to fail to recognise the plethora of culturally important detail essential for the appreciation of performance (Edwards and Sienkewicz 1990:2-3). Each society must be studied in terms of its own particular orientations. Regional variation of narratives can reveal a sense of landscape, a feeling of belonging, an awareness of shared history and an accent on human values; it is a type of cultural register. Such a broader view needs to be applied to understand the cultural specificities of stories told by the close-knit communities of the English Romanichal Gypsies of the late nineteenth and early twentieth century and their massive contribution to the English folktale corpus.

References

AARNE A tr. S Thompson 1973 2nd revision *The Types of the Folktale: A Classification and Bibliography* FF Communications, Helsinki

ACTON T 1979 "The Ethnic Composition of British Romani Populations" *Roma* Vol. 4(4) pp. 43-53

BENFEY T 1859 *Pantschatantra: Fünf Bucher indischer Fablen, Märchen und Erzählungen* 2 vols. Leipzig, cited in Thompson (1977)

BRIGGS K 1970 *A Dictionary of British Folk-tales in the English Language incorporating the E. J. Norton Collection* Routledge and Kegan Paul, London

CLINCH A J 1982 "The TW Thompson collection of Gypsy Folktales" PhD Thesis University of Leeds

COTTEN R 1954 "Gypsy Folktales" *Journal of American Folklore* Vol.67 pp. 261-266

CSENKI S 1974 *A cigány meg a sárkány* Europa, Budapest

DÉGH L 1972 "Folk Narrative" in Dorson R ed. *Folklife and Folklore* Chicago University Press, Chicago

DOBOS I 1981 *Gyemantkigyo* Europa, Budapest

DUNDES A 1963 "Structural Typology in North American Indian Folktales" *Southwestern Journal of Anthropology* Vol. 19 pp.121-30

DUNDES A 1965 *The Study of Folklore* Prentice-Hall, Englewood Cliffs, New Jersey

EDWARDS V and SIENKEWICZ T 1990 *Oral Cultures: Past and Present* Basil Blackwell, Oxford

ERDÉSZ S 1968 *Ámi Lajos mésel* Akademiai Kiado, Budapest, 3 vols.

GEORGES R A 1969 "Towards an understanding of storytelling events" *Journal of American Folklore* Oct/Dec Vol LXXXII

GRIMM, J and W 1975 *The Complete Grimm's Fairy Tales* Routledge and Kegan Paul, London

GROOME F H 1888a "Mr Groome's Theory of diffusion of folktales by means of Gypsies" *Journal of the Gypsy Lore Society* Vol I No 2 October pp.113-16

GROOME F H 1888b "Gipsy Folk-Tales: The missing link" *National Review* Vol. II, pp. 659-73

GROOME F H 1879 "Gipsies" *Encyclopaedia Britannica*, Vol. 10, pp.611-18

GROOME F H 1899 *Gypsy Folktales* Hurst and Blackett, London

GÖRÖG-KARÁDY V ed. 1991 *Contes d'un tzigane hongrois: Janos Berki raconte* Editions du CNRS, Paris

HYMES D 1975 "Folklore's Nature and the Sun's Myth" *Journal of American Folklore* Vol. 88

JACOBS J 1979 *English Fairy Tales* Hurst and Blackett, London

JONES M O 1967 "Francis Hindes Groome: Scholar Gypsy and Gypsy Scholar" *Journal of American Folklore* Vol. 80

KOVACS A 1985 "Jegyzetek" (Notes), in Berki J. *Berki János mésel Cigany es magyar nyelven* Academie des Sciences de Hongrie, Groupe de Recherches Ethnologiques, (Hungarian Gypsy Studies 3), Budapest

LANG A 1886 "Myths and Mythologists" *Nineteenth Century* Vol 19 January, pp.50-65

LÉVI-STRAUSS C 1955 "The Structural study of Myth" *Journal of American Folklore* Vol. 68

LUTHI M 1970 *Once upon a time: On the Nature of Fairy Tales* Indiana University Press, Bloomington

MAYALL D 1988 *Gypsy-Travellers in the Nineteenth-Century Society* Cambridge University Press, Cambridge

NAGY O 1978 "The Persistence of Archaic Traits among Gypsy Story-telling Communities in Romania" *Journal of the Gypsy Lore Society* 4th ser. Vol 1 (4)

OLRIK A 1909 "Epische Gesetze der Volksdichtung" *Zeitschrift fur Deutsches Altertum* Vol. 51 pp.1-12

ONG W 1982 *Orality and Literacy: The Technologizing of the Word* Methuen, London

PHILIP N ed. 1992 *The Penguin Book of English Folktales* Penguin, London

PROPP V 1984 *Theory and History of Folklore* Manchester University Press, Manchester

SAMPSON J 1892 "Tales in a tent" *Journal of the Gypsy Lore Society* 1st Series, Vol.3

SAMPSON J ed. Yates D 1933 *XXI Gypsy Folktales* Gregynog, Newtown

SAWYER R 1962 *The Way of the Storyteller* Bodley Head, London

STEINER G 1975 *After Babel: Aspects of Language and Translation* Oxford University Press, London.

TEDLOCK D 1975 "On the Transition of Style in Oral Narrative" *Journal of American Folklore* Vol.88

THOMPSON S 1977 *The Folktale* University of California Press, Berkeley

THOMPSON T W 1914 "English Gypsy Folktales and other traditional stories" *Journal of the Gypsy Lore Society* New Series Vol VIII (3) January

THOMPSON T W 1922-3 "The Gypsy Grays as Tale-Tellers." *Journal of the Gypsy Lore Society* 3rd ser. Vol I-II

TONG D 1989 *Gypsy Folk Tales* Harcourt Brace Jovanovich, New York

VEKERDI J 1968 "Gypsy Folklore" *New Hungarian Quarterly* Vol. 30, pp.150-153

VEKERDI J 1976 "The Gypsy's Role in the Preservation of Non-Gypsy Folklore" *Journal of the Gypsy Lore Society* 4th series Vol. 1(2) pp.79-86

Chapter 3 Scottish Gypsies/Travellers and the folklorists

Willie Reid, Educational Welfare Officer, Gloucester, and Co-founder, Scottish Gypsy Traveller Association

It might be thought that the identity of the Travellers is derived from their origins. Whatever the truth of this, theories of their origins held by folklorists derive pretty much from their current perceptions of Traveller culture and identity. From what has been written about the origins of Scotland's Travelling People (discounting the countless more obscure myths) there emerge three main theories. These lines of thoughts can best be described as the indigenous, Indian and fusionist theories.

Those who hold the indigenous theory believe Gypsies/Travellers were not immigrants like 'pure Gypsies' into the country but aboriginal people. Tim Neat summed up this indigenous theory in 1971 in the BBC documentary *The Summer Walkers* when he said:

> "Far from being the fluxion of the ages, a kind of drop-outs anonymous, the Travellers are heirs of a cohesive social structure whose origins almost certainly lie in the pre-Christian era. Evidence suggests that they are either the heirs of a caste of nomadic metal workers who rose to play an important part in high Celtic society or older still, the heirs of aboriginal hunter-gatherers who were pushed into northern Europe in the Neolithic period."

Secondly, the Indian theory presents Gypsies/Travellers as immigrants to Scotland and that their ancestry lay in the north-west of India. Linguistic scholars of the eighteenth and nineteenth centuries gathered evidence to support this view. The first reference to Gypsies in Britain was made in the records of the Lord High Treasurer of Scotland in 1505 (McRitchie 1894). Scottish Gypsies/Travellers have intermarried and mixed with similar Irish, Welsh and English Gypsy/Traveller groups. Gypsies/Travellers throughout Scotland are members of Gypsy organisations based in England.

Thirdly, there is the fusionist theory that believes there was fusion between the indigenous and immigrant groups from the sixteenth century. Even those who advocate the indigenous theory are forced to admit that "there was undoubtedly a certain degree of socio-biological fusion – and it is consequently safe to say that there cannot be many Scots travelling folk today without a dash of gypsy (sic) blood in them" (Henderson 1992:174).

No matter to which of these theories writers cling, Gypsy/Travellers are depicted as people who descended the social scale with the passing of time. As Henderson (1992) continued:

> "... the travellers [fell] from being quite high in the social scale, ricocheted down it with the passing of the centuries. In the Celtic society the black and white smiths (cairds = tinkers) were exceptionally valuable members of society. The cover languages ... cut them off from the ordinary clansmen."

The Indian theory too holds that Gypsies/Travellers descended the social scale from being welcomed at the Royal court to being social outcasts. In 1530 the Egyptians danced before the King in Holyrood Palace. In the latter half of the sixteenth century Gypsies/Travellers enjoyed protection from the Roslin family, they were given lodgings in the towers at Roslin called 'Robin Hood' and 'Little John' and they "acted several plays" during May to June each year (McRitchie 1894).

As a Gypsy/Traveller myself I am made painfully aware that we have always been defined by outsiders. Countless names and descriptions have been foisted upon us. The language used to describe Gypsies/Travellers is constantly changing and has more to do with government policy than ethnic identity. In their Sixth Report (1991:14) the Secretary of State's Advisory Committee on Scotland's Travelling People recommended a redefinition of the description of 'traveller'. Society has an incurable urge to label us so that they can painfully squeeze us into a corner of society.

Arguments relating to the nature and characteristics of the 'true Gypsy/Traveller' are tiresome, outdated and misdirected and, like the search for the 'true Scot', are easily reduced to absurdity.

Although Gypsies/Travellers have a strong identity that we defend fiercely, we are just as confused as others as to our origins. And the words used to describe Gypsies/Travellers do nothing to convey the ethnicity of groups; for example, the word 'Traveller' itself is misleading inasmuch as it is arbitrary. Although the word 'Traveller' was used by the group for many years, it was not until the 1970s that the authorities adopted it for official purposes. Gypsies/Travellers were ready to accept this new description because words such as 'tinker' or more commonly 'tink' had been used as a degrading form of abuse.

Regardless of theories of origin, Gypsies/Travellers remain a distinct ethnic group and are aware of the distinctive nature of the group. For the sake of cultural survival Gypsies/Travellers have always adopted and changed as society has developed. Others are bent on defining us according to how we travel or what we do rather than accept our full ethnic identity.

For Scotland's Gypsies/Travellers the word 'Traveller' is full of cultural connotations that go far beyond travelling although Gypsies/Travellers who do not travel are not recognised by the Secretary of State's Advisory Committee. One cannot choose to belong to the group, it is not something that can be opted in and out of – one is born into the culture and heritage – there is no choice.

Oral tradition

"The only satisfactory definition of a 'folksong' is a song that has been transmitted orally. That is, learnt by word of mouth without the assistance of the written word. That definition could be applied to ballads in this country but for the fact that there has been no such thing as purely oral transmission here for the last four hundred and fifty years ... Purely oral transmission can exist only among an illiterate community, cut off from all contacts with book-learning, and such a community has hardly existed in England or Scotland during the recorded history of ballads – which begins only in the late Middle-Ages" (Hodgart 1950, 1964:11).

When Hodgart first expressed this view in 1950 he could have been speaking for the entire academic establishment. About this same period, the early 1950s, Hamish Henderson was carrying out some field study for the School of Scottish Studies. In a recent interview he told me the aims of his early research:

"...the research as I envisaged it was to put on record the living traditions of as many of the various groups in Scotland as we could come across and this was not antiquarianism; it is looking at culture that exists in the present day" (Henderson, personal communication 13 February 93).

The most exciting find for Henderson and the School of Scottish Studies was the enormous wealth of oral cultural tradition to be found among the Gypsy/Traveller community. Writing of the much celebrated Jeannie Robertson, Angus Calder said in his introduction to Henderson's (1992) collection *Alias MacAlias* that "she rose up like the middle-ages in person". We must bear in mind Jeannie Robertson was only twenty-four years old when Henderson 'discovered' her. Researchers from the School of Scottish Studies recorded major ballads from the mouths of children as young as five years old. Henderson had indeed 'discovered' a living tradition that some had thought lost. He gives a vivid account of the vast oral tradition to be found at the berry-fields of Blairgowrie:

"Then the singing would begin, or else a melodeon might be fetched out of a tent, and one of the gypsies (sic) would give a brilliant display of step-dancing on a bit of board laid down for the purpose, encouraged by hooches and admiring cries. By this time four or five ceilidhs might be going on in the one berry-field, and the excited collector would have to decide whether to stay on at the first camp-fire of his choice, or move to another ... from which maybe, he could hear tantalising fragments of a rare 'Child' ballad, or the high flamenco-like cadences of a Gaelic tinker love lament. Recording in the berry-fields in fact, was – and is – like holding a tin can under the Niagara Falls; in a single session you can hear everything from ancient Ossianic hero-tales, whose contents reflect the life of primitive hunter tribesmen, to caustic pop-song parodies thought up by Clydeside teenagers that same afternoon" (Henderson, 1992:102).

Henderson still maintains that the greatest achievement of the School of Scottish Studies "was to put on record the enormous folk culture of travellers" (personal communication 12 February 93). Social barriers had prevented earlier collectors like John Francis Campbell and Gavin Greig from studying the folklore of Gypsies/Travellers. Henderson entered the Gypsy/Traveller world when it did "not pay to let informants know that one has been consorting socially with tinkers" (Henderson and Collinson, 1965). No one has done more to uncover and bring social and academic respectability to the Gypsy/Traveller oral tradition than Henderson. Because he dared to break the social barriers he discovered a world of folk culture that had never been touched by the respectable classes. Henderson put the Gypsy/Traveller folk culture in perspective when he wrote:

"Until comparatively recently, the number of folktale versions in English and Scots which had been put on record was surprisingly small, but the fieldwork of the School of Scottish Studies among the Scots-speaking 'Travellers' (or tinkers) has disclosed an enormous folktale treasury until now hidden away in their own secret world. Examination of this vast corpus of narrative artistry, and comparative study of the same or similar tales on record as being in the repertoires of storytellers as far away as Turkey, Iran and India, make it clear that we are dealing with an inter-nation *Marchengut* going back at least as far as the Middle Ages and, in the case of maybe a hundred tale types, probably a good deal further" (Henderson in Gifford 1988:267).

Perhaps I should make it absolutely clear that whereas I may be critical of the way folklorists interpreted Gypsy/Traveller identity, in no way do I demean the importance of folklore. The ballads and the tales found among Scottish Gypsies/Travellers are worthy of the most earnest academic study.

Before the 1950s there was hardly any interest in Scottish Gypsies/ Travellers at all. The founding of the School of Scottish Studies in Edinburgh in 1950 coincided with the Folk Revival in Scotland (Munro 1984). Gypsies/Travellers did not seek or even know of the School of Scottish Studies or of the Revival but were sought out because they were believed to be "one of the most authentic folk cultures in Western Europe". Since that time Gypsies/Travellers have remained a curiosity and even yet folklorists and folkscryers seek them out with bemused admiration.

All this interest raised the profile of the Gypsy/Traveller community and played upon the social conscience. The discovery of the oral traditions brought with it a degree of respectability and social admiration. For the first time there was a national interest in Gypsies/Travellers, and even though the 'discoverers' denied our full ethnicity they recognised our cultural distinctiveness.

I would suggest that this focus on the folklore was the inspiration behind the most comprehensive report ever made: *Scotland's Travelling People* (Scottish Development Department 1971). This report would lead to the setting up of the Secretary of State's Advisory Committee whose task was to advise the Secretary of State on policies covering Gypsies/Travellers. Although this Committee had no real power, and had only token Gypsy/Travellers on it and was always patronising towards Gypsies/Travellers, it did encourage the setting up of a network of sites throughout Scotland. Whether this was for the better or the worse is another matter.

Another positive point that sprang from the Folk Revival was that it gave a platform for 'new talent discovery'. A few Gypsies/Travellers found eager customers for traditional music and story. This brought the Gypsy/Traveller folk culture to a wider audience. The recording on tape and in print of these tales and songs ensures their survival. It is unlikely that such oral culture could otherwise have survived the barrage of mass media in the technological world.

This interest in Gypsies/Travellers came from the School of *Scottish* Studies and the Folk *Revival*. This focus on our community was not with the intention of studying Gypsy/Traveller identity but came from a search to discover Scottish identity and roots. The oral tradition found among Scottish Gypsies/Travellers represented an ancient oral form that was thought to be 'authentically Scottish'. Since the Union in 1707 Scotland has always had problems coming to terms with its national identity. From time to time there is a revival to re-assert Scotland's national identity. This fascination with the oral tradition brought nationalists back to a time before the Union, even to medieval times. Gypsies/Travellers were viewed as a living reminder of a Scots oral tradition that remained untainted from Anglification. We must bear in mind that it was folk culture that was so distinctive during the Scottish Enlightenment. The folk voice of Burns, Hogg and the revival of Gaelic poetry asserted a strong organic impact upon the Enlightenment.

So when Tim Neat (1971) talked of the origins of Gypsies/Travellers lying in the "pre-Christian era" and "high Celtic Society" and speculated as far back as the Neolithic period, and when Henderson talks of the "fallen Cairds" and writes of finding "ancient Ossianic hero-tales" they are clearly in search of an organic oral tradition/culture that would explain the nature of Scottishness.

Quite innocently Gypsies/Travellers wandered upon the scene and were overwhelmed with all this attention. A few were more than willing to clad themselves in tartan and play the part. To this day a few Gypsies/Travellers are making a living from the oral craft. In earlier times Gypsies/Travellers could profit from the myth that they were noble refugees and victims of the Highland Clearances. Every year in the most scenic glens of Scotland you can hear the sound of pipers wooing the tourists. Many Scots Gypsies/Travellers are patriotic to their country and even propagate the myth that their families once belonged to the great houses of Scotland.

All this concentration on the ancient, however, presented a very unfair, unbalanced and distorted image of the Scottish Gypsy/Traveller. We were viewed as noble savages who took no heed of the boundaries of time. We were seen as an ancient people whose culture and lifestyle was static. Of course, this limited and crude analysis led to stereotypes of the primitive tinker dancing and telling tales around his camp-fire – poor but contented, unlearned but happy, dirty but pure in heart. We were admired as wild social outcasts associated with the supernatural and mysteries and even dangerous and criminal. Such images fed the preconceptions and preoccupations of the researchers. What was happening was that we were being reshaped and remoulded with nationalistic characteristics that denied any Gypsiness (otherness) in our character. All this focus constantly reduced our identity down to the primitive.

In reality, these researchers created for us the culture of nostalgia: a Golden Age, a culture that had its day, a culture that was fast disappearing. A Traveller that was housed, informed and educated was rejected; only those who wandered with tents and were non-literate were accepted as 'true Travellers'. This stereotype seems ingrained upon the Scottish psyche. We must bear in mind that the folk researchers' focus was on the primitive and they only had a few Gypsy/Traveller informants. From these few they built up a distorted picture of Traveller/Gypsy life.

As they were seen as 'experts' their theories of the indigenous/ primitive went unchallenged by Gypsy/Traveller informants. Some Gypsies/ Travellers relied on them for knowledge about their own past. It is frustrating that there have hardly been any writers or researchers at all who wish to challenge the 'accepted' notions that sprang from the 1950s. Debate concerning the identity of Scottish Gypsies/Travellers is stifled and stagnant. Perhaps in time Gypsies/Travellers will re-examine our past and write a critical analysis of our history – but that is yet to be done.

Where the School of Scottish Studies and the Revival claim that Gypsies/Travellers were the custodians and tradition-bearers of a Scottish culture, I would wish to argue that such folklore belongs to the Gypsy/ Traveller community. Folklore has the power to transcend national and cultural boundaries and makes a distinctive home where it is most cared for; the folklore found amongst the Scottish Gypsy/Travellers has been shaped by the values and preoccupations of that community. It is one more strand of identity that makes up the intricate web that forms the Scottish Gypsy/Traveller. In almost every souvenir shop in Scotland you will find the books of Betsy Whyte and sometimes the stories of Duncan Williamson and Stanley Robertson. How ironic it is that these books should come to represent a strong Scottish identity. Writing of the identities communities create, Abrams (1979:393) made it clear when he wrote:

"As with any object or concept, every work of folk creation or transmission is an artefact potentially capable of providing great insight into the story of its culture, because that work, in both its form and its functions, reflects the preoccupations and values of those who reflects the functional unity which an in groups can create for himself. This unity is not decisive, one which speaks for all time and permanence, but rather represents a constantly shifting, but nonetheless effective, dialective unity – one that relies for its existence on contraries, on balanced oppositions."

Researchers have tended to examine the Scottish Gypsy/Traveller oral culture in isolation. There has been a desire to see this oral culture as indigenous, organic, but most of all Scottish, even though such oral ballads and tales can also be found among Gypsy/Traveller communities in England, Wales and Ireland (cf Gmelch and Kroup 1978, Kennedy 1975, McColl and Seeger 1977, Acton and Lee 1989) and elsewhere (Tong 1989, Riordan 1986). Yet this approach is based on incomplete analysis.

Most of the material collected is stored in the archives of the School of Scottish Studies and has not yet been thoroughly investigated. Surely we need to consider Scottish Gypsy/Traveller lore alongside other European Gypsy/Traveller lore to assess the significance of their role in retaining traditions for host societies, at the same time as they define their own identity. In fact we need to consider how far, as Europeans moving among other Europeans, selectively taking and rejecting cultural elements from others, the re-presentation of European folklore was the legitimate assertion of their own culture.

Travellers are not aware that they are the custodians of traditional culture. To us it is not a question of historic origin or artistic merit.

As Antonio Gramsci put it:

"... that which distinguishes folk-song in the framework of a nation and its culture is neither artistic fact nor historic origin; it is a separate and distinct way of perceiving life and the world, as opposed to that of 'official' society". (Gramsci 1950, translated and cited by Henderson, 1980, 1991:14)

It is this "separate and distinct way of perceiving life and the world" that is the most important point to bear in mind when considering folklore. Betsy Whyte (1990:183) reinforced this point when she wrote: "We have an entirely different way of looking at life".

From the first page of Whyte's first book to the last page of her second book she attempts to show the distinctiveness of Gypsy/Traveller culture and identity. The emergence of Gypsy/Traveller literature alongside the oral tradition clearly demonstrates that Scottish Gypsy/Travellers reject all attempts of assimilation and absorption.

The four faults of folklore

To summarise the criticisms that I have made of the way folklorists have treated the subject and Scottish Gypsies/Travellers:

1 They created a culture of nostalgia. Folklorists saw Gypsies/ Travellers as a primitive people frozen in time, an archaic tribe out of place in modern society.
2 The study of Gypsy/Traveller folklore got caught up in the search for Scottish national identity.
3 There was/is a general ignorance of the values beliefs, customs and traditions of Gypsy/Travellers.
4 There was/is an outright refusal to accept the 'Gypsouners' of Scottish Gypsy/Travellers.

The identity of the Scottish Gypsy/Traveller was one manufactured by folklorists who had a limited knowledge of the group. Unfortunately, these images perpetrated by School of Scottish Studies and the Revival have stuck – and it will take enormous efforts from Gypsies/Travellers to free ourselves from these mainly negative images. Those few Gypsy/Travellers who were overwhelmed and 'bought' into the folk circuit continue to perpetrate these myths.

Gypsies/Travellers did play a significant role in the folk renaissance. It has been said that they 'revolutionised' the folk scene. Their impact upon the folk scene, however, was mainly a passive one becaus￼ ￼ y were unaware of the motives for their involvement and it is ￼ ￼ more true that they played a passive role in the Revival. Our or￼ ￼ has or is an oracle that has carried us this far and cradled ￼ ￼ ￼eness throughout the ages. In robbing us of our oral cultur￼ ￼ s have taken oral treasures that have been preser￼ ￼ ￼he centuries. It is time Gypsies/Travellers reclaimed th￼ ￼ ￼mined them and buil￼ ￼pon the oral tradition.

This oral art form was not static but dynamic. Our oral culture is something that belongs to us and is the heritage of our children. Is it too late to develop, maintain, define and redefine the whole oral craft within the culture? Famous folksingers boast that they had learned songs from 'resource singers' at Gypsy/Traveller firesides and, indeed, many grew from and built upon the tradition. Given similar opportunities, Gypsies/ Travellers could take the classic oral tradition and create new art forms.

References

ABRAMS R B 1979 "Folklore in culture; notes towards an analytic method" in Brunvand J H ed. *Readings in American Folklore* Norton, New York

ACTON T A and LEE N A 1989 "The Present and Potential Impact of Romani Language and Culture on the School Curriculum in the United Kingdom – Sadašne i moguče djelovanje romskog jezika i culture na nastavne planove u Velikoj Britaniji" in Šipka M ed. *Jezik i Kultura Roma–Romani Language and Culture* Svetlost/Institute for National Minorities, Sarajevo

CHILD F J 1906 English and Scottish Popular Ballads David Nutt, London

GMELCH G and KROUP B 1978 *To Shorten the Road* O'Brien Press, Dublin

GRAMSCI A 1950 Letteratura e Vita Nazionale (Opere Vol. 6) CPI, Rome

GIFFORD D ed. 1988 *The History of Scottish Literature* Vol.3, Aberdeen University Press, Aberdeen

HENDERSON H 1980 "'It Was In You That It A' Began' – Some thoughts on the folk conference" in Cowan E J ed. *The People's Past* EUSPB, Edinburgh, 2nd. ed. 1991, Polygon, Edinburgh

HENDERSON H 1992 *Alias MacAlias* Polygon, Edinburgh

HENDERSON H and COLLINSON F 1965 "New Child Ballad variants from oral tradition" *Scottish Studies* Vol. 9 (1)

HODGART M J C 1950 1964 *The Ballads* Hutchinson, London

KENNEDY P 1975 *Folksongs of Britain and Ireland* Cassell, London

McCOLL E and SEEGER P 1977 *Travellers' Songs from England and Scotland* Routledge and Kegan Paul, London

McRITCHIE D 1894 *The Scottish Gypsies under the Stewarts* Douglas, Edinburgh

MUNRO A 1984 *The Folk Music Revival* Kahn and Averill, London

NEAT T 1971 *The Summer Walkers* BBC documentary, Edinburgh

ROBERTSON S 1988 *Exodus to Alford* Balnain, Edinburgh

SCOTTISH DEVELOPMENT DEPARTMENT 1971 *Scotland's Travelling People* HMSO, Edinburgh

SECRETARY OF STATE'S ADVISORY COMMITTEE ON SCOTLAND'S TRAVELLING PEOPLE 1991 *Sixth Term Report* HMSO, Edinburgh

TONG D ed. 1989 *Gypsy Folktales* Harcourt Brace Jovanovich, New York

WHYTE B 1979 *The Yellow on the Broom* Chambers, Edinburgh

WHYTE B 1990 *Red Rowans and Wild Honey* Cannongate, Edinburgh

WILLIAMSON D 1985 *The Broonies, Silkies and Fairies* Cannongate, Edinburgh

WILLIAMSON D 1987 *Tell Me a Story for Christmas* Cannongate, Edinburgh

WILLIAMSON D 1989 *May the Devil Walk Behind Ye* Cannongate, Edinburgh

Chapter 4 The construction of identity through narrative: folklore and the travelling people of Scotland

Donald Braid, Researcher, Indiana University, USA

The people who call themselves the Travelling People of Scotland have been known by many names. They have been called tinkers because some Travellers used to make and sell tinware, the term tink being linked to the sound of hammer on tin (Grant and Murison 1974:9, 338-39). Their nomadic life inspired names such as the "Gan-aboot folk" (the going about folk) or the "mist-folk" (Whyte 1979). Some scholars have used the term tinkler-gypsies, a term that emphasises possible ties to the Gypsies found in other parts of Europe (e.g. Henderson 1992:229; McCormick [1907] 1973). Some Travellers, bothered by how the term tinker has come to be used pejoratively by non-Travellers, and by how the term Traveller seems to reduce culture to a function of nomadic lifestyle, are contemplating adopting their own cant term *Nawkins* as a way of avoiding the problematic meanings of earlier terms.

These names are important for two reasons. First, they identify a group of people who, no matter how loosely tied, frequently identify themselves culturally with other Travellers and contrast themselves, as a group, with the settled folk. In this sense they might be said to have a sense of shared identity. Implicit in this sense of identity is a shared sense of difference with respect to non-Travellers.

These names are also important because they evoke social and historical contexts within which the motivations and boundaries of this sense of identity are not arbitrary. Although Traveller identity is in many senses defined by the Travellers themselves, their sense of group identification is influenced by the social environment within which Travellers have lived for generations. The 'Travelling People of Scotland' are a minority cultural group in Scotland. They are perceived by many settled folk as an unwanted and troublesome other and have consequently been the focus of legal and social discrimination that threatens their way of life. Travellers have isolated themselves from settled communities but have survived for centuries by exploiting the cracks in the settled economy. For a general overview of this social environment see Gentleman and Swift (1971) and Gentleman (1993).

Because of their hostile social environment and because of non-Traveller misconceptions of Traveller culture, the Travellers are strongly motivated to comprehend and deal with issues of cultural identity and difference (cf. Reid, this volume). But what does it mean to have a sense of cultural identity? What factors, characteristics, or processes underlie the perception of identity and difference? How is a sense of cultural identity and difference constructed and communicated?

A legacy of anthropological and folkloristic study suggests that culture and identity are not predetermined by race, genetics, or language (e.g. Boas 1940; Stocking 1982). Nor are culture and identity synonymous with superficial artifacts of lifestyle; for example, Travellers living on the road, on government sites, or in fixed housing may all share equally the same cultural identity. Surely legal definitions, such as the Travellers being of nomadic habit of life, do not capture the essence of cultural identity (cf. Acton 1993; Clements 1994).

I suggest, for Travellers and in general, that conceptions of identity are motivated by perceptions of difference. In this sense, identity fundamentally involves a continuity in perception of similarity or difference between self and other (cf.Burke 1969, 22; Erikson 1968, 50; Dundes 1983, 23739; Mathisen 1993; Oring 1994). Identity is a perception based in time and history. It requires a continuity of interaction among people over time. Through the temporal unfolding of individual experience with the world in relation to community interaction, members of a society develop shared ideational systems, belief systems or webs of signification (Geertz 1973:330) that might be referenced by the more inclusive term 'worldview' or 'ideology' (cf. Geertz 1973:193-229, Hill and Mannheim 1992:81-2). Though not determinative, worldview is centrally implicated in the interpretation and creation of meaning. Worldview is a resource that informs an individual's perceptions, actions, ideas, and interpretations and therefore influences the dynamics of interaction in the world. Given the centrality of worldview to meaning and action, I suggest the perception of worldview is a potent factor in perceptions of identity and difference. A person who approaches or interprets his or her world in a similar way is perceived to have a similar identity. Someone who behaves and interprets the world differently is perceived to have a different identity.

In suggesting that worldview is formed through the temporal unfolding of individual experience with the world in relation to community interaction, I mean to imply that worldview, and therefore identity, only exist as emergent personal constructs that are formed through interactions with other people over the course of time. These personal constructs are not necessarily systematic or coherent but pragmatic, providing an essential framework that orients individuals to their world and to their community. Worldview and identity are therefore not superorganic, homogenous or static. It is only possible to talk about cultural identity and worldview as being shared by the members of a community because these personal constructs are formed, negotiated, and attuned or shared through the continuity of interaction between individuals. This does not imply that identity is a superficial or easily manipulable construct. Identity is not a simple lifestyle choice that can be altered by the introduction of alien discourses about assimilation or sedentarisation. Identity is deeply intertwined with the perception of meaning in an individual's world. It is rooted in a continuity of experience that begins at birth and integrates both personal experience and symbolically mediated associations with other people and ancestors. Where attunement does take place individuals may come to identify with a cultural group and contrast this cultural identity with outsiders, whether perceived as individuals, members of distinct communities or as homogenous groups.

It does not follow, however, that the perception of a similarity or difference in worldview implies a comprehension of the origins and implications of such a difference. Because the ideational systems, belief systems or webs of signification on which worldview and identity are based, remain unquestioned at a deep level of common sense it may not be apparent that the present world is open to very different, though equally viable, interpretations. When members of one culture try to understand those of another, differences are often interpreted from within the framework of the interpreter's own worldview. It is therefore not unusual for differences to be explained by arguing the other somehow inhabits a different world or a different temporal reality (cf.Fabian 1983). This is certainly the case with many non-Traveller conceptions of Travellers (cf.Reid this volume). An early government report, for example, suggests that Travellers are an immigrant race representing a stage of human development different from that current in the society into which they intruded (Departmental Committee on Tinkers in Scotland 1918:22).

The academic literature on Travellers also carries a lingering notion of cultural and temporal stagnancy. For example, Farnham Rehfisch argues that the persistent persecution of Travellers has given rise to the conservatism that he argues is necessary for the survival of Traveller values:

> "Scots travellers have existed in a very hostile environment for many centuries ... they have maintained themselves primarily by holding tight to values and attitudes which are often in conflict with those of the mass society. Very simply if they had not done so they would no longer exist and would have merged with the Flattie [non-Traveller] group" (Rehfisch 1975:283).

It is possible to interpret this conservativism not as a positive, creative assertion of differential identity but as cultural stagnancy. It is as if Travellers were caught in time, barely managing to maintain themselves as they have always been. This sense of stagnancy is particularly prominent in arguments about Traveller origins. Without going into the arguments in detail, I can characterise two proposed origins of the Travellers (apart from those that link them to the Gypsies): that they are the heirs of a caste of nomadic metalworkers who rose to play an important and integrated role in High Celtic Society and that they are heirs of the aboriginal hunter-gatherers who settled in northern Europe in the Neolithic period (Neat 1979:42; cf. Henderson 1992:229). While such origins may give the Travellers historical status or some claim to aboriginal rights, these arguments also suggest that Travellers maintain an archaic quality that explains their inability to integrate themselves with the modern world. Timothy Neat develops this theme of stagnancy by suggesting the parallels that can be drawn between the Highland travellers and the Paleolithic Peoples and concludes: "If the Highland travellers are not descendants of pre-agricultural, aboriginal Britons, their lifestyle and their psychology retain remarkable similarities" (Neat 1979:42).

Popular notions of the Travellers also carry a sense of temporal distancing. For example, an article titled "Scotland's Colorful Tinkers" in *The Highlander,* a magazine for Scots in America, sums up Traveller existence by commenting:

"Today the classic tinkers of Scotland have all but vanished. There's a breed of folk who call themselves Travellers who turn up for the berrypicking and others ape the old time Gypsies when it suits them, to extract money from the public. But the tinkers who sat by road, loch, and burn mending tin pans have gone and with them the colorful ballads which told of their colorful mysterious ways" (Lamont-Brown 1994).

Not only does this article situate Travellers in a romanticised past, it denies any connection between current day Travellers and this past.

Temporal distancing also derives from other typological factors such as the categorisation of Travellers as illiterate, a distinction that often comes packaged with assumptions about inferior cognitive ability (cf.Chafe and Tannen 1987:391-92). Non-Travellers frequently comment that Travellers are lazy and incapable of working a steady job, presumably because they do not know how to use their time properly. All of these characterisations, made by non-Travellers, work together to construct a vision of the Travelling people as a stagnant and unchanging other who exist in a separate time.

Even the positive attitudes expressed toward the Travellers as custodians of the colossal wealth of folk tradition of every conceivable kind (Henderson 1992:219) can be problematic. Folklore is often associated with that which is old, with tradition as conservation of the past. In this sense Travellers might be viewed as uncreative vessels of tradition, without the capacity to change what has been passed on to them. In temporal terms, if Travellers possess folklore they must maintain direct connections with the past and therefore they must not be living in the same temporal reality as the rest of us. They survive anachronistically in the modern world.

It might be argued that Travellers characterise themselves as backward and past-oriented, as the following remark quoted by Neat (1979:40) implies in making a distinction between Travellers and tramps:

"To differentiate himself from a windmilling tramp from Donegal, an Aberdeenshire Traveller remarked, that kind of lad's not one of us – Charlie Doyle just lives from day to day – but we, we live entirely in the past".

As another example, here is the response I got in asking Traveller Duncan Williamson why Traveller stories never seem to end with the hero marrying the princess (a characteristic of many European Märchen):

DW They never, no never married the princess and lived happy ever after in my stories. You see the Travelling tales, Travelling stories, there were no ever happy ever after or once upon a time. There were no once upon a time.

DB   Hmm.

DW You'll never find any of my stories once upon a time or happy ever after.

DB   Is that the Travellers' way (?)?

DW That was the Travellers' way.

DB   With the future?

DW You were na, you see, the Travellers didna live for one day.

DB   Mhmm.

DW Who was going to know if they were gonnae live happy ever after. See what I mean?

DB   Yeah.

DW So according to the Travellers they only lived one day at a time.

SG   Hmm.

DW They never looked forward to the future.

(Interview, October 1987)

Non-Traveller portrayals of the Travellers do not arise from any objective factor of cultural identity, but rather from typological fallacies and assumptions that derive from a failure to treat the Travellers as coevals or equal participants in the present time (cf.Fabian 1983). Further, the Travellers' comments about themselves can not be taken as a corroboration of some typological status, nor as a reflection of inferior cognitive abilities or their ability to understand those around them. Rather, these comments should be seen as an intentional casting of their own beliefs and identities in a way that stands in opposition to the beliefs and identities of the settled folk. My point is that any consideration of Traveller identity must not fall into ethnocentric traps. It must be based on the assumption that Travellers are creative human beings fully engaged in the modern world and perfectly capable of participating in a dialogue on issues of cultural identity.

How can such a cross-cultural dialogue about identity take place? Building on recent discourse-centered and performance-centered approaches to culture that arise from "an understanding of social life as communicatively constituted, produced and reproduced by communicative practice" (Bauman 1989, 177; cf. also Sherzer 1987; Urban 1991), I suggest that the expressive forms and traditions of folklore, as forms of symbolic discourse, play a key role in constructing, embodying, negotiating and attuning the individual constructs of worldview and identity for members of a given culture. An analysis of how folklore is used by members of a culture should therefore give valuable insight into the process of constructing and negotiating issues of cultural identity.

Folk narratives are a central expressive form in Traveller culture, a form Travellers use in their interactions to tell each other who they are (cf.Braid 1996a). While not all Travellers would consider themselves storytellers, oral narrative forms are highly valued among Traveller communities and virtually everyone tells personal experience narratives. I suggest the centrality of narrative forms within Traveller lives makes narrative a natural resource for Travellers to invoke in negotiating issues of identity and difference both within Traveller communities and in interactions with outsiders.

This chapter therefore focusses attention on the intersection between Traveller narrative discourse and issues of cultural identity. Drawing on specific examples of oral narrative, I will investigate how individual Travellers use narrative performance to construct, communicate and negotiate aspects of their identity. Because conceptions of identity are fundamentally based in perceptions of similarity and difference, a study of Traveller narrative performances can give insight into individual perceptions of not only who Travellers think they are, but also who Travellers think they are not, and who they think settled folk are (cf. Basso 1979). I should emphasise that I in no way intend to create a new and better definition of Traveller identity. Nor do I believe that Travellers are a homogeneous community where one voice can claim to speak for all Travellers. My goal is to let individual Travellers speak for themselves about identity through their own narratives.

My approach to Traveller narratives builds on a conception of narrative in which narratives are not static but are emergent constructs which are transformed and adapted through the agency of the performer to the needs of the performance event. I believe that Travellers are conscious agents in creating the formal features of narrative performance that develop complex fields of referencing and meaning in their narratives. I have convinced myself of this ability many times in examining the use of narrative in relation to the ongoing social interactions within which they are performed and within which they often play a central role (e.g. cf. Braid 1993, 1996a). Before I begin my analysis, however, it is important to clarify the basic assumptions of my performance-centered approach.

Performance, narrative and identity

The idea that narrative and folklore are somehow related to an essential identity of the people who maintain cultural traditions is not new (cf. Oring 1994). Yet the relationships between folklore, culture and identity are complex and are often oversimplified. Folklore is not a static expression of homogenised identity but is dynamically motivated by and expresses, issues of differential identity (Jansen 1965; Bauman 1972). A focus on performance, rather than isolated texts, builds on the understanding that the form, function, meaning and use of folklore forms are not fully fixed but partly generated in the act of performance within situated events. (For overviews of performance approaches to folklore see Bauman 1977, 1989; Bauman and Braid in press; Bauman and Briggs 1990; Fine 1984.)

There are two senses of the term performance that are relevant to understanding narrative use in social interaction. The first is the sense in which performance is agent-centered. This use of performance implies the situated use of folklore in the accomplishment of social life (Bauman 1989:177) literally the doing of folklore. The second sense of performance focuses on the role of the performer as creative agent:

"The second and more marked sense of performance centers on

performance as a special, artful mode of communication, the essence of which resides in the assumption of responsibility to an audience for a display of communicative competence, subject to evaluation for the skill and effectiveness with which the act of expression is accomplished (Bauman 1977; Hymes 1975b).

This focus on the poetics of performance highlights the act of artistic communication within situational contexts of social interaction, with an emphasis on form-function-meaning interrelationships. Individual artistry is a central concern, though always by reference to the dynamic tension between the socially given and the emergent, between the conventions of performance on the one hand, individual creativity and situational uniqueness on the other, in the use of a proverb, the telling of a tale, the delivery of an oration and so on."
(Bauman 1989:177)

Performance approaches challenge static notions of the origin, ownership and meaning of folklore forms. They raise questions about the conservativism and homogeneity of folk groups, suggesting instead that folk groups are characterised by innovation, creativity and differential identity (Jansen 1965; Bauman 1972). They also challenge conceptions of tradition as static informational load, as cultural baggage to be carried (Bauman 1972; cf. Ben-Amos 1984). Tradition is not an intrinsic quality inherent in some texts and not others. Dell Hymes (1975a, 353-5). argues that tradition must be understood as an active process of traditionalisation through which individuals create the connections to a meaningful past that are essential to personal and social life. In many senses, the meaningful past is itself the product of traditionalisation.

From this perspective, folklore forms are constitutive of identity. The important question becomes not: how does folklore reflect identity? But how is folklore used as a symbolic medium in which issues of identity are not only represented, but constructed, embodied, negotiated and transformed? The process of traditionalisation plays an important role in establishing and legitimating the continuity of both individual constructs of worldview and the attunements of worldview formed among individuals who perceive themselves to be members of collectivities. Meaningful events and interactions, for example, may be traditionalised through their repeated performance as narrative. Specific personal experience narratives, family stories, folktales and legends traditionalised in this way can be used to teach or remind individuals who they were and therefore who they are. In this sense narratives can become symbolic constructs of identity that can play an important role in constituting, maintaining and negotiating identity.

Most importantly performance approaches recognise the creativity of performers in terms of how and when they communicate identity in performances of folklore. The narrative forms and genres passed down through the generations are, in fact, resources a narrator can adapt through performance to the needs of the performance event. They are "equipment for living" (Burke 1941). Although these narratives may carry some forms of meaning with them as they are recentered in a performance event, their full meaning and function are emergent out of the interaction; they cannot be fully interpreted without reference to the situational and cultural contexts of performance (cf.Malinowski 1953; Bauman and Briggs 1990, 66-72). The poetics and stylistics of performance are essential resources performers use in the construction and communication of these situated meanings. Who is present, what is happening in the event and why the story is being told will influence how it is told and therefore the meanings that are communicated. Traveller performances among community members, for example, will call forth differing expressions of identity than will performance interactions that include outsiders such as folklorists or government officials.

The analysis of individual folklore performances can therefore give valuable insight into a performer's own constructions of identity. But such an analysis must be undertaken carefully. Américo Paredes (1977), for example, points out how serious misunderstandings can arise if an ethnographer fails to understand the artistic modes of another culture's language use, such as joking or insult.

The creative act that underlies performance makes narrative an ideal source of data for studying Traveller constructions and negotiations of worldview and identity. In telling a personal experience narrative, for example, the narrator selects and shapes the flux of experience into a coherent and followable whole. The narrativisation process is not arbitrary. While many divergent narrativisations might be possible, narrators will tend to narrativise the flux of experience in terms of their own beliefs, understanding and point of view and therefore, to them, the narrative may appear to reference past events accurately. The coherence that informs narrative as sequence and gives it meaning, is dependent on worldview. As I argued above, each individual's worldview is a pragmatic construction that is rooted in a continuity of individual experience in relation to community interaction. It is linked to the need for continuity of connection to a meaningful past and in this sense may be attuned to the constructs of other community members.

Although it is not fixed and immutable, the continuity in worldview that informs an individual's narrative expressions can be interpreted from narrative performances – if the dynamics of performance are included as part of the interpretation. Analysing narrative performances should therefore make it possible to gain insight into the way Travellers comprehend dimensions of their own experience and that of others and therefore their conceptions of worldview and identity.

The process of narrativisation, however, is not fully determined by worldview. If the agency of the narrator is recognised, the interpretation that takes place in narrativisation need not be seen as a passive act. It can have political dimensions as well. Richard Bauman (1986:5-6). points out that not only does narrative have the potential to make the flux of experience comprehensible: it may also be an instrument for obscuring, hedging, confusing, exploring or questioning what went on, that is, for keeping the coherence or comprehensibility of narrated events open to question

In this sense, narrators can creatively construct and perform narratives as intentional negotiations of identity. Following a narrative performance requires the listener tentatively to accept the coherence with which the narrative is constructed. This tentative acceptance of coherence opens the listener up to the inherent narrative logic and can enable a persuasive exchange of meaning and experience (cf.Braid 1996b). Where narratives deal with aspects of worldview and belief through, for example, narrating the words and actions of individuals, these narratives can be used persuasively to negotiate the validity of the narrator's worldview and identity.

Narrative negotiations of identity

I use the term negotiation in describing the dynamic relationship between narrative and identity because I mean to suggest that narrative performances, as situated communicative acts, are part of ongoing exchanges between participants. While many of the narrative analyses I present in this study explore how individual narrative performances reflect or embody expressions of identity, it is important to recognise these narrations may be part of long-term negotiations. Many of the narratives I present in this work are stripped of ongoing discourse exchanges that extend well beyond the specific performance event in which they were narrated. For example, my interactions with the narrators extend over many years. A specific narrative performance may therefore be a move in an ongoing dialogue that builds on previous exchanges and understandings as much as on the dynamics of the current performance event.

A second way in which narrative performances can be considered to be negotiations of identity builds on the fact that narratives are doubly grounded in human events, in the narrative event and narrated event (Bauman 1986:2). A performer can narrate events that are themselves negotiations of identity. Alternately the performer can transform narrated events into negotiations of identity by metanarratively focusing on issues of identity that are expressed in these events.

Narrative performances can also function as negotiations of identity since they can keep working long after the face-to-face interaction has ended. They can persist in memory as entextualised wholes that are carried away from the performance interaction and can be thought with and thought through in attempts to understand the world. As I write now, for example, I reflect upon the stories I was told during fieldwork encounters. These stories retain their persuasiveness as I try to understand Traveller life experience, worldview and identity.

While all Traveller narratives might embody facets of their identity, one genre of Traveller narratives is particularly effective in communicating issues of identity and worldview. I term these narratives interaction narratives because they narrate interactions between Travellers and non-Travellers. By focusing on observable actions in the real world, these narratives negotiate identity in pragmatic terms, as it is actually expressed through the actions of individuals, not as it is conceived in some abstract or ideal world. This anchor in the real world additionally suggests these narrative representations of identity have some objective validity.

When interaction narratives are performed in events with non-Traveller participants, both the dynamics of the narrative event and the narrative content become particularly relevant to understanding cross-cultural negotiations of identity. In these events, issues of cultural identity are frequently foregrounded. During my field interviews, for example,

I asked questions about Traveller life and Traveller interactions with the settled folk. Many of these questions were answered through the use of narratives. I suggest these narratives must be interpreted as embodying communications about identity as part of a dialogue between Traveller and non-Traveller researcher. Similarly, public performances put a performer on display and highlight the performers unique repertoire and identity. These events can therefore provide opportunities for identity to be strategically packaged and presented to outsiders.

Performance of interaction narratives allows Travellers the opportunity to creatively construct and communicate their own images of identity. Because of the agency of the narrator and the creativity involved in the selection and presentation of what happened in the narrated event, the incidents narrated in these stories are marked as significant since they have been selected and narrativised for performance by the Travellers themselves. How these events are portrayed and the stylistics of performance can therefore give insight into how Travellers creatively interpret and traditionalise events in the world through their narrative artistry. These performances may embody diverse communicative strategies that present Traveller identity and argue for its validity or which contrast Traveller and settled identities. These strategies may parallel strategies used among groups of Travellers or they may take advantage of differences in order to communicate effectively.

I have identified five strategies Travellers use in negotiating issues of cultural identity by selecting and performing interaction narratives during events when non-Travellers are present:

1 the use of narrative to report actions or speech that indexes key facets of identity
2 the recontextualisation of narratives as a focus for evaluations and interpretations of identity in the narrative event
3 the use of narrative to report evaluations of identity from participants in the narrated event
4 the use of fictional narrative to suggest conceptions of identity as listeners follow the interactions of fictional characters and
5 the use of metaphor in fictional narrative as a commentary on differential identity.

These strategies are often combined in any given performance.

I have explored all these possibilities in detail elsewhere (Braid 1995, 1996a). Here I present several representative examples of how narrative performances can be used to negotiate issues of identity. I recorded the experience narratives during interviews or conversations that focused on Traveller life and experience. "The Fox and the Dog" was recorded during a public performance. Since my focus in this paper is on exploring how identity is negotiated through interaction narratives I have made no attempt to fully explore other aspects of function and meaning in my analyses. I end the chapter with some thoughts on how narrative negotiations of identity can transcend face-to face interactions. In particular I will comment on the effect of media presentations of Traveller narrative.

Reported speech and action

One key to the potency of experience narratives in constructing and negotiating identity comes from the ability of narrative performance to re-create events or interactions for those present during the performance event. Narrative re-creations can function to expand the boundaries of the performance interaction and therefore the data that are available within these interactions for individuals to use in constructing their senses of worldview and identity (cf.Braid 1996a). In cross-cultural interactions this ability of narrative becomes particularly important for it allows a narrator to present events and experiences the non-Traveller may never experience in any other way (cf. Braid 1996b). This allows non-Travellers insight into how and why Travellers view the world the way they do.

The simplest form of this re-creation might be seen in terms of brief narratives that relate reported speech or reported actions. I recorded a large number of these narratives in response to my questions about relations between Travellers and non-Travellers. For example, I recorded the following narrative from Betty Townsley during an interview session with Betty, Dr. Thomas Burton, Susan Grizzell and myself. Our conversation was generally about Traveller life and occupation. I asked a question about Travellers moving in groups for safety in response to harassment from non-Travellers. Betty commented: "So if you've got safety in numbers it's okay. You live with it. You've got to live with this sort of fear as well. You – there's a fear there as well." The following exchange came shortly after Betty's comment:

DB Do you get a lot of problems with that when you go door-to-door selling things?
     That people are very upset with you?
BT Mhmm.
TB Have you had any bad experiences yourself?
BT Mhmm.
     One woman chased me down the driveway with a knife.
     [laughs]
     (All the way?)
     I went up and she says,
     "I'm sick fed up with people coming to my door,
     I'm fed up with tarmackers.
     I'm fed up."
     I said,
     "I only come to ask you the time," You know?
     I wasn't really.
     I was going to sell her some peat.
     I said,
     "All I want to do is ask you the time."
     Well down the road –
     She had this big knife
     and she's chasing me down the drive.

(TS92025)

I can imagine this story being told among Travellers as a warning about how crazy the settled folk can be. In the interview context, however,

Betty's re-creation serves as graphic evidence of who the settled folk are and the irrationality of their response to Travellers. Thomas Burton's question prompts Betty to shift from talking abstractly about the kinds of harassment Travellers might endure to talking concretely about an interaction that she did endure. Betty does not just tell us she feels uneasy around settled people. She shows us why she feels it. Her narrative re-creates the interaction in a way that all present in the performance event can formulate their own understanding of what happened and why.

In understanding how this narrative works to communicate Traveller identity it is important to consider the experience of following the narrative performance. By following Betty's performance I can experience what it must be like to be suddenly chased down the drive with a knife while knowing I need to keep ringing doorbells to survive economically. By putting myself in Betty's position, I can therefore gain insight into the ongoing sense of hostility Travellers have to deal with throughout their lives.

In this example and in others, tellers use narrative to show events, actions or words from the past. These events are strategically selected as examples that speak for themselves. The narratives focus on non-Travellers and their actions. In this sense, they are not so much presentations of Traveller identity as presentations of the context within which Traveller identity is formed and maintained. This is an important foundation for understanding Traveller identity. If outsiders can understand the fears and prejudices that permeate Traveller interactions with non-Travellers, they can better understand how Travellers understand and respond to the world.

A complementary group of narratives presents an image of Traveller identity through the narration of their words and actions. Like the fictional narratives I discuss below, these narratives provide an overt characterisation of Traveller identity (for an example see Bauman and Braid, in press).

Evaluations of narrated action
In other performances, my Traveller consultants used narratives not only to re-create events but also to provide a context for their interpretations and evaluations of identity. Through narrative performance, narrators effectively recentered past interactions within the narrative event as a common focus for exploring the contrasts between Traveller and non-Traveller identities.

I recorded the following narrative, for example, during an interview with Betty Townsley. Worried by a recent government proposal to change the Caravan Sites Act of 1965 (Department of the Environment 1992), Betty, Susan Grizzell and I were talking about problems that derive from government policies about Traveller camping. Betty commented on some problems of government Traveller sites and some of the successful struggles Travellers have undertaken to establish sites. We discussed the ongoing harassment of Travellers despite the non-harassment policy that is in force in many parts of Scotland (cf.Secretary of State's Advisory Committee 1982, 18-19). During this discussion, Betty narrated a number of brief examples of harassment. Then, following a comment by Susan about the stereotype that all Travellers and Gypsies are thieves, Betty commented that she has to keep receipts for everything she owns so that the police will not confiscate her possessions under suspicion of theft. She then narrated the following experience:

Well I mind that we were,
they nearly took our trailer from us
More or less about,
maybe about two year ago.

5   They come in a landrover
and about – ten – detectives.
Just because one man on the motorway passed by
and thought it was his.
    Thought it was his.
10   It looked like his.

Now, how many cars look alike?
You can't just go and point,
    "that, thats my trailer,
        that's it.
15   I want it." [DB – yeah]

Now this trailer was only, what,
months old.
And he come down with this big landrover
and just reversed it in./

20   And Willie said, "What are you doing?"
He said, "We got a report that this trailer is stolen."
And he said, "What proof have you got?" /
He said, "Well we've got some numbers here." /
"Well", Willie said, "There's my number there."
25   He said, "Check it."

Right.
One letter was the same.
One!   [DB laughs]
    It was a eight,
30   I remember eight was the same.
        One eight.

Right.
He says, "Well, eh" –
Now this young boy he was really cheeky –
35   "I think we should take it away
to go through it proper."

And (?) the one who was above him said, "No."
"No," he says,
"Its okay," he says.

40   And then the boy, it was supposed to be his trailer that was stolen,

he says, "Well,"
"I've got reflectors." /
You know how you've got orange reflectors along the big sides?
He said, "the middle one,"
45 he said, "I had a hole in it."
He said, "And I filled it with paste,"
he said, "And put the reflector on it."

"Oh that's okay," the policeman said,
"Okay."
50 RRRIP.
Ripped it off.
Broke it off.

There was nothing behind it because it was new.

And he said, "I don't think it was that one, I think it was that one."
55 So he ripped that one off.

And were standing [laughs]
and (he?) said, "Just tear it in." /
I'm watching this.

So I went down to the phone,
60 and I phoned a lawyer.
because we've got a lawyer (?).

And they followed me to the phone.
Knocked on the [Betty knocks on the table] phone
and I pulled the door open.
65 "You don't have to phone your lawyer.
We decided we are not going to do it.
We'll come back in the morning.
We won't take it away."
Followed me to the phone. [laughs]

70 Hmm?

That was horrible that.

(TS92031)

Betty's performance brings her example into the narrative event and anchors it with respect to our emerging understanding of Traveller identity and the Traveller problem in Scotland. Through her narration Betty tells us what happened and lets us understand what it is like to experience an event like this. But in this narration Betty actively evaluates what happened from a Traveller perspective through how she tells the story (cf. Labov 1972). Through metanarrative commentary and other formal features of her performance, Betty suggests an interpretive framework that highlights the assumptions that underlie the police action. This, in turn, implicates aspects of settled worldview that inform these assumptions.

In lines 7-8, Betty suggests the whole event is motivated by one man's conclusion that Betty and her husband must be in possession of his stolen trailer because he thought it was his. Betty emphasises the absurdity of this conclusion through her repetition "Thought it was his. / It looked like his" in lines 9-10, her metanarrative question "How many cars look alike?" in line 11, and her re-enactment of frivolous claims of ownership in lines 12-15. Yet the flimsiest suggestion of theft is apparently believed by the police who arrive with no fewer than ten detectives ready to haul the trailer away without any further evidence. Even the fact that only one number of the serial number matches the stolen trailer – a point Betty again emphasises through repetition in lines 27-31 – is not sufficient to awaken the authorities to the thought they may have made a mistake. One supervisor notes they might have made a mistake in lines 37-39, but the detectives continue to assume that the trailer must be stolen and rip parts off the trailer to prove the theft. Implicit in the police actions is an exoteric conception of Traveller identity in which the police are so sure that all Travellers are liars and thieves that contradictory evidence does not register opposition to this assumption. They have trusted the word of a non-Traveller as to theft but entirely ignore the Traveller's (assumed) comments that the trailer in fact belongs to them. Implicit in the police actions is the belief that all Travellers are lazy and never work. All money or expensive possessions must therefore be the product of theft. I should note that many Traveller trailers I have seen are quite elaborate, spotlessly clean and surely expensive. This fact probably plays into the police assumption that no Traveller could legitimately afford such an expensive trailer.

In contrast to the actions of the police, Betty portrays the Travellers as incredulous but sane participants in the event. Upon being told that the police suspect their trailer is stolen, Betty's husband sensibly proposes they check the serial number before hauling it away (lines 20-25). It does not come close to a match since the trailer is not stolen. When parts of their nearly new trailer are ripped off to prove the theft, Betty and her husband do not go wild but stand and watch in civilised horror (cf. lines 56-58). Where any other citizen might call the police to prevent these outrageous acts, Betty cannot, since it is the police themselves who are doing the acts. Instead, Betty goes to the phone to call her lawyer. This act awakens the detectives to the fact that they are not dealing with what they have assumed is an unintelligent, passive thief. Betty is well aware of the law and her rights under the law. Perhaps the courts will even overlook any prejudice against Travellers and understand the absurdity of the police actions. It is not the rights of the Travellers that force the detectives to back-off, but the police fear of the potential consequences of legal action.

Because of her creative selection and presentation of this narrative, Betty's performance functions as a unit of ideological negotiation within the performance event. It brings a real event into the focus of our discussion of Traveller harassment by police. Her narrative is also a move in an ongoing dialogue that focuses on Traveller identity in relation to the identity of the settled folk around her. Through following Betty's narrative performance, Susan, and I gain insight into Traveller and settled worldviews and identities. While Betty's evaluative comments certainly influence how we comprehend the event, it is difficult to imagine how this event might be narrated differently in order to validate the police actions in the interaction. It is, in fact, doubtful that any non-Traveller present at the interaction would choose to narrate this event.

The effective use of narrative as a focus for evaluations of identity requires careful selection of the event to be narrated. If the narrated event invokes symbols that play meaningful roles in non-Traveller worldview, the reinterpretation of these symbols in the presentation and evaluation of Traveller identity can enhance the potency of the narrative negotiation by suggesting a parallel depth of meaning in Traveller lives. Betty's narrative, for example, invokes symbolic associations with truth, justice and home. The contextualisation of these symbols from a Traveller perspective forces a re-evaluation of both the meaning of these symbols and Traveller identity.

Reported evaluations of identity

The stories I have analysed above negotiate aspects of identity through the presentation and interpretation of events in which actions index underlying worldviews and identities. This is only one possible strategy for negotiating issues of identity in narrative performance. Another strategy involves the presentation of narrated events in which non-Travellers themselves evaluate the identity of the Traveller participants in the event.

This approach to negotiating identity is exemplified in a narrative I recorded from Bryce Whyte during an interview on 25 October 1992. Also present during this recording were Susan Grizzell and Dr. Thomas Burton. During a conversation that focused on Bryce's memories of Traveller life on the road, he talked about the Travellers' need for independence and contrasted this with the experience some Travellers had in the British army during World War II. He then narrated an incident that took place during his own training in the army. The narrative is too long to print here in its entirety and so I have summarised all but two brief segments of the narrative – the parts most relevant to this example. A full transcription of this narrative can be found in Braid (1996a, 227-33).

[Bryce described how he was included in a group that was marched up onto a bleak hillside for a survival training exercise. It was a very cold and windy day with intermittent snow showers. The commanding officer, a captain who had served in the 1914 war, instructed the men that they were to take rations, make a fire and cook their own supper. The captain was to sample the food before they could eat. Bryce teamed up with Hughie, another Traveller, and they worked together, making a small Traveller-style tent out of their groundcloths and some branches. Inside this tent they built a fire to cook their stew. Bryce commented about the other soldiers, who were running around looking for stones to build a fireplace.]

I says, "Poor buggers." [laughs]
I says, "They'll never make it."
I says, "They'll never make it."
I said, "They'll have tae want meat the day."

[When Bryce and Hughie finished cooking they called over the captain. He was startled they had finished so quickly, but was impressed by their ingenuity and the good taste of the food. Bryce and Hughie commiserated with the captain about how incompetently the rest of the soldiers

approached the exercise. The captain states that he would like all of his
men to be like Bryce and Hughie.

When they returned to the base, the captain calls Bryce and Hughie
into his office.]

> We went intae the office
> and he says tae,
> says eh,
> "Youse two", he says, "that eh," he says, "that was a lovely grub,"
> he says, "youse made," he says.
> He says, "Youse has done that," he says, "quite a few times." /I
> says, "Well" – / He says, "Are you Travellers?"
> He says, (are you?)
> "What we call tinkers," he said.
> I says, "Yes sir, and proud o' it."
> He says, "And so am I."
> He said, "I wish to hell," he says, "all my company was tinkers,"
> he says.
> He says, "I remember," he says, "in the 1914 war,"
> he says, "I had three or four of them in my company,"
> and he says, "They were just like youse."
> He said, "All the rest o them (you see?) were starvin," he says,
> "And they survived."
> Says, "They survived."
> So.
> That was a good thing for us.

> (TS92030)

Bryce's story is crafted as a statement about Traveller identity but the
evaluation of identity in this story does not come from a Traveller. It is
reported from someone a non-Traveller would consider a respected member
of society, an army captain. Bryce's narration also re-creates the event that
provides the captain's motivation for making his evaluation. The captain is
responsible for training soldiers to fight to defend the freedom of all British
citizens. He fought in the 1914 war and knows what it will take to survive
and successfully defend the country. The captain's evaluations of Traveller
identity and skills are therefore made by a competent judge. These
evaluations are also made with reference to abilities that profoundly affect
all who are touched by World War II. By selecting and contextualising his
experience as he does, Bryce draws on our knowledge and experience to
interpret the narrated event for ourselves. But he also reports the captain's
words thereby suggesting that, in following the actions of the narrated
event, we should reach the same conclusions as does the captain.

Fictional portrayals of interaction
From a performance-oriented perspective, any narration necessarily
implies choices must be made concerning how the story is to be narrated.
Narrators are creative agents in choosing the words, timing, intonation,
emphasis and so on, as they recontextualise their narrative within the
performance event. Unless a story is memorised and I have seen no
evidence of this among the Travelling People, the text of a narrative will be

emergent in performance. When narratives are performed as negotiations of identity in interactions with non-Travellers, this freedom in how a narrative is performed becomes a resource that can be mobilised to enhance the efficacy of the negotiation. While this freedom can be effective in the performance of experience narratives, it reaches its full potential in the performance of fictional narratives. Within any constraints of the plot of a traditional narrative the narrator has full licence to create character, personality, words and actions as needed to negotiate issues of Traveller and non-Traveller identity.

Presentational freedom of expression can result in an overt statement of identity by, for example, casting a Traveller in the role of a wise character in a traditional narrative. As the narrative hero demonstrates his or her wit and wisdom with respect to some non-Traveller, a suggestion is made concerning Traveller identity in the real world.

Another strategy for negotiating identity in narrative makes use of metaphor to present interactions that comment on facets of differential identity. As an example of this strategy I present a narrative that relates a fictional encounter between a fox and a dog. This story is a version of Aarne and Thompson Type 112, "Country Mouse Visits Town Mouse" (Aarne and Thompson 1961:45). A version of this story can be found in many collections of Aesop's Fables (e.g. Handford 1954:43; Grossett and Dunlap 1947:22-4). Here I transcribe a performance by Duncan Williamson that was recorded at the National Storytelling Festival in Jonesborough, Tennessee, on 9 October 1987. At this time Duncan was in America as part of a brief storytelling tour I arranged for him. The audience were primarily adults who knew little about Traveller culture, a piece of data that will become relevant in my analysis that follows the transcription.

The Fox and the Dog

And this story
is about a little fox too.

For he had been hunted for many days
with the gamekeeper and the farmers.
5   For he had stole a chicken the day before from a farm.

And he lay there in his den in the rocks
and the sun was shining
it was very very warm.
And for two days he lay there
10   afraid and terrified to come out from his den.
And the heat was terrible inside these rocks.

And he said to himself,
You know,
I must find something to eat
15   or something to drink
         or I'm going to die.
I've only got two choices
       stay here and die

or go out and be shot. [laughter]

20 So finally,
    he crawled from his den hungry and thirsty.
    But there was no one around.
    And he travelled across the moors.
    All the streams had dried up
25   with the sun.
    He couldn't find himself a dead bird
        or a rabbit
           or nothing to eat.

    But he looked down there in the valley and he saw the farm.
30 He said, I would love to go down there, he said.
    But, if I do they might catch me this time.

    But, he said, I've an old friend down there
    whom I haven't saw for many years.
    The old dog.
35 And he lies there behind the farm.
    And he might have something in his dish
    that he could spare for me.

    So he crawled down
    the best way he could.
40 Trying to conceal himself among the bushes
    and finally he came behind the farm.
    There was nobody around.

    There lay the old dog
      with his paws crossed.
45   Asleep in his barrel
           among the straw.
    Before him stood a large dish, of beautiful food.
    Scraps and bones and milk
    everything that was needed.

50 The fox crawled up and he said, "Cousin Dog?"
    Are you awake?
    The old dog got up
      and he opened his eyes
        and gave himself a stretch.
55 And he says, "Of course it's your old sel ol Mister Foxy.
    What are you doing here?"
    He said, "I'm hungry."
    He said, "You know what happens if the farmer finds you here?"

    He said, "You'll be shot."
60 "Well," he says, "It's either be shot or die with the hunger."

    He says, "What do you want from me?"

He said,
"Whed something from that dish."
The old dog says, "Help yourself
65   take the lot
        I'm not hungry," he said.

So quickly the old fox, Foxy he gobbled up everything
   licked his lips
      and said,
70   "Doggy," he said, "I really enjoyed that."

And the dog said, "Foxy," he said, "Look,
you'll have to change your ways." [laughter]
He said, "You can't go around stealing from people," he said,
"And expecting to survive the way you do." [laughter]
75   He said, "Why don't you get a job for yourself?" [loud laughter]

He said, "A job?"
"Yeah," he says, "Like me.
Be a guard dog." [laughter]
He said, "Cousin who would take a fox for a guard dog?" [laughter]
80   He said, "Have you ever tried?" [laughter]
"No," said old Foxy, "I never had the chance to try."

"Well anyhow," he says, "Look what I've got, here."
Foxy says, "What have you got?"
He said, "I've got my barrel
85   and my straw.
And," he said, "I lie here
all day in the sun.'

Foxy said, "That sounds good. [laughter]
But," he said, "What else have you got?"

90   "Well," he said, "I have my chain,
   my collar."
Foxy said, "What did you say?" [laughter]
He said, "My chain and my collar of course."
Foxy said, "What do you need a chain and a collar for?"
90   He said, "To tie me up."
Foxy says, "You mean to tell me that you get tied up all ti all day
long?"
"Well," he says, "Sometimes my master lets me loose –
but not very often."

"Ah well," old Foxy said,
100 "Look," he said,
"It wouldn't be for me."
Said, "You keep your barrel,
  and keep your straw.
      And keep your dish.

105 And," he says, "I'll go on my way."
    He said, "I might be hungry
    but I'll be free."
    He said, "Freedom and hunger for me."
    And then the old fox was gone.

110 The old dog lived for a long long time on that farm.
    But he never saw his old cousin Foxy again.
    [applause]

                           (TS87008)

At the surface this narrative performance appears fairly straight-forward. The narrative event is clearly identifiable with the performance on the stage of the storytelling festival. The narrated event is an encounter between a fox and a farm dog that is projected into the past. The audience presumably follows this projection and hears the action as if it was a real event that took place at some point in the past. The use of reported speech in, for example, lines 13-19 and 30-37, strengthens the suggestion that Duncan is narrating a past event. These lines are clearly framed as what was said in the narrated event. They reproduce the prosody and paralingual features of the narrated event in the moment of performance. John McDowell (1982:128-9) argues that these moments of reported speech can function as cases of marked ostension which give the illusion of collapsing the boundaries between the time of narrative event and the time of the narrated event in a making present that allows the listener the illusion of a more direct experience the events being narrated.

Within Traveller culture this internationally known folktale has been transformed into a metaphorical commentary on Traveller-settled relations. Duncan first heard the story from his father (SA76.108). He has told this story many times to his own children, two of whom, now in their forties, remembered hearing this story as youngsters and associating their identity as Travellers with that of the fox in the story (TS93017, TS93025). On several occasions Duncan has commented that this story is a real Traveller story (e.g. Fieldnotes 9/20/94; TS92034). When I asked him during an interview why this was a Traveller story he responded:

"Because it is the idea of someone wanting to be free. I mean the Travellers don't have a 9-5 job like the dog. The dog had a 9-5 job in that barrel. And he was a guard dog in the barrel. . . . The Travellers regard themselves as the fox. You see what I mean? The Dog is a non-Traveller. See what I mean? ... The Travellers prefer freedom than have a 9-5 job. They would rather go hungry than have a job that tied them down where they couldn't wander and see what they wanted to see. And this was their idea. You see? That's why they compared themselves to the fox. The idea of the fox played an important part in Travellers lives because the fox wanted to be free. He would suffer, be hungry, be wet, be cold, but he would be free. No one would tell him what to do. You see what I mean? He was a free spirit. The dog was tied up wi' a chain and a barrel. He was a dog right enough. And he done his job and he had his food and he had his warm bed. But what in the hell else did he have? NOTHING! Do you see what I mean? So that's why its called, classed as a Traveller story."

(TS92038)

Direct parallels to this attitude can be found in the ways that other Travellers value their time. This is expressed, for example, by Betsy Whyte in her autobiography when she refers to the departure of another family from a communal camping site: like all Travelling people they just had to keep moving. It is only with this sense of freedom that they can get any joy out of living and they are willing to bear discomfort, even hardships, to keep that freedom" (Whyte 1990:183).

During another interview Duncan commented the fox is, in fact, an common metaphorical substitute for Travellers. He said that the character of the fox was like a Jack among the animals (TS92034). Jack is a common folktale hero in Traveller stories. Duncan commented that fathers were telling ... Jack stories to their sons because, in a way, they would probably want their sons to grow up like Jack (TS92034). He noted that animal tales, including those involving foxes, are similarly teaching stories. The metaphorical connection between Traveller and fox works because of parallels in the lives of foxes and Travellers. Still later in the same interview, Duncan commented:

"The only animal I am really sorry for is the fox. Among all the animals that is protected, the fox is the one that is hunted for no reason at all. What does he do? He only hunts for a little to eat. And once he has his belly full he will go off and sleep."

(TS92034)

These observations parallel Traveller feelings that they are similarly persecuted for no reason at all. They also parallel Traveller beliefs that a poached salmon or a few stolen potatoes from a farmers field are not really theft but justified acts since they are based on the need to survive and not on greed.

For non-Traveller audience members these deep cultural associations with foxes do not exist as a key to story meaning. But I suggest the metaphorical framing of the narrated event is still supported by the content and formal features Duncan uses to develop this dialogue. In addition to adding an ostensive experience of the narrated event, Duncan's use of reported speech presents some interpretational problems. Foxes and dogs do not normally talk. The content of their talk does not seem very fox-like or very dog-like. This becomes most evident beginning at line 71 where the conversation turns to issues of jobs, lifestyles and their relative benefits. These interpretational problems hint at a narrative meaning that transcends reporting an amusing conversation between a fox and a dog. The ambiguity in referencing that is inherent in reported speech provides the possibility that the present tense narrative dialogue is anchored in the narrative event where a Traveller performer is speaking to an audience of non-Travellers. If these words belong to Duncan himself then the expressions of identity in the narrative are representative of some more general expression of Traveller identity. This suggests a parallel framing to that of fictional encounter, one in which the narrative dialogue should be interpreted metaphorically as part of an ongoing dialogue that comments on the differential identity between Travellers and non-Travellers. In this interpretational frame the fox represents Travellers and the dog represents non-Travellers in a prototypical encounter between Traveller and non-Traveller identities.

There are therefore two parallel interpretive frameworks generated in this narrative. One in which the time of narrative sequence references fictional past events and another that references the ongoing within-timeness of Traveller life. The two frames are linked by metaphor and these links are keyed by the symbolic associations of the fox and by the ambiguities of reported speech. Within each of these frames there is an implicit contrast between the stable but constrained lifestyle of the dog, his gainful employment, his food dish and his collar and the uncertain but free lifestyle of the fox. The ambiguity and indirectness of metaphorical referencing allows these contrasts in identity to be developed with some independence from the associations and stereotypes the listeners may have about Travellers. The metaphorical link between the two frames also enhances the richness of the negotiation of identity. For example, there is an equation between the traditional cleverness of the fox, as conveyed in many other stories and in direct observation, with the creative abilities of the Traveller to exploit the system without being dominated by it. This metaphorical connection also suggests that Traveller identity and world-view are just as logically sound as the identity of the fox that is shown in the fictional narrated event to be in agreement with nature or the natural way of things.

The use of fictional narrative has expanded the resources available for the negotiation of identity. Through narrative re-creations, fictional characters that metaphorically stand for representatives of different cultural groups become participants in the encounter. In following the narrative, listeners interact with these characters and extract experiential meanings from their interactions. In this way performers and listeners can form and negotiate issues of identity with respect to these fictional events and characters. The fox may confirm deeply held values for a Traveller listener. For a non-Traveller listener the same narrative may introduce a suggestion that Travellers are not so crazy after all.

Negotiating identity beyond the interaction order
Throughout this work I have focused on the perception and negotiation of identity through narratives told in face-to-face interactions in what Erving Goffman has termed the interaction order (Goffman 1983). But the influence of narrative performances in negotiating identity can transcend the performance event. This is true in the sense that following a narrative performance can generate experiential resources for listeners that can be thought with and thought through in listeners' struggles to understand the world (Braid 1996b). When I contemplate questions of Traveller identity, for example, I recall these narrative performances. They are resources that exemplify how Traveller identity is played out through interaction. They provide me with valuable and dynamic references for my own constructions of Traveller identity. In effect, they have been incorporated into my own sense of worldview as it relates to the Travelling People.

The modern world provides other channels through which narratives of interactions between Travellers and non-Travellers can transcend face-to-face situations. This involves mediated communications through radio, television, film and print media. Whether news stories that focus on problems of illegal camping or fictional stories that involve some Traveller characters, most of the narratives about Travellers told through these media are the constructions of non-Travellers. These stories tend to derive from non-Traveller beliefs and therefore to perpetuate non-Traveller conceptions of Traveller identity. Several of my Traveller consultants commented on the inaccuracy of the portrayals of Travellers in the media. Willie MacPhee complained during one interview with me that the BBC interviewed him for over an hour and that he "tellt them a lot of things about the Travellers". In the broadcast they only used three or four words out of all he said. Willie commented: "I was actually telling them the truth. But they werna broadcasting the truth." (TS92023) Edie MacPhee and Tracy Donaldson commented that the portrayals of Travellers they had seen on television were "always inaccurate" (TS93025). Two studies of the depiction of Gypsies and Travellers in children's literature tend to confirm this continuity in use of stereotyped images of the Travellers (Binns 1984, Kenrick 1984). Beyond these studies little research has been undertaken to establish the content or effects of these non-Traveller constructions of Traveller identity.

There are occasions when Travellers get to tell their own stories through the media. A number of documentary films and videotapes have been made and broadcast, although these tend to be conceived and edited by non-Travellers. Radio and television interviews have provided some opportunities for Traveller commentary and the performance of ballads and stories. Published books and articles of Traveller storytelling provide another communicative medium (cf. Robertson 1988, 1989; Williamson 1985, 1992; Douglas 1987). These mediated narratives reach a wide audience and move negotiations of identity from face-to-face encounters to a larger political arena.

It is my belief, though, that mediated communications dilute the efficacy of narrative negotiations of identity. I suggest this dilution arises from a lack of involvement or engagement with the act of performance. For both performer and listener the interaction is indirect. There is little or no audience feedback. The performer cannot contextualise his or her performance for an unknown audience. The audience has a restricted channel of information that may not extend beyond the verbal text of a narrative as in the case of a narrative printed in a book. Yet some Travellers I interviewed suggested mediated communications about Travellers might have a positive effect by exposing non-Travellers to aspects of Traveller culture and belief. Willie MacPhee, for example, said that television programmes such as Peggy Seeger and Ewan MacColl's 1982 broadcast *Go! Move! Shift!* might have a positive effect on non-Travellers by telling part of the truth of what has happened (TS92023). Others commented that the compromises made by performers in addressing the media and the non-Traveller world in general, dissociated any potential benefits of mediated communications about identity from the reality of Traveller life on the road.

Understanding differences in how face-to-face and mediated narrative performances function to negotiate identity and assessing the possible effects of these performances, requires extensive field research that lies well beyond the focus of the present work. I do hope that my models as to how experiential and fictional narratives can function in face-to-face interactions might be of some use in addressing questions of mediated communication.

Note on transcriptions
The notational system I have used in the transcriptions has been developed to reveal specific features of the form and style of performance. I have broken the narratives into lines that are based partly on the pauses in delivery (cf.Tedlock 1972) and partly on syntactical structures (cf.B. Hymes 1981, 30941; V. Hymes 1987). Specific choices in preparing the transcriptions have been made with the goal of revealing formal patterning of the narratives while preserving a sense of the rhythms of oral performance. Transcriptions have been broken into syntactical units that are marked by blank lines. Sequences of narration that build on a single idea have been transcribed as a series of lines with increasing left indentation. I have used the symbol / to indicate brief hesitations in delivery that mark, for example, change of character but which do not interrupt the flow of delivery.

Words enclosed in parenthesis with a question mark (xxx?) represent my best guess at transcribing words or passages I found difficult to hear. In some cases where I cannot even guess what was spoken I have marked missing utterances with (?).

Comments in square brackets [ ] are my comments about non-verbal aspects of the performance. This might include comments on audience response, gestures of the narrator or my comments intended to clarify the narrative. They were not spoken by the narrator.

References
AARNE A and THOMPSON S 1961 *The Types of the Folktale; A Classification and Bibliography* Folklore Fellows Communications No 184, Helsinki

ACTON Thomas 1993 unpublished draft report to UNISAT/Etudes Tsiganes Research Project on *Gypsies and Travellers: What Future in the Europe of 1993,* partially published as "Les definitions legales du Tsigane au Royaume-Uni" in A Reyniers 1993 "Tsiganes dEurope: circulation et enracinement" *Études Tsiganes* 39:1 pp.23-26

AESOP see Handford S

BASSO Keith H 1979 *Portraits of "The Whiteman": Linguistic Play and Cultural Symbols among the Western Apache* Cambridge University Press, Cambridge

BAUMAN Richard 1972 "Differential Identity and the Social Base of Folklore" in Paredes Américo and Bauman Richard eds. *Toward New Perspectives in Folklore 3* University of Texas Press, Austin, pp.1-41

BAUMAN Richard 1977 *Verbal Art as Performance* Newbury House, Rowley, Massachusetts

BAUMAN Richard 1986 *Story, Performance and Event* Cambridge University Press, New York

BAUMAN Richard. 1989 "American Folklore Studies and Social Transformation: A Performance Centered Perspective" *Text and Performance Quarterly* 9 pp.175-184

BAUMAN Richard and BRAID Donald in press "The Ethnography of Performance in the Study of Oral Traditions" in Foley John Miles ed: *Teaching Oral Traditions* Modern Language Association, New York

BAUMAN Richard and BRIGGS Charles L 1990 "Poetics and Performance as Critical Perspectives on Language and Social Life" *Annual Review of Anthropology* 19 pp.59-88

BEN-AMOS Dan 1984 "The Seven Strands of Tradition: Varieties in Its Meaning in American Folklore Studies" *Journal of Folklore Research* 21 pp.97-131

BINNS Dennis 1984 *Children's Literature and the Role of the Gypsy*: Manchester Travellers' School, Manchester

BOAS Franz 1940 *Race, Language, and Culture* University of Chicago Press, reprint 1988 Midway, Chicago

BRAID Donald 1993 "The Traveller and the Hare: Meaning, Function and Form in the Recontextualization of Narrative" *Folklore Forum* 26,2

BRAID Donald 1995 "The Negotiation of Cultural Identity Through Narrative: The Travelling People of Scotland" in Joachim Knuf ed. *Texts and Identities: Proceedings of the Third Kentucky Conference on Narrative* 87-99 Narrative Studies Group, Lexington, Kentucky

BRAID Donald 1996a "The Negotiation of Meaning and Identity in the Narratives of the Travelling People of Scotland" PhD diss. Indiana University

BRAID Donald 1996b "Personal Narrative and Experiential Meaning" *Journal of American Folklore* 109

BURKE Kenneth 1941 "Literature as Equipment for Living" in Burke K *The Philosophy of Literary Form* Louisiana State University Press, Baton Rouge, pp.293-304

BURKE Kenneth 1969 *A Rhetoric of Motives* University of California Press, Berkeley

CHAFE Wallace and TANNEN Deborah 1987 "The Relation Between Written and Spoken Language" *Annual Review of Anthropology* 16 pp.383-407

CLEMENTS Luke 1994 "Gypsies Face a New Age" *The Times* January 11

DEPARTMENT OF THE ENVIRONMENT 1992 *Consultation Document on Gypsy Sites Policy and Illegal Camping: Reform of the Caravan Sites Act 1968* Department of the Environment, London

DEPARTMENTAL COMMITTEE ON TINKERS IN SCOTLAND 1918 *Report of the Departmental Committee on Tinkers in Scotland* HMSO, Edinburgh

DOUGLAS Sheila 1987 *The King O The Black Art: And Other Folk Tales* Aberdeen University Press, Aberdeen

DUNDES Alan 1983 "Defining Identity Through Folklore" in Jacobson-Widding Anita ed. *Identity: Personal and Socio-Cultural: A Symposium, Uppsala 1983* Humanities Press,Atlantic Highlands, New Jersey, pp.235-61

ERIKSON Erik H 1968 *Identity: Youth and Crisis* Norton, New York

FABIAN Johannes 1983 *Time and the Other: How Anthropology Makes its Object* Columbia University Press, New York

FINE Elizabeth 1984 *The Folklore Text: From Performance to Print* Indiana University Press, Bloomington

GEERTZ Clifford 1973 *The Interpretation of Cultures* Basic Books, New York

GENTLEMAN Hugh 1993 *Counting Travellers in Scotland: The 1992 Picture: Estimates of the number, distribution and characteristics of Travelling People in Scotland in 1992 based on a count undertaken for the Scottish Office* The Scottish Office Central Research Unit, Edinburgh

GENTLEMAN Hugh and SWIFT Susan 1971 *Scotland's Travelling People: Problems and Solutions* HMSO, Edinburgh

GOFFMAN Erving 1983 "The Interaction Order" *American Sociological Review* 48 p.117

GRANT William and MURRISON David D eds 1974 *The Scottish National Dictionary* The Scottish National Dictionary Association, Edinburgh

HANDFORD S A trans. 1954 *Fables of Aesop* Penguin Books, Baltimore

HENDERSON Hamish 1992 *Alias MacAlias: Writings on Songs, Folk and Literature* Polygon, Edinburgh

HILL Jane H and MANNHEIM Bruce 1992 "Language and Worldview" *Annual Review of Anthropology* 21 pp.381-406

HYMES Dell 1975a "Folklore's Nature and the Sun's Myth" *Journal of American Folklore* 88 pp.345-369

HYMES Dell 1975b "Breakthrough into Performance" in Ben-Amos, Dan and Kenneth Goldstein eds. *Folklore Performance and Communication* Mouton, The Hague, pp.11-74

HYMES Dell 1981 "Discovering Oral Performance and Measured Verse in American Indian Narrative" in Hymes D *"In Vain I Tried to Tell You": Essays in Native American Ethnopoetics* University of Pennsylvania Press, Philadelphia, pp.309-341

HYMES Virginia 1987 "Warm Springs Sahaptin Narrative Analysis" in Sherzer Joel and Woodbury Anthony C ed. *Native American Discourse* Cambridge University Press, Cambridge, pp.62-102

JANSEN Wm. Hugh 1965 "The Esoteric-Exoteric Factor in Folklore" in Dundes Alan ed. *The Study of Folklore* Prentice-Hall, Engelwood Cliffs, New Jersey, pp.43-51

KENRICK Donald 1984 "The Portrayal of the Gypsy in English Schoolbooks" *Zeitschrift des Georg-Eckert Instituts* 6 pp.38-47

LABOV William 1972 "The Transformation of Experience in Narrative Syntax" in *Language in the Inner City: Studies in the Black English Vernacular* University of Pennsylvania Press, Philadelphia

LAMONT-BROWN Raymond 1994 "Scotland's Colorful Tinkers" *The Highlander* 32 pp.40-42

MALINOWSKI Bronislaw 1953 "The Problem of Meaning in Primitive Languages" in Ogden C Kand Richards A I eds. *The Meaning of Meaning* Harcourt Brace, New York, pp.296-336

MATHISEN Stein R 1993 "Folklore and Cultural Identity" in Anttonen Pertti J and Kvideland Reimund eds. *Nordic Frontiers: Recent Issues in the Study of Modern Traditional Culture in the Nordic Countries* Nordic Institute of Folklore, Turku, pp.35-47

McCORMICK Andrew 1907 *The Tinker-Gypsies* 1973 reprint, Norwood Editions, Darby, Pennsylvania

McDOWELL John H 1982 "Beyond Iconicity: Ostension in Kamsá Mythic Narrative" *Journal of the Folklore Institute* 19 pp.111-39

NEAT Timothy 1979 "The Summer Walkers" *Seer 42* Duncan of Jordanstone College of Art, Dundee, pp.40-48

ORING Elliott 1994 "The Arts, Artifacts and Artifices of Identity" *Journal of American Folklore* 107 pp.211-33

PAREDES Américo 1977 "On Ethnographic Work Among Minority Groups" *New Scholar* 7 p.132

REHFISCH Farnham ed. 1975 *Gypsies, Tinkers and other Travellers* Academic Press, London

ROBERTSON Stanley 1988 *Exodus to Alford* Balnain Books, Nairn, Scotland

ROBERTSON Stanley 1989 *Nyakim's Windows* Balnain Books Nairn, Scotland

SAYY.##. These numbers refer to recordings lodged in the Folklore Archives at the School of Scottish Studies, University of Edinburgh. YY refers to the year of recording and ## indicates the sequentially numbered tape within each year

SECRETARY OF STATE'S ADVISORY COMMITTEE 1982 *Scotland's Travelling People 1979-1982: Third Report* HMSO, Edinburgh

SEEGER Peggy and MacCOLL Ewan 1982 *Go! Move! Shift!* STV Production from Scotland, Scottish Television

SHERZER Joel 1987 "A Discourse-Centered Approach to Language and Culture" *American Anthropologist* 89 pp.295-309

STOCKING George W 1982 "Franz Boas and the Culture Concept" in *Race, Culture, and Evolution: Essays in the History of Anthropology* University of Chicago Press, Chicago

TEDLOCK Dennis 1972 "On the Translation of Style in Oral Narrative" in Paredes Américo and Bauman Richard eds. *Toward New Perspectives in Folklore* University of Texas Press, Austin, pp.114-33

TSYY### These numbers refer to my field recordings. 19YY refers to the year of the recording and ### indicates the sequentially numbered tape within each year

URBAN Greg 1991 *A Discourse-Centered Approach to Culture* University of Texas Press, Austin

WHYTE Betsy 1979 *The Yellow on the Broom* 1986 2nd edition, Futura Publications, London

WHYTE Betsy 1990 *Red Rowans and Wild Honey* Canongate Publishing, Edinburgh

WILLIAMSON Duncan 1983 *Fireside Tales of the Traveller Children* Canongate Publishing, Edinburgh

WILLIAMSON Duncan 1985 *The Broonie, Silkies and Fairies* Canongate Publishing, Edinburgh

WILLIAMSON Duncan 1987 *A Thorn in the King's Foot* Penguin, Harmondsworth, Middlesex

WILLIAMSON Duncan 1987 *Tell Me a Story for Christmas* Canongate Publishing, Edinburgh

WILLIAMSON Duncan 1989 *May the Devil Walk Behind Ye: Scottish Traveller Tales* Canongate Publishing, Edinburgh

WILLIAMSON Duncan 1990 *Don't Look Back Jack* Canongate Publishing, Edinburgh

WILLIAMSON Duncan 1991 *The Genie and the Fisherman: and Other Tales from the Travelling People* Cambridge University Press, Cambridge

WILLIAMSON Duncan 1992 *Tales of the Seal People* Canongate Publishing, Edinburgh

Chapter 5 Australia: sanctuary or cemetery for Romanies?

Ken Lee, Lecturer in Sociology and Anthropology, University of Newcastle, Australia; Founder, Romani Association of Australia, Inc.

"Ethnic identity and difference are socially produced in the here and now, not archaeologically salvaged from the disappearing past" (Smith 1992:513)

This chapter examines conceptual and methodological difficulties associated the study of ethnic identity in general, and Romani ethnic identity in particular, especially the proposition that some measure of exclusionary opposition is a *necessary* condition for the maintenance of Romani ethnic identity. It also considers the implication for Romani identity if exclusionary opposition *does not* occur.

An account is given of the development, continuation and present situation of Romani identities in Australia. It is argued that the situation in Australia is such that the exclusionary opposition seen as a necessary condition of Romani identity formation is not found. Hence, it would appear that the current situation in Australia not only offers possibilities for the constructive continuation of Romani identities and Romani life, but also simultaneously presents risks that specifically Romani ethnicity may be submerged in a 'multicultural' society. Banton's comment over a decade ago still holds good: "the relationship between the Gypsies (sic) and the majority society does not fit well into any of the categories used in sociology for intergroup relations." (Banton 1983:158).

Approaches to identity

Academic discourses over the last forty years have tried to explain the origins and strength of ethnic identity, the source and degree of attachment to a particular ethnic group. Three broad approaches can be distinguished.

The primordialist view

The primordialist view, beginning with Shils (1957), holds that ethnic identity is *a priori*, ineffable and affective, that it springs from

> "...congruities of blood, speech, custom and so on [which] are seen to have an ineffable and at times overpowering coerciveness in and of themselves" (Geertz 1973:259 cf. also Eller and Coughlan 1993).

Alleged atavistic traits have long been seen as defining Romani life and culture; one has only to read Grellmann, Hoyland, Crabb, Paspati, or any of the nineteenth century Gypsylorist writers to be aware of this. The alleged primordialism of Romani identity is reinforced by the clear evidence for an Indian origin; there are demonstrable links, linguistic, cultural and phylogenetic to an original 'homeland'. The persistence of Romani 'culture' is seen as evidence of the strength of primordialist ties, their overpowering coerciveness.

The circumstantialist or constructivist view

In contrast to the primordialist view is the circumstantialist view (variously also called constructivist, situational, structuralist or instrumentalist) which essentially argues that ethnic identity is a product of social interaction in particular circumstances and has no necessary basis in some primeval ineffable atavistic coercion.

Barth's work on boundary maintenance added a new dimension to the study of ethnic identity when he argued that it was "the ethnic *boundary* which defines the group, not the cultural stuff which it encloses" and that this boundary needed "continual expression and validation" (Barth 1969:16).

Barth's seminal work emphasised the mutually reinforcing *inclusionary* and *exclusionary* processes involved in the separation of groups (Barth 1969). Boundaries can be characterised by an *opaqueness / transparency* dimension (i.e. the degree to which the characteristics beyond the boundary can be seen) and a *permeability / impermeability* dimension (i.e the ease with which the boundary may be crossed.) The relative proportions of these dimensions will determine the strength and functioning of the boundary.

Barth also addressed the position of Romanies as a pariah group:

> "[Pariah] groups are actively rejected by the host population because of their behaviour or characteristics positively condemned, though often useful in some specific practical way. European pariah groups of recent centuries (executioners, dealers in horse-flesh and leather, collectors of night-soil, gypsies (sic), etc.) exemplify most features: as breakers of taboos they were rejected by the larger society. Their identity imposed a definition on social situations which gave very little scope for interaction with persons in the majority population, and simultaneously as an imperative status represented an inescapable disability that prevented them from assuming the normal statuses involved in other definitions of the situation of interaction. Despite these

formidable barriers, such groups do not seem to have developed the internal complexity that would lead us to regard them as full-fledged ethnic groups: *only the culturally foreign gypsies* [sic] *clearly constitute such a group*" (Barth 1969:31 emphasis added).

The inference that can be drawn is that the ethnic identity of the Romanies must be explained not just by local pariah status but by some other culturally foreign characteristics that have allowed internal complexity to develop. In a footnote, Barth (1969:38) states that the behaviour for which Romanies are condemned

"rests prominently on their wandering life, originally in contrast to the serf bondage of Europe, later in the flagrant violation of puritan ethics of responsibility, toil and morality."

Thus, for Barth, what expressed, validated and reinforced the Romani/non-Romani boundary and provided a focus for group identity was not some coercive property of the 'ties of blood', but rather was the continued practice of nomadism. That is to say, it was a specific cultural practice within specific historical and spatial contexts. By extension of Barth's arguments any ethnic attachment is based on continual construction, modification, reinforcement and validation of identity.

The oppositional view
Over twenty years ago Spicer attempted to synthesise the primordial and circumstantial viewpoints in what he called an oppositional approach. (Spicer 1971). He argued that some groups of people with some affective attachments to cultural symbols have persisted, under different conditions, for long periods; these groups he labelled as persistent identity systems, having the following characteristics:
- they had outlived several types of state organisation
- they had experienced pressures for assimilation or incorporation
- they had successfully resisted such pressures
- they had developed well-defined symbols of identity.

He focussed on *continued opposition* as an important explanatory factor for a persistent identity system, stating that:

"Its formation and maintenance are intimately bound up with the conditions of opposition ... a continued conflict between these peoples and the controllers of the surrounding state apparatus." (Spicer 1971:797)

He argues that flexibility and responsiveness to opposition characterises both the symbolic content *and* the mechanisms for persistence of a group. These concepts were expanded and illustrated by Castile and Kushner (1982:xix). They argue that:

"Too much opposition can stimulate the majority population to undertake pogroms, exile, forced apostasy, and, in the ultimate case, genocide. Too little opposition and the membership may be absorbed into the larger society through an inability to define a group identity distinguishable from that of the dominant population"

How exactly this 'inability' would arise and operate under conditions of 'too little opposition' and how much is 'too little' are not made clear.

More recently, Scott has developed and extended Spicer's approach, arguing that the degree of cohesion or solidarity in an ethnic group is *directly* related to the degree of opposition encountered and further, that such causation is circular; the more the opposition, the greater the solidarity; the greater the solidarity, the more the oppression (Scott 1990).

Jenkins (1994) has also argued that externally located processes of categorisation (i.e." a class whose nature and composition is decided by the person who defines the category" (Mann 1983:34))is important in the reproduction of social identities. He states:

"The experience of categorisation may strengthen group identity through a process of resistance and reaction. Thus, the experience of being categorised may contribute to the formation of group identity... Similarly, group identification is likely to proceed, at least in part, through categorising others..."
(Jenkins 1994:203).

Implicit oppositionalism

Within these three broad categories, there are many variations of emphasis and explanation such as, for example, the attempt by Bentley (1987) to utilise Bourdieu's concept of *habitus* to explain the affective focus of ethnicity, the response from Yelvington (1991) and the counter response from Bentley (1991). Each category, and each attempt to combine categories, or to offer new modalities of explanation results in more problematics. Indeed, Liebkind has argued that: "... the problem of [ethnic] identity is one of the most difficult challenges to which social science is called to respond. No single heuristic device is likely to conquer the whole problem" (Liebkind 1992:147)

I would argue that *each* of the three approaches outlined above assumes some degree of opposition to explain the existence of an ethnic identity. The Oppositionalist approach, of course makes this quite explicit; the Circumstantialist view is based on boundary maintenance and a boundary, by definition, separates; the Primordialist view appeals to a set of opposed 'coercive congruities' that makes one identity different from another.

Even post-modernist approaches to ethnic identity contain an implicit assumption of opposition:

"In post-modern social analysis, the subject is decentred...[to]... produce a 'self' experienced not as a single, completed identity, but as multiple, incomplete and partial identities, formed in historically specific relation to the different social spaces that people inhabit over time." (Smith 1992:501)

Part of that fragmented selfhood includes ethnic identity, which is:

"... a dynamic mode of self consciousness, a form of selfhood reinterpreted if not reinvented generationally in response to changing historical circumstances. As a deeply emotional component of personal identity, ethnic identity is socially constructed and reconstructed as people respond to the changing material conditions, semiotic codes, power relations and relations among groups shaping a specific place and time."
(Smith 1992:512)

For Romanies, semiotic codes, intergroup relations and power relations have historically included some form of exclusionary or discriminatory practices, such that the social spaces they have inhabited have incorporated 'opposition' (cf. Fraser 1992; Hancock 1987).

Each of the various approaches to examining ethnic identity outlined above, implies that some degree of opposition is *necessary* to maintain ethnic identity. The history of Romani presence in Europe provides a wide range of discriminatory and persecuting practices, from bureaucratic harrassment to outright genocide. The Romanies have always been 'opposed' to a degree that suggests hostility towards them is an essential component in their construction of ethnic identity.

We can then pose the question: how will Romani identity be constructed and maintained, and what forms will it take, if exclusionary opposition is minimal or non-existent?

I would like to examine some implications of this possibility by examining the presence of Romanies in Australia.

Romani presence in Australia
Romani presence in Australia can be conveniently categorised into three historical periods, although within each era, there are a variety of different contexts for Romani experience and validation of identity.

1788-1868: The first Europeans to the end of the convict era
The first permanent European presence in Australia occurred on 26 January 1788 with the landing of the so-called First Fleet, a naval and military garrison, guarding a group of convicts. (There is considerable controversy in Australia over the correct term to use to described the arrival of the Europeans; some Aboriginals insist that 'invasion' is the appropriate term, whereas some non-Aboriginal Australians prefer 'settlement', or 'occupation'. I have used the hopefully neutral term 'presence'.)

It is claimed that there were three Romani convicts recorded on the First Fleet; only about twelve other specific mentions of 'Gypsies' (sic) occur in records of subsequent convict shipments to the end of the convict era in 1868 (Donohoe 1988). Given that vagabonds and itinerants were a target group for the Draconian transportation laws of late eighteenth and early nineteenth century England, and the fact that over 162,000 convicts were shipped to Australia, this figure for 'Gypsy' (sic) convicts (about 0.01per cent) seems very low. Since Romani identity, however, was not necessarily recorded in records of sentencing, nor convict shipment manifests, it is possible that there were more Romani convicts than were recorded. Not all convict records have survived and there is no way of knowing from the available records whether the use of 'Gypsy' in the historical record is an unequivocal identification of a 'real' Romani ethnicity, or simply a matter of a generic term for vagrants and nomads. Thus, the precise number of Romani convicts is not known, nor ever likely to be known.

As often occurs with incomplete and inadequate historical data, one has to fall back on speculation. Recent studies of convict records do show some identification of 'Gypsies' (sic) from sentencing records (Tipping 1988), and many more occurrences of names and occupations associated with English Romanies (cf. Tipping 1988, Chapman 1986, Robinson 1988, Erickson 1979). Because of the considerable research conducted, there are perhaps more documentary records about Romani presence in the convict era than any other period of Australian history.

Some of the Romani convicts were soon absorbed into the life of the struggling convict settlement, and records exist of their family and occupational activities, for example, James Squire (Donohoe 1988:63-4). Of others, little is known except for the details of their arrival, for example, Elijah Elliot (Donohoe 1988:66).

In the context of a struggling convict settlement, there would have been little likelihood of a continuation of *anyone's* ethnic identity, as the miscellany of convicts were subjugated to the labour demands of an imperial convict garrison and a new settlement. It should be no surprise, then, that there are no documentary records of any expression of Romani identity in the convict era. For Romani convicts, transportation meant social and psychological death; exiled, they had little hope of returning to England to re-establish the family ties, cultural roots, continuous expressions and validations that would have revived their Romani identity, although there is one record of a Henry Lavello or Lavell (Lovell, perhaps?) who did return to England, after a full pardon, with a son born in Australia, probably to an Aboriginal woman. This son later returned to Australia; his sister (born in England, apparently to the same Aboriginal woman) was later sentenced to transportation to Australia. There is no record of the brother and sister being re-united in Australia (Donohoe 1988:65).

1868-1945: The free settlers arrive
The convict 'era' was actually a series of periods, depending on the colony; for example, the last convict shipment to New South Wales was in 1849; South Australia, not founded until 1836, never had any convict population; in Western Australia, free settlement preceded convict settlement which did not begin until in 1848 for juvenile offenders and 1850 for adults, continuing until 1868. This was the year of the last convict shipment from England.

Free settlement occurred simultaneously with convict settlement, eventually surpassing convicts in number; virtually nothing, however, is known of free Romani migration to Australia during the period from 1868 to 1945.

There are some scattered references: for instance, Borrow's account of the transportation of 'The Fighting Gypsy', Jack Cooper, to Australia (Borrow 1874 [1908]:212) and Boswell's recollection of relatives of his great-grandfather being transported to Australia (Boswell 1973:17).

There is some evidence that a small number of English Romanies emigrated voluntarily in the late nineteenth century. For example, one

William Roser, alleged to have been a Romani who travelled in the south of England, emigrated to Western Australia in 1842 as an indentured farm labourer (Young 1982).

This information is based on an extended period of genealogical research by Roser's descendants, whilst undertaking a general family history; although not searching specifically for Romanies, their investigations revealed Roser's Romani identity. It seems clear, then, that whatever Romani identity Roser and his immediate family may have projected and whatever practices they followed, specifically Romani identity did not flow on to his descendants.

Similar generalised family history searches are increasingly revealing Romani ancestry of some degree amongst present day Australians. A scattering of Romani emigrants has been found from the 1870s up to the 1970s. What is *not* found though, is any clear evidence for the perpetuation of a distinctive Romani lifestyle or identity.

The 'Second Wave' diaspora of Eastern European Rom has been well documented, and again, Australia was a destination: "In 1898 a group describing themselves as 'Greek Gypsies' landed near Adelaide and remained in Australia for five years before vanishing from record." (Gilchrist 1992:262).

Although Gilchrist says that they "vanished from the record", in fact some descendants of these 'Greek Gypsies' still survive in Australia, have maintained their ethnic identity and many of their cultural practices. The traditional burial of a 'Gypsy (sic) Queen', a descendant of these Greek Gypsies, was widely reported in both the print and electronic media in Australia in 1982. *(Sydney Morning Herald, Sydney Telegraph-Mirror, Sydney Sun, 1982).*

Little is known about Romani migration to (or from) Australia during the latter half of the nineteenth century and the first half of the twentieth century. As in the convict era, there are no documentary accounts of expressions of specific Romani identity.

1945-1994: The post-war immigrants
Following the Second World War, Australia was a major migration destination as the Australian Commonwealth Government sought to manage its labour market shortages by a programme of massive immigration. Australia became a haven for European emigrants, refugees and 'displaced persons' (and, some have argued, Nazi war criminals; see Aarons 1988).

This pattern of international migration continued into the late 1970s, when the demand for immigrant labour diminished and immigration policies became much more restrictive. From 1945 to the present, some 4.5 million immigrants have come to Australia, and they and their first-generation descendants now account for some 40 per cent of the Australian population of 18 million (Collins 1988).

Romanies appeared within this large migration stream. Some European Romanies came as refugees or displaced persons; others came as emigrants, declaring their identity as the nationality of their country of origin. Some English Romanies emigrated as 'Ten-Pound Poms' under the Australian Commonwealth Government assisted passage schemes; others came at their own expense. Since there is no official category of 'Romani' for immigration purposes, there can be no accurate record of the numbers of Romanies who may have arrived since the Second World War and hence there can be no accurate data on the numbers of Romanies currently in Australia. The 1986 census indicates that 1,034 people revealed Romani ancestry; in the 1991 census, the question relating to ethnic origin was removed, and only thirty seven people identified as Romani. Any figures would only be guesstimates, or wild speculations, depending on point of view, but a population of 20,000 has been suggested – but this could be wrong by plus or minus 25 per cent.

Here I refer to those people who have a *definite* knowledge of Romani descent and who would identify as Romani. There are, of course, many more who have some degree of Romani ancestry – the remote descendants of the convicts, for example – but who are not aware of it. Australians, in common with many descendants of emigrants, have a fascination with their roots and origins and many genealogical searches have unearthed both distant and recent Romani ancestry.

In summary, there are Romanies in Australia, and they have been there since the first European settlement, but very little is known about them; neither their numbers and distribution, nor patterns of movement, nor economic activities, nor the proportions which are nomadic or sedentarised, nor those who retain 'traditional' (sic) occupations and those who work in normal jobs, nor their experiences of emigration, their degree of identity retention or abandonment, their degree of ethnic cohesion. The information to be presented below has been gleaned from a variety of sources through personal contact; much of it is anecdotal rather than the result of rigourous investigation; most must, of course, remain guarded and confidential.

Much more rigorous investigations are needed to give a more rounded (but never complete) picture of the situation of the Romanies in Australia.

Types of Romani identity in Australia

In present-day Australia, the construction, reinforcement, expression and validation of Romani identities will broadly depend on the interaction between the prior specificities and intensity of Romani identity in the immigrant's source location and the perceived potential for constructing and expressing identities in the Australian context. The extent to which prior Romani identities are reproduced and modified in the Australian context requires considerable ethnographic investigation. For example, virtually nothing is known about the extent to which the rhetoric of assimilation and integration in the *gaje* community, both at an official and policy level, and amongst immigrant groups, influences Romani perceptions of their own position and their own practices in identity construction. For the past five years, however, I have been conducting research amongst various Romani individuals and groups on their construction of Romani identities in the Australian context. This remainder of this paper is a brief and preliminary survey of some of that research.

We can as an initial step broadly distinguish a number of different types of Romani identity, depending on the intensity of identification as a Romani, and on the specificities related to the source area. In other words, the complexity, variety and dynamism of Romani identities in the main European and British source areas are reflected in Australia.

Firstly, there are those whose Romani identity is firmly and unproblematically lodged in the interlocking specifics of Romani descent, Romani dialect, Romani culture and Romani lifestyle and for whom the move to Australia is merely a change of location. These may vary from English Romanichals who continue a nomadic lifestyle, pursuing a similar pattern of existence to that they followed in England to Macedonski Roma who continued the urbanised and sedentarised lifestyle of their source country.

Secondly, there are others of Romani descent, with knowledge of Romani culture, dialect, and lifestyle who have chosen gradually to integrate into the non-Romani community, and who are gradually modifying, losing or discarding their prior Romani identity. These are naturally predominantly sedentarising or already sedentarised.

Thirdly, there are those who know of Romani descent, either directly or through discovery following genealogical searches, but who have no knowledge of Romani culture or lifestyle. For some in this group, Romani descent may be a quaint but unimportant element, no different to having some other 'exotic' ancestor, with no resultant expression of a Romani identity. Others, though, may actively seek out Romani relatives and other known Romanies or other people like themselves, in order to extend their knowledge of Romani culture and lifestyle in an effort to create some form of Romani-related identity which incorporates an expression of their biological descent.

Fourthly, there are those who, although having Romani ancestry, do not know of this and know nothing of the culture and lifestyle, and hence for whom Romani identity is not an issue. Included here would be many of the descendants of the convicts and nineteenth century settlers. It is possible that on discovery of Romani descent, people in this group may shift into one or other of the types in the third group.

There is nothing unique to Australia about these categories: they can occur in any situation. What *is* unique, I believe, is the facility with which these options can be expressed.

Potentials for identity construction in Australia

In addition to the usual factors of descent, socialisation and culture inherent in identiy construction there are several factors peculiar to the Australian context that must be considered.

In contrast to Europe, the United States, or even Latin America, where there have been a centuries-long Romani presence and visibility, Australian non-Romanies have little knowledge about Romanies, beyond the crude media stereotypes and vague childhood recollections or experiences when visiting Europe. There are many Australian *gaje* who have *never* actually seen, or recognised, a Romani. I once met a fourth-year sociology student who did not even know what a 'Gypsy' (sic) was!

Since the Australian *gaje* are generally so ignorant of Romanies, there is little overt harassment or persecution, and Romanies can if they choose, generally remain successfully hidden in the host society. Regretfully, it must also be said that the *Koori* (Aboriginal) population often provides the ideological labour of functioning as the dirty, idle, shiftless, hedonistic, fringe-dweller scapegoat, thus diverting attention away from Romanies. Thus, the context of identity construction for Romanies is significantly different from virtually all other locations in Europe and the Americas.

For nomadic Romanies, particularly those from the British Isles, Australia offers significant attractions. During the settlement of Australia's frontiers, mobility and nomadic living, from cattle drovers and camel-drivers to travelling peddlers, were an accepted part of life. Even today, it is acceptable for Australians to adopt a caravan-based nomadic lifestyle; it is the dream – and reality – of many *gaje* from adventurous youth to retirees and superannuants to 'travel round Australia in a caravan' before finally settling down.

For British passport holders, assuming a visa can be obtained, and there is enough money for the fare, Australia is accessible, either as a visitor or as a permanent migrant. English is the official language and so there are no language barriers; it is possible to travel over most of the country without restriction. There is an extensive network of caravan parks and the vast majority of these provide sealed roads, individual concreted sites with power, running water and sullage drainage serviced showers, toilets and laundry blocks, barbeque facilities and picnic tables. Many have swimming pools, TV and recreation rooms, and on-site stores.

Romanies are not excluded from these caravan parks.

They may sometimes be segregated within them, separating the 'recreational' caravanner from the obviously 'commercial' nomad. This is not a discrimination based on race or ethnicity but on the practicalities of caravan park life and it applies equally to the many Australian *gaje* who are commercial nomads. The climate is such that it is possible to travel and work the entire year; the UK problem of diminished income in the winter is avoided. And the Australian population is sufficiently well off to provide a reasonable source of income for the nomadic Romanies.

Thus in the general absence of overt hostility and harrassment, nomadic Romanies can continue to express a specifically Romani identity, adapted to local conditions.

There are many Romanies and Travellers of British origin who continue to follow a nomadic lifestyle on the roads of Australia, and many who say that Australia is the best contry in the world for Travellers, and the last place where they can continue a truly nomadic existence.

On the other hand, the lack of overt harrassment and discrimination means that it is also possible for Romanies *voluntarily to sedentarise* relatively easily. The diversity of the ethnic mix of post-war immigration has produced a greater tolerance of difference amongst native Australians; Romanies are but one small and virtually unknown immigrant group amongst many. It has also meant, when needed, a greater ease of concealment of Romani identity; amongst Italians, Yugoslavians, Greeks, Lebanese and Turks, the English Romanies can appear not too different in physical appearance, language and culture to the Australian host society.

There are also several other features of the Australian situation that make the option of voluntary sedentarisation possible. Home ownership in Australia is seen as a desirable and worthwhile goal, to be actively encouraged. Hence, many Romanies (sedentarised *and* nomadic) have been able rapidly to acquire houses and land. It is also much easier to buy land and have housing built. The average Australian house is on a quarter-acre block, allowing ample room to store a caravan or two if a semi- sedentary lifestyle is desired. There is also a movement in Australia towards housing built on small acreages (2-5 acres) as a 'hobby farm', which allows room for not only a house and caravan but also swimming pool, stables, and horses; some Romanies have settled in such a situation.

Sedentarisation also means access to education for children, again this can occur without the negative stereotyping and harrassment that occurs in the UK. Some Romanies emigrated from England *precisely* so their children could attend school without harrassment. Indeed, English speaking Romani children may be at an *advantage* compared to immigrant children from a non-English-speaking background. I know of several instances of Romani parents who sedentarised in Australia only within the last twenty years; some have children who are now graduates of Australian universities. There is one case of a child of sedentarised Romani parents who completed one degree then simultaneously completed a further bachelor's degree *and* a master's degree at two different universities!

For the sedentarised Romanies, a wide range of quasi-traditional occupations, such as car-sales yards (Australia has the second highest rate of vehicle ownership in the world after the USA), spray-painting, roofing, seasonal agricultural work and, of course, fortune-telling are undertaken. Other opportunities for self-employment are also taken advantage of for instance, in garden care and maintenance, swimming-pool maintenance, market trading, small-scale manufacturing and various kinds of retail trading. *Gaje* occupations are also taken, particularly by the educated children of Romani parents.

Again, it is argued that in Australia, the lack of widespread overt opposition to Romanies, coupled with some positive advantages, allows the choice of sedentarisation or semi-sedentarisation to be made relatively easily. The construction of Romani identity by these groups is, of course, much more problematic than for those who have continued a nomadic existence, but nevertheless, some form of Romani identity continues. As in the European and English situations, the importance of nomadic activity to Romani identity is a matter of negotiation between those who are fully nomadic and those who are sedentary. In Australia, however, the range of possible combinations of nomadism and sedentarism allow a much greater flexibility, and thus much more room for manouevring in identity construction, than in Europe.

Thus Romani identities in Australia are negotiated over wide range in a spectrum of nomadism/sedentarism, from a wide range of prior positions.

Multiculturalism: State support for ethnic identity

Since 1945 immigration to Australia has brought 4.5 million immigrants from 130 countries resulting in firstly, a large proportion of both foreign-born immigrants and first-generation Australian born children of immigrants in the population – currently estimated at 40 percent, and secondly, a pronounced ethnic mix – ranging from the early European arrivals to later Asian and Latin America arrivals.

One effect of these phenomena has been a shift from a government policy of assimilation (that is, all immigrants, and specifically their native-born children, were expected to become 'Australian' and to discard any previous ethnic or national attachments) to one of 'multiculturalism' (that is, immigrants were encouraged to retain their ethnic identity, as well as to develop an 'Australian' identity).

Multiculturalism is now Government policy; there is an Office of Multicultural Affairs attached to the Prime Minister's Department, as well as a Federal Department of Immigration, Local Government and Ethnic Affairs, and Departments of Ethnic Affairs in the various states. Bob Hawke, a former Prime Minister stated:

"A multicultural Australia is one in which Australians have an equal right to participate in all aspects of the nation's life... The policy of multiculturalism... recognises the fact of diversity in Australia and the socially enriching value of diversity."
(Advisory Council on Multicultural Affairs 1988:2)

In theory, any ethnic group, including Romanies, has an equal right to participate in all aspects of the nation's life. And this is not merely empty rhetoric, since in spite of funding cuts, considerable provision is made for ethnic groups, including a nationwide network of Migrant Resource Centres, which provide interpreter facilities, counselling and access to social, welfare and educational facilities for ethnic groups.

Two examples of Romani responses to this policy will be given. Firstly, in Perth, Western Australia, a group of Macedonian Rom from the former Yugoslavia migrated over a period of years in the late 1960s. They formed a group in Perth and eventually developed their own traditional dance troupe, Romani football team, had their own Romani dialect community radio programme and developed good relations with the local state ethnic affairs commission (Dean-Oswald 1988). Originating from the same area in Macedonia they tend to be confined to the Perth area and are a small, tight-knit community which has substantially reproduced the sedentarised, urban-based life of their Yugoslavian origin.

In 1990 in New South Wales a small group of English Romanies formed the Romani Association of Australia, Inc. (hereafter RAA). Although the membership is small (less than 100) there are members in every state. Being allowed (in fact, encouraged) to form this legally incorporated Association in New South Wales, is a recognition of the right of Romanies to identify themselves as an ethnic group. RAA is registered in the Ethnic Communities 1994 Reference Book, and as such is circulated by Government departments with relevant material.

A sample of recent Government circulars includes an invitation to a book launch for *Growing up Italian in Australia*; an invitation to a Migrant Employment Taskforce meeting on '*Newly Arrived Migrants and Access to Welfare*'; a request from the Ambulance Service of New South Wales for submissions relating to servicing local ethnic communities; an invitation to contribute to a bibliography of Australian multicultural writers as well as regular newsletter from the anti-discrimination Board and Human Rights Commission.

RAA is also regularly approached by people who, having done genea-logical searches, discover an Romani ancestor and wish to discover more about the culture or even to trace relatives. Many discoveries go back to the late nineteenth century and as these genealogical discoveries surface, a better picture of the Romani diaspora to Australia can be developed.

Conclusion

In theory, Australia is a country where retaining ethnic identity and cohesion is not just encouraged but actively supported by the state. Under these circumstances, then, Romani identities could be reconstructed under a benevolent government that recognises and celebrates diversity. The brief examples of the Perth Roma and RAA Inc attest to this. Apart from this open display of Romani identity, there are many other Romanies, both nomadic and sedentarised, from a wide range of backgrounds and source countries, living under a wide range of conditions, who are perpetuating some form of Romani identity without fear of harrassment or negative stereotyping. In other words, Australia appears to offer a sanctuary for Romanies, a situation almost unprecedented in Romani history. This is not to say, however, that the Australian situation is entirely benevolent. For example, in 1994 a children's book about Romani bear handlers in Turkey was published in Australia which contained text and illustrations that could be interpreted as anti-Romani racism; recently introduced anti-vilification legislation, however, may mean that if this publication is found to be racist, then there are avenues to correct the situation. This matter is currently a matter of correspondence between RAA and the publishers.

On the other hand, if we accept the implicit and explicit arguments outlined earlier, that the dynamic balance of exclusionary *and* inclusionary processes is a *necessary* element in maintaining internal cohesion and ethnic identity, what happens when those hostile external pressures are removed? Is it possible that in a seemingly benevolent Australia, the removal of external pressures on Romanis will affect *internal* cohesion to such a degree that the flexibility, adaptation and responsiveness that have been effective for a millennium will wither away? Will this relative benevolence make the absorption of Romanies into a *gaje* culture easier and painless? In other words, could the apparent sanctuary become a cemetery?.

Already other ethnic groups in Australia are questioning the policies of 'multiculturalism', arguing that the ethnic identity that the state allows to persist and be displayed is merely the superficial traits of 'dress, dance, diet and dialect'. Any element of ethnicity that would threaten state structure and state control, it is argued, is subjugated and only the diversion of harmless display is tolerated.

It is, of course, far too early to say whether this apparent threat to Romani identity is just another one of the dire predictions of demise that have been current for two centuries.

What we have in Australia, within the broad framework of a liberal-democratic-welfare state, is a wide array of potentialities for constructing a range of Romani identities, and within this broad framework it seems likely that Romani identity will continue to be the diverse, fluid and evolving self-ascription that it always has been.

> "Defining the context of opportunities and constraints upon social action ... is itself a continuous process of contest and struggle in which the historical practices of people are actively inserted as *articulations*, which mediate, and in turn modify, the permissions and constraints."
> (Smith 1992:503)

Romanies have for centuries persisted by defining the context of opportunities and constraints and actively articulating their identity through their historical practices. I see no reason why this process should cease in Australia.

A note on terminology
Throughout this paper, wherever possible, I use the self-ascriptive ethnonym of Romani (or one of its variants). Wherever the exonym 'Gypsy' (or one of its variants) occurs, for example in quotations, I have used a parenthesised 'sic'. Although a cumbersome construction, it is a reminder that this term is usually considered derogatory and is an embedded racist use of language.

References

AARONS M 1989 *Sanctuary: Nazi fugitives in Australia* William Heinemann, Port Melbourne

BANTON M 1983 *Racial and Ethnic Competition* Cambridge University Press, Cambridge

BARTH 1969 *Ethnic groups and boundaries* Little, Brown, Boston

BENTLEY G C 1987 "Ethnicity and Practice" *Comparative Studies in Society and History* Vol 29 (1) January pp. 24-55

BENTLEY G C 1991 "Response to Yelvington" *Comparative Studies in Society and History* Vol 33 (1) January pp.169-175

BORROW G 1874 [reprinted 1908] *Romano Lavo Lil* John Murray, London

BOSWELL S G 1973 *The Book of Boswell: the autobiography of a Gypsy* Penguin, Harmondsworth

CASTILE G P and KUSHNER G [Eds] 1982 *Persistent Peoples: cultural enclaves in perspective* University of Arizona Press, Tucson

CHAPMAN D 1986 *The people of the First Fleet* Doubleday, Sydney

COLLINS J 1988 *Migrant hands in a distant land* Pluto Press, Sydney

CRABB J 1831 *The Gipsies' Advocate* Seeley, London

DEAN-OSWALD H 1988 "Roma" in Jupp (1988)

ERICKSON R 1979 *Directory of Western Australians 1829-1868* Vol. II University of Western Australia Press, Perth

DONOHOE J H 1988 *The Forgotten Australians; Non-Anglo or Celtic convicts and exiles* Privately Published by the Author, Sydney

ELLER J D and COUGHLAN R M 1993 "The poverty of primordialism: the demystification of ethnic attachements" *Ethnic and Racial Studies* Vol.16 (2) April pp.183-202

FRASER A 1992 *The Gypsies* Blackwell, Oxford

GEERTZ C 1973 *The interpretation of cultures* Basic Books, New York

GILCHRIST H 1992 *Australians and Greeks: 1 The early years* Halstead Press, Rushcutter's Bay

GRELLMAN H M G 1783 *Ein historischer Versuch über die Lebensart und Verfassung, Sitten, und Schicksale dies Volks in Europa, nebst ihrem Ursprunge,* private, Dessau and Leipzig

HANCOCK I F 1987 *The Pariah Syndrome: An account of Gypsy slavery and persecution* Karoma Publishers, Ann Arbor

HOYLAND J 1816 *A historical survey of the customs, habits and present state of the Gypsies* Wm. Alexander, York

JENKINS R 1994 "Rethinking Ethnicity: identity, categorisation and power" *Ethnic and Racial Studies* Vol.17 (2) pp.197-223

JUPP J ed. 1988 *The Australian People : an encyclopaedia of the nation, its people and their origins* Angus and Robertson, North Ryde, New South Wales and London

LEACH E 1954 *Political systems of highland Burma* G Bell and Sons, London

LIEBKIND K 1992 "Ethnic identity – challenging the boundaries of social psychology" in Breakwell G M 1992 *Social psychology of Identity and the self concept* Surrey University Press, London, pp.147-185

PASPATI A G 1870 *Études sur les Tchingianés ou Bohémiens de l'Empire Ottoman* A.Koroméla, Constantinople

SCOTT G M 1990 "A resynthesis of the primordial and circumstantial approaches to ethnic group solidarity: towards an explanatory model" *Ethnic and Racial Studies* Vol.13 (2) pp.148-171

SHILS E 1957 "Primordial, personal, sacred and civil ties" *British Journal of Sociology* Vol. 8 (2) pp. 130-145

SMITH M P 1992 "Postmodernism, urban ethnography, and the new social space of ethnic identity" *Theory and Society* Vol.21 (4) pp.493-532

SPICER E H 1971 "Persistent Cultural Systems" *Science* Vol.174, (4011) pp.795-800

SYDNEY MORNING HERALD 10-4-1982 to 16-4-1982

SYDNEY TELEGRAPH-MIRROR 10-4-1982 to 16-4-1982

SYDNEY SUN-HERALD 10-4-1982 to 16-4-1982

YELVINGTON K A 1991 "Ethnicity as Practice? A Comment on Bentley" *Comparative Studies in History and Society* Vol.33 (1) pp.158-168

YOUNG J 1982 *In Search of Elizabeth* Chatterbox Press, Armadale

Chapter 6   The puzzle of Roma persistence: group identity without a nation

Michael Stewart, Researcher, London School of Economics

"... the Gypsy identity to which these young people cling is no longer the same as that of their elders ... [we may be] witnessing the last flickering of the Gypsies' centuries-old resistance to assimilation" Charlemagne (1984:14).

Every age, ours as much as its predecessors, believes that it will be the last to be blessed (and cursed) by the presence of the Gypsies. Well-wishers and hostile commentators, romantics and cynics alike are of fixed opinion that the 'wanderers of the world' have at last been 'domesticated', their way of life finally outmoded and that 'the time of the Gypsies' has run out. Such assertions like many made about Gypsies are based on no more than casual acquaintance with the realities of Gypsy life. In truth Gypsies all over Europe have been remarkably successful in preserving their way of life, adapting to their changed conditions in order to remain the same.

Gypsy blacksmiths may no longer be in demand but competitively priced builders are rarely redundant; the age of the horse has gone and with it the great horse-fairs at which Gypsies excelled but the second hand car-market provides new opportunities; mass-produced plastic clothes pegs have long replaced hand-made wooden ones but the housewife who no longer even has a washing line may still buy 'lucky' flowers from a Gypsy hawker at her doorstep or even have her fortune told. Within the feudal division of labour some Gypsies probably prospered since non-agricultural craft activities such as smithing, tanning, music-making were classified as infamous, or polluting occupations and were reserved for outcasts like the Gypsies. But for the past two centuries, at least in North-Western Europe, Gypsies have been economically marginalised and have lived often in considerable poverty (cf. Tomka 1984). As anyone who has carried out serious research among Gypsies will tell you they continue to find economic and social niches in which to make a living and maintain their way of life.

It might be suggested that resistance to the notion that the Gypsies are in decline is to be expected from an ethnographer, a person professionally ill-disposed to hear any suggestion that 'her' or 'his' people (as it is put in trade talk) are unfit in evolutionary terms for the modern world. Maybe. But consider, for a moment, another possibility: that it is our way of thinking, our deep seated pre-suppositions which lead us to assume that Gypsies are in permanent culture-crisis. The source of this illusion lies, I suggest, in the way we think about nations and their members. As Ernest Gellner (1983) has put it, nowadays it seems "a man must have a nationality as he must have a nose and two ears .... having a nation is not [in reality] an inherent attribute of humanity, but it has now come to appear as such".

Homes, nations and homeless peoples

When we think of our national identity or that of other European peoples (with or without states) we imagine a near mystic assimilation of territory, language and people. A nation's language may provide the clearest expression of its identity, a compelling symbol of enclosure, but a nation's land anchors that language to shared experiences and history, providing a marker of where one people begins and another one ends. Apart from physically establishing a putative discontinuity between cultures, the land in its unchanging features also provides an image of the continuity of each culture: persisting into the future of course, but more importantly through its territory a culture reaches back uninterruptedly into the past, into its past. And back there, in the depths of nationalist-phantasmagoric time, is an autochthonous beginning of each nation, a mythical origin which links the two legitimating charters of national integrity: genealogy and territory.

When, as has happened recently, groups of ethnic Germans who have lived divorced from their ethnic kin for centuries in the Volga basin in Russia, begin a return migration to their *vaterland*, or when the Pontic Greeks who likewise maintained language and distinct identity for 2,400 years in the Turkish and then Soviet Empires declare a desire to see their 'homeland' we are at one level amazed at the tenacity of ethnic identity. But at a deeper level we are prepared for this sort of event: it lies (ideo-)logically within the canons of national self-expression. As a leading British commentator (Ascherson 1991) put it, when faced with this kind of national awakening we are reminded that "those who feel homeless have to believe in a place where they will be at home". In terms of this 'naturalised' dream of homeland the stubborn determination to remain Greek or German (whatever this really means) seems comprehensible to us, because these people came from a land and desire to return to it.

Such can never be the case with the Gypsies, a nomad people who have no homeland to dream of, no original territory to reclaim. The various names by which they are known tell us as much: in France they were originally known as Bohemians but there could hardly have been a less likely representative of the Slavonic populations of historical Bohemia. In England their name Gypsy originally meant a person come out of Egypt although gradually people decided that they probably migrated from India – Egyptians who came out of India, perhaps. Elsewhere in Europe they are known as Tsiganes or some cognate term (Zigeuner, Cigany etc.), that is, quite probably, the nominal descendants of an obscure medieval Greek mystic sect. In the face of this uncertainty the Gypsies have appeared supremely unruffled.

The Gypsies of Europe have not thought of themselves as a diaspora population, eking out an existence of exile until blessed by the chance to return to the homeland. They are homeless and quite happy thus. But by appearing to have so carelessly lost their home they put themselves beyond our pale of reason. It seems to us that without a home, if only an imagined home, the preservation of identity is a sisyphean task. We know that Gypsies (many of them at least) share a language but this seems to those of us enchanted by the nationalist spirit a poor soil in which to hold sustainable cultural roots. Gypsies transmit their culture from generation to generation but they do not construct their society in the image of a lineage preserving its patrimony.

Lacking even the desire for a shared territory, the basis of a nation, Gypsies constitute a kind of awful historical mistake, a blot on the parsimonious schema of 'one people, one state' with which we try conceptually to order Europe today. Nonetheless, however difficult it is for us to understand and accept, survive the Gypsies do. In this short chapter I try to give some sense of how a group of Hungarian Gypsies endured the last fifty years of economic, social and political repression and emerged in sometimes thriving communities. If Gypsies can go through this kind of gruelling survival test we can safely assume that they are likely to outlive less punishing regimes in the future.

Gypsies in a communist society
Living in Hungary there are several groups of Gypsies but my story concerns only one of them, the so-called Vlach Gypsies who make up some 20 per cent of the wider Gypsy population. These Gypsies who speak Romani have, since their arrival in Hungary some 100 years ago, been thought of by non-Gypsy Magyars as the most Gypsy-like of the Gypsy groups. Vlach Gypsies had been slaves in Moldavia and Wallachia to monasteries and Boyars for six centuries before being liberated in 1860 (Beck and Gheorghe, nd.). They were soon dragged, like their peasant compatriots, westwards as the great population migration began from the Balkans towards the New World. The Hungarian speaking Roma who live inside Hungary's present borders are relatives of those Gypsy groups in Poland, Romania, Slovakia and the Czech republic who today speak the Carpathian dialect of Romani. The question as to why the Rom inside Hungary's present borders should have abandoned their language, it would appear since 1918, has never been answered.

Because they unashamedly rejected the values of the majority society they were subject to more or less overt repression both before and during the socialist period. After the Communist take-over the majority of Gypsies were assumed to be on the road to integration and assimilation; but the Romani speaking Vlach Gypsies with a language of their own, distinctive dress, an alternative economic morality and separate communities seemed to the authorities to have their faces turned towards the past. Particular efforts were therefore made to encourage them to assimilate and abandon their way of life.

The very existence of autonomous Gypsy communities apparently quite beyond the influence of state organs was construed as a threat to political stability and ideological hegemony, a carnivalesque incitement to disorder. As such these communities were the object of a concerted campaign at all levels of the state, the aim of which was their elimination, and the subsequent assimilation of the Vlach Gypsy population into the dominant Magyar ethnic group.

However, despite the fears of some sections of the Hungarian intelligentsia the motives for the Communist campaign were for the most part less nationalist/ethnic than socio-political for in almost every way the Vlach Gypsy way of life ran against the grain of Communist social and economic ethics. At the XXX Congress of the Hungarian Communist Party one of its 'experts' on the Gypsy question argued that allowing ethnic movements hindered the struggle of the Hungarian people to achieve 'national unity', but he belonged to a particularly populist current of opinion, opportunistically attached to the party. Gypsies had traditionally sought out forms of self-employment or short term contractual labour in preference to wage-labour but Communist social policy insisted that all citizens have registered work places and live from a fixed wage. So while the state wished families, for instance, to send their sons to work in a shipyard along with other labourers, a Gypsy family would much rather have contracted to remove the rust on the hull of a ship for a fixed fee using all the labour available to them as they saw fit in their own time. Secondly, the Vlach Gypsies had made a speciality of trading and marketing the products of non-Gypsies, but the Communist regime was set upon eliminating all forms of private trade. Convinced by their strain of Marxist theory that trading middlemen were modern day usurers, making money out of time and other people's labour, the Communists had set out to eliminate all forms of private commerce including that of the Gypsies. Finally, the Communists wanted to see a unified, homogenised society of workers but Gypsies resisted assimilation into a Magyar working population most of whose members were openly contemptuous of them. So great was the hostility at times that when offered the chance to take council housing on advantageous terms many Gypsies continued to prefer the difficulties of ghetto life.

A cultural vacuum

Communist theory of social change aimed to achieve radical social transformation by making a clean break from the past. Only through a rupture with the past would the mental *tabula rasa* be created onto which the Communists would then write their scientifically derived formulae for a good social life, uncorrupted by the false consciousness and false identities induced by previous class society. Gypsy identity was one such false-consciousness waiting to be replaced, an unfortunate hangover from the feudal and capitalist divisions of labour.

Since the Gypsies' distinct identity was thought to arise from their social excommunication, Gypsy 'ethnicity' as far as the Communists were concerned was characterised more by absences than presences. It is slightly anachronistic to talk here of Gypsy 'ethnicity' since it was only in the 1980's that the Hungarian Socialist Workers' Party was able to admit that Gypsies constituted an ethnic group at all: previously they had maintained that the term Gypsy referred to a sociological problem, not a culturally distinct people (cf. Guy 1975, and Erdös 1960). To state officials Gypsies presented a virtual blank board waiting to be written on. By breaking up Gypsy communities and the cycle of deprivation thought inherent in them and providing regular 'socialist' waged-work Gypsies would be set upon the path away from profligacy and spendthrift behaviour towards a sober work ethic having both the means (wages) and ends (a home) to accumulate the necessities for a 'civilised' way of life.

In October 1985, a good thirty-five years into the Communist period, I began my research on a Gypsy settlement in northern Hungary. There I found a burgeoning community of Gypsies determined to maintain their cultural identity and social distinctiveness. In trying to manage their circumstances under the socialist regime these Gypsies were able to draw on three strengths: their communal organisation, their attitude to the creation of wealth and most curiously the importance they attach to sharing speech and song. This chapter discusses primarily the first of these resources.

A 'state of siege'

On the settlement where I lived, a half-hour walk from the centre of a prosperous agricultural town, a large extended family of Gypsies (some thirty separate households) had gradually bought up small peasant houses with gardens. They had converted the productive land into yards for their horses and were using their isolation from the town as cover for a range of semi-licit 'second economy' activities. Although their economic circumstances were better than those of the majority of Gypsies in Hungary the problems these Gypsies faced in maintaining a community and the solutions they found to them were typical of fellow Romani-speaking Gypsies throughout Hungary.

For as long as we have records it is clear that Gypsies in modern Hungary have lived in a 'state of siege' under which the outside world has constantly sought to break down the cohesiveness of their communities and assimilate Gypsies piecemeal as individual families (the image comes from Luc de Heusch's traveller-style account of Gypsy life in central Europe, (de Heusch, 1961). Under Communist rule, as any one family showed itself capable of leading a non-Gypsy life by, for instance, maintaining good work records, building itself a slightly better than average house, and accumulating domestic goods within the house, they would be offered the chance to assimilate 'up' into the Hungarian population through the offer of a flat in a better area of town. The state in other words was always on the look out for the individual Gypsy family which showed itself capable of diverging from the norm of Gypsy life.

Now, Gypsies themselves tend to be intensely egalitarian and individualistic. Partly in response to their regular subordination to the *gajos,* Gypsies are unwilling ever to be, or appear to be, bossed around by another Gypsy. There are no institutional structures in Gypsy society nor corporate property arrangements which would give some Gypsies authority over others. Individual identity and character are also given great rhetorical and practical stress in all kinds of minor and major ways in Gypsy culture. However, this kind of economic and social individualism leads to differences among individuals and families which envious Gypsies can always interpret as the result of a desire of the successful to cut themselves off from their relatives and friends and move upwards into the *gajo* world. In other words, the very powerful individualist current in Gypsy culture appears to pose a threat to the continuity of community. Kertész-Wilkinson is wrong to suggest in her chapter (apparently on the basis of a reading of my 1988 thesis,) that in north Hungary the Rom make no distinction among the *gajos*. What I say is that for the Rom all *gajos* are categorically 'peasants', but this does not mean that they do not recognise social distinctions among the *gajos*. The confusion arises because the Rom use of the Hungarian term '*paraszt*' is metaphorical, as I made clear (1988, Ch. 7) and does not directly correspond to the Hungarian descriptive usage, with which Kertész-Wilkinson is familiar, to describe a class of people. So for the Rom I know, and unlike other Hungarian speakers, there is no necessary contradiction between being a 'peasant' and being 'genteel' (*uri*).

Gypsy community organisation testifies to the success with which they have resisted the attempt by the outside world to lever members out of the groups, but this has not been done without a constant struggle. In response to their effective enclosure in a hostile world the Gypsies developed a battery of communal devices to protect themselves, summed up in the term *Romanes* – a term which refers both to Romani, the Gypsy language and to 'the Gypsy way of doing things'.

The Gypsy way
In so far as 'the Gypsy way' concerns relations with the outside, official *gajo* world matters are fairly straightforward. The Gypsies construct the world around their settlements as a place full of dangers for themselves. Thus people will rarely leave the settlement alone. A man making a trip into town will always be accompanied by another: men especially should never be allowed in town alone for fear that they will fall into trouble with the non-Gypsy authorities, especially the police. Again when a member of a community is ill in hospital a near constant presence of visitors is maintained and at official visiting hours up to a score of Gypsies may arrive to re-create the atmosphere of the settlement within the hospital – all in order not to leave one's fellow Gypsy alone among the *gajos*. This ethic of caring for one's own sort is extended to Gypsies one doesn't know (*streina Rom*). If one comes across 'stranger Gypsies' in trouble, broken down on the roadside for instance, then one should stop and offer assistance.

However, in daily relations within the settlement the 'Gypsy Way' is a more demanding ethic. Inside a settlement a fundamental aspect of *Romanes*, the 'Gypsy way', is an ethos of sharing with and thereby helping each other (*zhutis ame*). As a Gypsy woman once put it to me: "Gypsies help each other out. If a Gypsy has lots of money and somebody else needs some then he'll give it to him. If one Gypsy woman sees another who hasn't got anything to eat or cook, she says to the other one, 'Come to shop with me and we'll buy some food to eat'. They help each other out ... unlike the non-Gypsies. That's not the custom with the non-Gypsies".

This account is undoubtedly romanticised but it fairly reflects the rhetorical stress which Gypsies put on a willingness to share the necessities of life. It is this rhetorical stress which largely accounts for the legitimate restrictions and limits imposed on the expression of the potentially divisive individualism.

Commensality and food

Food is not usually served by Gypsies for what would appear to them to be an exclusive family meal. Gypsy cuisine, while close to its Hungarian counterpart, is considered by Gypsies as specific to themselves.

Though in practice most people eat in their own homes, each house cooks much more food each day than it will consume itself – so as to have some food to offer to visitors. Because there is no formal family gathering, nor set time to eat, food that is offered to a visitor never seems like the remains of a private family occasion but rather like that which a house provides for anyone who passes through it to eat as and when they see fit.

When food is served it is placed in a bowl on the floor or on a stool in the middle of the room and any men present will be enjoined to sit down together around it. The women will eat either at once from a different bowl or later from the same bowl. Since commensality is such an emotive sign of sharing, of being Gypsies together, if any Gypsy goes into a house where another is eating the very first thing offered to him is food: "Come! Eat!" (*Av! Xa!*).The offer will be repeated with astonishing persistency until the guest accepts since Gypsies profoundly dislike eating while another sits in the room without joining in. The significance of this derives in part from the fact that the *gajos* are notoriously unwilling to sit down and eat food with a 'dirty' Gypsy.

Not to have food to offer is a cause of mortifying shame and opens a household up to the accusation that it is tight-fisted with its food. For a similar reason no one should ever be told to hurry while eating.

This is, the reader may feel, a minor example of the commitment to sharing but if you consider that most Gypsy families are reduced to a diet of bread and potatoes by the end of the wage-month it is a clear sign of the greater value accorded to hospitality over personal gratification.

Being open to the needs of others

Going beyond the boundaries of hospitality in the house there is a constant flow of minor goods and services between households. Women frequently ask each other for domestic articles so that to borrow the broom from a neighbour may take one on a trip round three of four houses following its path as it has been lent from house to house. A woman who buys large quantities of food will find herself giving some of it away as her friends send their children round to ask for some of it. (Gypsy larders are in consequence bare of food other than that day's comestibles).

Gypsy men demand hay for their horses from one another's supplies, help each other with shoeing or breaking a horse, all without expecting any direct return. Men and women will happily lie (*xoxaven*) for each other to the *gajos* and in the petty pilfering that goes on in the daily market women also help each other out without expecting a part of the other's takings. In principle men should be willing to lend money to their 'brothers' when they are wealthy but in practice men try to hide their money (by giving it to their wives, putting it in the bank or handing it to the *gajo* anthropologist) and so save it from the claims of relatives.

A further expression of 'sharing' can be seen in the manner with which children are treated. For instance, adults are not restricted to making demands on their own children to go to the shops for them or do other domestic work. More significantly adults often take responsibility in raising other people's children. Many Gypsy children spend a considerable portion of their childhood being looked after by non-parental relatives. In such cases the parties to the informal adoption refer to each other as 'parents' and 'children' (*dad, dej/chav,chej*). One aspect of the ethic underlying this is given almost ritual form in the way elder relatives jokingly 'kidnap' children, taking them off on a trip for a few hours without telling their parents – thereby playing symbolically with the ambivalent rights of the community over its children.

Through all this sharing Gypsies create an image of a people open to the needs of others and willing to pool its resources. Typically, throughout the winter, when each family tends to spend its time cooped up in its home, Gypsies complain frequently and then as the warmer spring weather comes they enthusiastically welcome the first opportunity to shift all of domestic life, especially cooking out of doors. The image of the Gypsies as 'poolers' also receives striking symbolic elaboration, in frequent swaps (*paruvel*) of clothing and jewellery between Gypsies. I remember often seeing elderly and respected Gypsy men agreeing during a drink at a bar to swap a piece of clothing, a jacket, a hat, a pair of boots and then as they struggle to fit on their new boots proudly announcing to each other and the world at large their 'brotherly' feelings for one another. Gypsy clothing is in any case remarkably standard, even uniform so the result of such swaps is a kind of symbolic re-doubling of the 'sharing' of dress.

The ethic of sharing and the image of brotherhood

This activity brings to light an even more important aspect of sharing: a tendency to homogenise activities. So long as all Gypsies do the same, look the same, eat the same they appear equals. Waves of fashion sweep across a settlement like the one I lived on and then pass a few weeks or months later: one winter everyone buys bantam ducks, another year pigeons are all the rage. One week a man buys gravel to lay in his yard and the next week the head of every self-respecting household has done the same. In this way no differentiation is allowed, no family gets ahead of the others.

In a world where Gypsies were stigmatised at the bottom of the Hungarian social pile and where the state was offering inducements to individual Gypsy families to give up the Gypsy way of life and assimilate 'up' into the Magyar working class, the commitment of each individual and family to his fellow Gypsies was put permanently in question. In the face of this, the demand made by Gypsies of one another was that they constantly affirm their intention to remain a Gypsy by doing the same as each other and so levelling their unique and individual characters to a common standard. *Romanes*, the Gypsy way, is an exacting regime but by demanding that the Gypsies all face in one direction, as it were, it created the conditions in which Gypsies resisted a society far more powerful than their own.

The injunction of ethnic and communal solidarity is buttressed by the moral idiom, an idiom of brotherhood, within which communal relations are conceived and talked of. There is no extension of the concept of 'sister' to encompass large social groups as there is with the notion of 'brother'. Women and men may feel great affection towards a sister or other woman but there are few or no contexts where this emotion can be publicly manifested in the way that brotherly sentiment is constituted as a basis of the Gypsy social order. It is typically a group of brothers who are said to found a settlement and in an ideal world it is brothers who live and work together. Among the Gypsies brotherhood is an egalitarian idiom: not only is there no kinship term for elder or younger brother there are also no significant social roles attached to relative seniority. In settlement life fathers have little authority over their sons and there is no stigma attached to a son who shouts orders back at a bossy father. Gypsies address men as "Boys!" (*chavale!*, i.e. unmarried men).

The idiom of brotherhood results further in a devaluation of descent and inherited identity. Hungarian Gypsies tend to emphasise identity which comes from one's relations with one's ('classificatory') siblings with whom one grows up as much if not more than identity derived from one's parents and connections to the past. One's inherited identity is only peripherally a guarantee of one's moral worth and so being a Gypsy requires regular, practical re-affirmation of one's sense of connection with one's fellow brothers. Gypsies who give up the Gypsy way thus effectively cease to be Gypsies and *gajos* who marry a Gypsy and adopt *Romanes* are treated as fully assimilated Gypsies. During the Communist period pressure from Gypsy intellectuals resulted in the granting of a legal status to the Gypsies as an 'ethnic group'. The Gypsies I know were largely uninterested in this change and feel very little link with the intellectuals who claim to speak on their behalf. While for the intellectuals the common ethnic origin of the Gypsies is genuinely felt and imagined, this is not so for ordinary Gypsies. For them only an identity rooted in joint action in the present is significant. Thus they know that their ancestors are said to come from India but display no interest in this fact.

Brothers against households
The concern with establishing and re-establishing identity in the present is not simply the result of the political pressure on Gypsy society from without. It arises as importantly from an internal contradiction at the heart of Gypsy communities: the ideology of brotherhood (almost self-evidently) can never provide a charter for all of Gypsy social life since in effect it excludes or at least devalues the role of the women and those activities which Gypsy men and women share. Most dramatically the ideology of brotherhood exists in de facto contradiction to the domestic organisation of Gypsy communities into independent households headed by a marital couple.

It is in this context that one can make sense of the rhetorical and ritual stress which Gypsies give to sharing in such acts as the kidnapping of children: they represent a desire to render permeable the walls of the household and to suggest that Gypsies can be open to one another independently of household ties.

Such ritual gestures do not, however, resolve the intensely practical problems that arise as a result of the existence of households for a community ideologically conceived as a 'brotherhood'. Whatever the ideology of sharing, households are the site of any accumulation of wealth that does go on. Moreover, individual households face the world of the *gajos* rather diversely and from such variations disparities of wealth and comfort arise among the Gypsies. As a result quarrels break out when a son objects to the constant demands for hay from his father or a daughter-in-law protests about always buying food for her mother-in-law. As I see it, such conflicts over sharing result from the irreconcilable demands of communal life and life in households. Because of this conflict one finds oneself as an outsider observing a continuous shifting between an image of the Gypsies selflessly helping each other and an image of them mercilessly counting the cost of their relatives' demands.

For the Gypsies, however, it is mostly possible to avoid facing this contradiction. At moments of conflict an individual resists the implication that he/she has refused to subordinate his or her household interest to the welfare of the Gypsies in general, by reinterpreting the demands made by a particular individual as the unreasonable, personal needs of a wayward father/mother-in-law/brother, etc. Very commonly, moreover, conflicts between men about the allocation of material and symbolic resources are played out between female members of a family, between sisters-in-law and a daughter and mother-in-law, so the locus of disagreement does not appear to be the male members of the community (Stewart forthcoming, ch.5).

Nonetheless, while able to reinterpret particular quarrels so as not to upset ethnic ideology, the social implications of inequalities among households are always divisive: difference, specificity and individuality can all be interpreted as an attempt to stand apart and above from the Gypsies, as an attempt to leave one's fellow Gypsies behind. Since getting rich goes hand in hand with developing good relations with powerful *gajos* it often seems to less successful Gypsies that the rich are breaking their ties with the Gypsies. So, the ethic of sharing and brotherly feeling among the Gypsies are far more than symptoms of an intense communal sentiment – they reflect an attempt, successful so far, to preserve the very basis of their communities and identity.

The free lunch

It is not only in matters of communal organisation that Gypsies have asserted their autonomy from the surrounding non-Gypsy society. As important has been their distinctive approach to the matter of gaining a livelihood. Gypsies, however, are an impoverished and multiply dis-advantaged people, living on the periphery of Hungarian society and so their attempts to establish economic autonomy are fraught with contradiction.

The fact is that the vast majority of Romani-speaking Gypsies in Hungary today are wage-workers, that is to say, are 'objectively speaking' a part of the Hungarian 'working class'. For as long as the Vlach Gypsies have lived in Hungary, that is five generations or more, they have relied on waged and other dependent labour relations for the bulk of their income. However, they have never allowed this real dependence to undermine fatally their struggle for an independent mode of life.

That independent way of life is represented for the Gypsies above all by trade and in the communities that I know best, by horse-dealing. This horse-trading cannot be understood in isolation but reveals its full significance in contrast to the work ethic of the surrounding non-Gypsy, especially peasant population, an ethic which was taken on lock, stock and barrel by the Communist regime. While the peasant/socialist ethic urges self-sufficiency and moral elevation through work, for the Gypsies the good life derives from deals in which one puts no work into the horse. If they 'work on' anything it is the human parties to the deal, not the horse. For the peasants/socialists work refers only to heavy, physically exhausting, sweat-expelling, earth-shifting effort. Through such punishing toil the peasant makes a 'proper' person of himself and provides the means for an independent life for himself (cf.Bell 1984: 170, Fél and Hofer 1969 and Stewart 1993).

In dealing the Gypsy tries to achieve a similar moral elevation, only in his case by making money grow without effort and labour. If the 'peasant' ethic amounts to a belief that you can only harvest what you have sown, the Gypsies seem determined to prove that in reality there are always things to harvest which they have not 'sown'. Through a rhetorical celebration of economic cunning they present trade as a means to live 'well' and 'lightly' (*laches*) in the world. As Gypsies put it: "We make money turn around for us, turn around and come to us". They do this by organising, persuading or manipulating others into doing business. The Gypsy's role on the market is managing people. A Gypsy once told me that anyone can be a trader 'if they have the words', that is, the style that is necessary to convince people to part with their money or possessions and do business.

In trade it is through words that the Gypsy affects the world around him. As another man put it, "I need to have speech (*vorba*). If I don't have that then I can't do anything. You see, most people don't have this ... You have to talk someone into buying a horse. You have to talk the horse up [lit. beside it], so someone will buy it. You have to take a person's hand to make them do business – otherwise they won't come together".

Through trading Gypsies try to assert a degree of control over the outside world, or at least a rejection of the control which outside forces exert over the Gypsies. Their efforts do not meet, however, with immediate success. Horse-trades are for most Gypsies a risky, even loss-making enterprise – most Gypsies can only afford to buy older horses and so have difficulty recovering their investments. However, the capital for buying horses comes from the sale of pigs which have been reared without monetary cost by Gypsy women and so precise accounting is rarely carried out. Secondly, all deals with *gajos* are classed as 'sales' (as against 'swaps' with fellow Gypsies) and so a deal can in most cases be represented as profitable. This profit won is money gained without having to give of oneself (as one must in wage-labour) and so without having to recognise dependence on the non-Gypsy 'other'. Earnings from wage-work, although more important economically, are ideologically devalued as being fit only for private accumulation in the household. The money which Gypsies 'win' in trading, provides a basis, ideologically at least, for cycles of feasting and celebration in which Gypsy brotherhood (and thereby community) is ritually established. In dealing and creating money which feasts one's fellow Gypsies, a man is directly serving the social good. So it is the fact of dealing, rather than the amount of money made which establishes a deal as good: the proof of the dealing lies in the drinking! In horse fairs macro-economic forces and micro-level powers which shape Gypsy lives are thus effectively denied.

Brothers in song
Gypsies have no land nor any other significant means of production. Although in the medieval and early modern period their professional

specialisations as blacksmiths and musicians gave them a certain power and prestige in non-Gypsy society, nowadays it is only through successful speech that Gypsies make their mark on the *gajos*, so it is entirely appropriate that it is through a celebration of particular forms of speech that Gypsies ritually constitute their communities as brotherhoods.

On the major public festivals of Christmas, New Year and Easter, as well as at personal rites of passage such as christening, request for a bride, conscription, release from prison and so on Gypsies celebrate their shared existence. These celebrations, known as *mulatshago* (from the Hungarian *mulatni*, to enjoy and entertain oneself with abandon), provide an occasion for the enactment of an ideal of Gypsies (almost entirely men) sharing their wealth with fellow Gypsy (men) drinking and singing together. During the *mulatshago* the ethic of hospitality embodied daily in small gifts of food and drink to guests is expressed most dramatically and publicly.

But the point of these celebrations and their climax is when the men pause from their conversations and sing together. These songs which must always be 'true' are laments about the conditions of Gypsy life, the poverty, the suffering of imprisonment, the pain of leaving one's mother or being betrayed by one's wife and above all the centrality of the 'brothers' in Gypsy life. As important as the content of the songs is the style in which they are performed. Each song is said to belong to someone and its rendition is initiated by this man. However, his voice is soon lost in the mass of voices as all the Gypsies present join in together in a virtual monody that is technically known as 'heterophony'.

Kertész-Wilkinson introduced me to the technically correct term ('heterophony'). I am not clear, however, why Kertész-Wilkinson's chapter in this volume adopts a straw man approach to my earlier argument. She implies that I talk in a technical fashion of the Rom singing in 'unison'. In a footnote to a 1989 article I made a misleading reference to medieval choral music (following up an interest in exploring the notion of 'brotherhood'), but the article itself, far from suggesting total unanimity of performance (unison singing) deals with the way the 'lead' singer's role is or is not integrated with that of all the other 'brothers'. Indeed in that original article I include an example of a song in which the individual variations of the lead singer are marked! Here again, then, it is at least gratifying to see that Kertész-Wilkinson agrees with and re-affirms the points I made in 1989.

At such a moment when all the Gypsies sing together, act in concert, they achieve an ideal of brotherly behaviour which inspires them to accept the egalitarian demands of the ethic of sharing brothers outside the context of *mulatshago* when relations are often more fractious. In their songs Gypsy men 'become' brothers to one another, assert their unity both against the dominant *gajo* world outside, in contrast to their own normal divisiveness and in opposition to the world of women barred from the *mulatshago*. Here then is a paradox: by keeping the Gypsy women out of the ritual, Gypsy men represent an image of a successful, viable community; and this is one which the women too respect and attempt to sustain as the extended analyses of Gypsy song and its performance in Stewart (1989) and Kertész-Wilkinson's chapter in this this volume shows.

Kertész-Wilkinson provides a complementary perspective on singing in less formal contexts in two Hungarian Gypsy communities, though she presents her contribution as a challenge to my own position. Kertész-Wilkinson's aim seems to differ from mine in that while I have tried to show the social effects of the most prominent form of verbal expression in the main collective activity of Hungarian Rom, Kertész-Wilkinson wishes to demonstrate the variety of musical expression in two Rom communities. Before the confusion of perspectives develops any further it is perhaps worth stressing that though Kertész-Wilkinson constructs part of her argument around a putative difference with my approach, hers and mine are, it seems to me, theoretically complementary and empirically rather closer than she suggests. The suggestion of difference derives in part from a misunderstanding about my argument taken over from Bloch (1974): the point of describing *mulatshago* as 'ritual' activity was not to set up an opposition between two entirely separate spheres of activity (public/private or whatever) but to show the effects of 'formalisation' *as a process*. For this reason the crucial axis of my argument has dealt with the way individual experience is aligned with collective interests through the practice of singing together. Empirically therefore, Kertész-Wilkinson recapitulates the essential thrust of my argument. Her summary of her case, "in performance individual and social identities ... are enacted and reconciled through the interaction between the communal and individual creativity ..." parallels rather closely my own earlier article (1989). So, far from suggesting that all individuality was suppressed in singing, as Kertész-Wilkinson asserts, I showed how the tension between the individual and collective aspects determines the actual performance of song in *mulatshago*. When successful, I argued, personal and collective perspectives were aligned through song. What seems to me new in Kertész-Wilkinson is the fascinating discussion of less formalised performance contexts, and above all the emerging contrast between what appear to be two rather different communities of Rom.

The persistence of Gypsy identity

Across Eastern Europe today ancient cultural differences remain important in part because they were, despite Communist Party intentions, re-enforced in the past thirty years. Through the 1960s and 1970s the Hungarian authorities believed that they were making an entirely original and unprecedented offer to the Gypsies of Hungary by allowing them for the first time to participate as full members of society, as members of the class that is nominally in charge of production. But the Communist state made the mistake of trying to integrate the Gypsies by persuading them to adopt the old peasant attitude to labour. Since Gypsies had defined themselves in opposition to just this ideology of work it was not surprising that they had difficulty taking it on when re-presented by the socialist state.

But if wheeling and dealing continued to be the ideal for Gypsy youth this was not just explicable in terms of their anti-labour ethic but also reflected an assessment of material chances in socialist Hungary. Gypsies entered the labour market as un-skilled or semi-skilled workers and were often given tasks peripheral to the main production processes. In a word they continued to provide cheap labour for the dirty jobs Magyars wouldn't do. On the other hand, they knew that if they could establish a niche within the 'free' second economy the road to wealth would be open. A fairly accurate, pragmatic assessment, therefore, of the different life-chances of 'worker' and 'trader' under Kadarite socialism also motivated Gypsies to resist assimilation of the dominant communist/peasant work ethic.

But neither cultural pre-disposition nor rational calculation could have substituted for the 'dream of a place where they could be at home' in keeping their hearts and minds firmly set during the ideological onslaught they suffered during the Communist period. National territory provides both a compelling image of enclosure and a set of powerful practices (borders, passports, currency, balance of payments) which together establish the image of a potentially self-sufficient people, independent of other nations. The Gypsies, lacking national territory, had to be able to create an image of self-sufficiency in other ways. One source of strength came from the representation of a means of making money without having to incorporate the outsider, the *gajo* 'other' through reciprocal relations with them. At horse markets Gypsies could continue to represent a domination of the *gajos* at an ideologically loaded moment. Profit, that which was won for nothing from the *gajo*, allowed the Gypsies to imagine that they can live by keeping to themselves. The other source of ideological strength came from the ritual representation in *mulatshago* of Gypsy political egalitarianism and the ethos of sharing. Here Gypsy men (supported by their women) again showed it is possible to live self-sufficiently, in this case without women and households. In ritual, as in horse-dealing, Gypsies engaged in an activity which reflexively established the truth of what it asserts (Gypsies are 'brothers', Gypsies 'live from dealing') and so were provided with an image of a viable way of life separate from the non-Gypsies.

All ethnic myths are inevitably ideologically biased representations as they have to claim a discontinuity between cultures that does not, cannot exist. This is all the more true for groups like Gypsies and Jews who live amongst a host population with whom they often share more similarities than they do with members of their own ethnic group elsewhere. The ability ideologically and practically to create a gulf between Gypsy and non-Gypsy and sustain an image of the world in which it is possible to live by 'keeping to oneself' are thus crucial prerequisites for the continuing construction of the Vlach Rom as a distinct ethnic group. Their achievement is all the more noteworthy in that not all Hungarian Gypsies fared so well. Some of the more powerful peoples of the world have managed to institutionalise this ancient ideological image in the form of territorial nation states; the feat of the Gypsies is to have done this with neither the ideological device nor the practical power of their host populations.

References

ASCHERSON N 1991 "When the Dead Awaken" *Independent on Sunday* May 12

BECK S and GHEORGHE N nd. "From Slavery to Co-inhabiting Nationality: The Political Economy of Romanian Gypsies" paper to the Symposium on the Social Anthropology of Europe I.U.A.E.S. Intercongress, Amsterdam

BLOCH M 1974 "Symbol, Song, Dance and Features of Articulation: is religion an extreme form of traditional authority?" *Archives Européennes de Sociologie* XV (1) pp.55-81

CHARLEMAGNE J 1984 "Bridging the Cultural Gap" *Unesco Courier* October (Special Issue on "The Gypsies") pp.15-17

BELL P 1984 *Peasants in Socialist Transition: Life in a Collectivised Hungarian Village* University of California Press, Berkely

ERDÖS K 1960 "Le problème Tsigane en Hongrie " *Études Tsiganes* Vol.3 pp.1-10

FÉL E and HOFER T 1969 *Proper Peasants: Traditional Life in a Hungarian Village* Viking Fund Publications in Anthropology, No. 46, Aldine, Chicago

GELLNER E 1983 *Nations and Nationalism* Blackwell, Oxford

GUY W 1975 "Ways of Looking at Rom: The Case of Czechoslovakia " in Rehfisch F ed. *Gypsies, Tinkers and Other Travellers* Academic Press, London, pp. 201-229

De HEUSCH L 1966 *A la découverte des Tsiganes: Une expedition de reconnaissance* Ed. de L'Institut de Sociologie de L'Université Libre, Bruxelles

KAMINSKI I-M 1980 *The State of Ambiguity, Studies of Gypsy Refugees* Anthropological Research, Gothenburg

OKELY J 1983 *The Traveller-Gypsies* Cambridge University Press, Cambridge

PIASERE L 1984 *Mare Roma: Categories Humaines et Structure Sociale Une Contribution a L'ethnologie Tsigane* Thèse pour le Doctorat du 3.ème Cycle, University of Paris

STEWART M 1989 "'True Speech': Song and the Moral Order of a Hungarian Vlach Gypsy Community" *Man* Vol 24, pp 79-102

STEWART M 1993 "Gypsies, the work ethic and Hungarian Socialism" in Hann C M ed. *Socialism* Routledge, London

STEWART M forthcoming *The Time of the Gypsies: poverty, cultural identity and resistance to proletarianisation in socialist Hungary* Westview, Boulder

SUTHERLAND A 1975 *Gypsies: The Hidden Americans* Tavistock, London

TOMKA M 1984 "The Gypsy Craftsmen of Europe" *Unesco Courier* October (Special Issue on "The Gypsies") pp.15-17

WILLIAMS P 1984 *Marriage Tsigane: une cérémonie de fiancailles chez les Rom de Paris* L'Harmattan/Selaf, Paris

Chapter 7 Song performance: a model for social interaction among Vlach Gypsies in South-eastern Hungary

Irén Kertész-Wilkinson, Lecturer in Ethnomusicology, Goldsmiths' College, London

The Vlach Gypsies or Rom, as they refer to themselves, form an identifiable social category among the three main groups of Hungarian Gypsies, the others being the Beash, who speak Romanian and Hungarian, and the Romungri, or older-established Hungarian Gypsy groups. The Vlach Gypsies are marked by three major cultural features: their own language, Romani, their own song repertoire and their own style of performing songs and dance. All three features are essential to any public event and thus to Vlach identity. This is reflected in the folk view that every 'true' Rom must be able to sing, dance or tell folk tales in the Romani way, at least to an acceptable degree.

Song and dance performances of the Hungarian Vlach Gypsies embody a range of symbol systems which constitute Rom identity. These performances externalise the Vlach Gypsy inner social structure through which the place and role of individuals and their interactions can be enacted and, albeit temporarily, re-structured. They also create an explicitly acknowledged boundary between themselves and non-Gypsy or other Gypsy groups.

The meaning of musical performances as a cultural phenomenon and a social fact cannot be understood without examining the social contexts in which musical activities take place. Such contextual investigations are all the more indispensable in cases such as that of Hungarian Vlach Gypsies where – in distinction to many other societies including the peasant cultures of eastern European within which they are embedded – more or less the same repertoire is performed in a wide range of contexts. In such circumstances it is misleading to assign a single meaning to song and dance performances. This is especially so because, as symbolic systems, they already contain multiple possible interpretations and therefore social context merely adds a further dimension to that complexity.

Social contexts of cultural manifestations have generally been grouped into two main categories: public and private. Of the two, the public contexts have gained greater attention from social scientists and ethnographers because, as Richard Baumann (1978:280) points out, they are:

"... the most prominent performance contexts within a community. They are, as a rule, scheduled events, restricted in setting, clearly bounded, and widely public, involving the most highly formalised performance forms and accomplished performers of the community."

However, as Baumann continues:

"The most challenging job that faces the student of performance is establishing the continuity between the noticeable and public performance of cultural performances, and the spontaneous, unscheduled, optional performance contexts of everyday life."

The study of performance, as Ruth Finnegan (cited in Baumann 1978) reminds us, is by no means simple or:

"... altogether straightforward, partly because this interest has been relatively undeveloped till recently compared to textual analysis, partly because of the unlimited number of possible components in performance given the variety of cultural, historical and generic conventions and the varying ways these are developed."

In my own field of Hungarian Vlach Gypsy song studies the contextual approach has been largely neglected until recently. Most researchers, following the model set by Hungarian folk music research, have had as their primary goal the collection of large samples of data in order to establish the characteristic features of a particular style before focusing on in-depth studies. This extensive survey method limited the time that was spent in any specific community and thus inevitably led to a neglect of contextual studies of performances.

Among the few who have changed this path is the English anthropologist, Michael Stewart, who conducted in-depth research of a north Hungarian Vlach Gypsy community in the mid-1980s. His anthropological background and the model of his teacher, Maurice Bloch (1974), led Stewart, rightly, to consider performance events as forms of ritualistic and symbolic communication in which singing and dance play essential roles. In the spirit of the structuralist approach his study brought out various binary oppositions of Vlach Gypsy life: between everyday speech and ritualistic performances of song, relationships between Gypsies and non-Gypsies and male-female gender oppositions, all of which Stewart showed, to some extent, have their parallels in the musical performance. Stewart's study is undoubtedly a significant development in Hungarian Vlach Gypsy song research. He was the first to study performance of the songs as an enactment of social life and to realise that their significance to the 'insiders' lay in their offering a vehicle for telling the 'truth'.

That entails a selection of values that are expressed in the song text which, according to Stewart's study, must be in Romani language and sung to a Vlach Gypsy melody.

Stewart's approach, however, is flawed by being limited to a single context of performance, the male-only *mulatsago*, and by viewing song as essentially only a verbal expression. This constrains him to the correspondingly limited conclusion that performance serves the purpose of expressing a traditional form of authority through which Vlach Gypsy men wish to establish equality between one another whilst asserting their domination over women. This echoes Bloch's verdict on the function of song and dance performance among the Merina of Madagascar as well as in other parts of the world. Ultimately, Stewart may have detracted from the undoubted value of his work by failing to consider whether his *a priori* model fitted the full diversity of the culture to which he applied it. As Ruth Finnegan (1992:100) pointed out in relation to the variability of social situations of performance, one has to be:

"... alert to this variety rather than just presupposing one model (most likely projected from personal preconceptions)."

Indeed, Stewart mentions that there are other events, such as weddings, during which women are present, but he omits them from his study on the ground that the folk terminology does not name them *mulatsago* (Stewart 1987:145). Whilst no one would argue about the importance of folk concepts in establishing valid categories, we must be wary about accepting them as the sole determinants. A consideration of all contexts may reveal aspects of folk classifications that in turn hide multiple functions of performances. Concepts and functions of performance are indeed significant aspects of any ethnomusicological and anthropological studies that enlarge our knowledge about human societies. Nevertheless, the aims of these two disciplines are also to show disparities which need to be recognised. As Blacking (1989:61) has noted:

"Studies of music and dance have been both helped and seriously hindered by the application of ideas and methods drawn from history and the social sciences, chiefly because they cannot account for the crucial fact that individual aesthetic experience frequently transcends time, place and social constraints. It has indeed been useful to examine the varieties of human creativity within historical and cultural framework but at the same time, the concepts of history and the social sciences can shift the emphasis away from the content of the music and dance and concentrate on *their uses* and their *extra-musical* and *extra-dance* meanings to those who use them, rather than on their *special qualities* and *musical* experiences... Using socio-political concepts to explain musical variety implies that artistic imagination is simply part of the superstructure of social life, determined by economic and political formations: musical variety is therefore seen as the product of political and ethnic differentiation rather than of a special kind of human creativity."

In order to study and understand musical performance as experience and as human creativity, many ethnomusicologists have urged the need for a special approach, namely, participation in music-making (for example Baily 1984; Blacking in Howard 1991; Feld 1982; Hood 1960; Kertész-Wilkinson 1994). Some anthropologists have offered similar advice. For example, Colin Turnbull (1990:77) has noted that:

"Few of us, for instance, pay nearly enough attention to the use of the senses of smell, taste, and touch, or to non-verbal sounds. Yet these, particularly sound, are often key elements in ritual and other religious behaviour. Sound alone provides a royal road to the liminal condition, and the feelings it evokes can be highly significant for the fieldworker if he allows them, if not sound itself, to move him both physically and emotionally, instead of confining himself to an exclusively conscious, rational framework."

Turnbull (1990,p.79) argues later that:

"The use of subjectivity, of total (including emotional, spiritual) participation ... is not unlike use of rational process by which we recognise without any discomfort that things are seldom, if ever, what they seem to be, and set about arriving at a more accurate, more complete knowledge of what they are by reconsidering them in light of other information, form different perspectives, and so forth. Anthropologists go to exceptional lengths, in fact, *not* to accept things for what they seem to be, but those lengths are entirely intellectual and, all too often, spectacularly acrobatic but ultimately meaningless."

This type of approach opens up the possibility of surmounting the limitations that result from regarding song and musical performance mainly on a verbal level, which is my second main criticism against Stewart's work. The researcher's physical as well as emotional participation in performance may result in the discovery of many processes of communication that take place at a non-verbal level. We may find that relationships between participants are not simply reproductive or counter-balancing social relationships but specific interactions or alliances that are based on the outcome of kinetic, affective and aesthetic experiences.

This chapter will show how Hungarian Vlach Gypsy song performance may gain different meanings according to a variety of social context. My aim is to show not so much how musical performance reveals a different reality from the "mask of appearance" of everyday reality, as argued by Michael Stewart (1989:79) but how, through a study of multiple contexts, we can "discriminate between the common mask [of musical performance] and the complex variations which it conceals" (Cohen 1984:74 [my parenthesis]). Because music operates simultaneously at different levels, not only can it accommodate the highly social and highly individual within the framework of a single context, it can also offer, as a form of symbolic expression, a perfect medium to enact the conflicting or paradoxical values and emotions which serve to affirm and re-structure social interactions.

My analysis will concentrate on the repertoire and performance rules of both the slow and dance song genres of the Vlach Gypsies within the dialectical movement of public/communal, the less formal and the private/individual contexts.

Social and economic life of the two communities under study

The fieldwork on which this chapter is based was carried out during two extended visits to Hungary. The first of the visits, from August 1987 to January 1988, was mainly among the Vlach Gypsies of Community A. It was in the course of this first period that I decided to make Community B the locality for the second phase which was completed between July 1988 and January 1989.

The two communities are situated in Békés County, in the south-east corner of Hungary, an area that lies between the Transylvanian mountains and the Great Hungarian Plain within easy reach of the Romanian and Serbian borders. It is an ethnically mixed area with significant populations of various Gypsy groups (Vlach Rom, Romungri, Beash), and Slovaks, Romanians and Serbs interspersed among the Hungarian majority. This diversity is experienced most obviously through the various languages one hears when travelling on the trains and buses, still the main means of transport between the county's settlements. The climate is continental with hot summers and often bitterly cold winters with heavy snowfalls. The hot weather and the rich soil favour agriculture. Besides grain crops, the co-operative farms of this region specialise in growing onions, paprikas and melons. Food-processing and the manufacture of shoes, clothing and bricks provide most of the limited opportunities for work in light industry.

In both communities seasonal work is an important means of subsistence. During springtime the Rom collect edible snails whilst in the summer they pluck geese, pick blueberries and cut sorghum. In the late summer and autumn these can be supplemented by gathering corn cobs left in the fields by the harvesting machines; some of these are sold, the rest are kept to feed the horses during the winter. With the exception of plucking geese, the work is carried out by entire family groups working together as teams. They work hard for four or five hours a day, sometimes more, but in keeping with the Rom tradition of not separating work and enjoyment, they treat it as a family outing with jokes and songs livening up every moment. The democratic nature of Vlach Rom society finds expression in the equal division of rewards for labour. Children get their fair share but they often spend it on household goods to help their mothers.

The combination of various factors, such as lack of heavy industry in this area, no land to join co-operatives, the general poor health of Vlach Gypsies and a gradual shift in Hungarian government policy on provision of social allowances and security for those who live below the official poverty line, has meant that in the south-east of Hungary most Rom men, after a longer or shorter period of state employment, revert to their traditional occupation of horse-dealing or set up their own private business. In accordance with Rom tradition, it is up to women to support the family on a day-to-day basis through whatever jobs the local economy offers. In Community A some women worked either in a factory making socks and tights or in poultry factories. Others received a state disability pension on grounds of poor health and/or child allowances which served to provide for the families' basic necessities including food, clothing and household requisites. The local council, including its chairman, was sympathetic to Gypsies and actively assisted improvements in the settlement as well as providing various supplementary welfare allowances including grants for outfitting the children at the start of the school year and for purchasing fuel during winter.

The council of Community B, by contrast, was hostile towards Gypsies. It not only resorted to every possible pretext for refusing assistance, which included setting absurd conditions for providing loans for improvement or purchase of properties, it also imposed punitive fines on Gypsies caught collecting wood on common lands. Nevertheless, the Rom women were in demand among Hungarians of the village and nearby towns for various occasional jobs such as domestic cleaning, white-washing walls and gathering onions, garlic or poppy-seed for which they were given goods in exchange or some money.

The difference between the two Vlach Rom groups is apparent in their economic and social structure. Whilst the Rom of Community A have higher incomes that advantage is offset by the fact that they must buy almost everything in the shops or from Hungarian neighbours. The minimal role of welfare assistance in Community B is compensated for by a continuing demand from Hungarians for traditional domestic help from the Gypsies. That makes the Vlach Rom of Community B more resourceful in finding means of subsistence but in the process they end up even more marginalised in the eyes not only of the Hungarian population but even of other Rom groups which tend to look down on them for their poverty.

As regards social structure, Community A comprises three core families who are allied through marriage. Through the loss of many kin members to neighbouring towns over recent decades, it is more open than Community B in that Rom men from outside are accepted for marriage. Furthermore, the main kin group in Community A is regarded as of higher standing in the Rom hierarchy of 'nations' than its equivalent in Community B. The Rom of Community B compensate for this by maintaining strong unity as a closed cognate group.

The inner structure of the two communities
The Vlach Gypsies in the two communities I studied have structured their inner life on the purity principle to create boundaries between gender and generation which also encompass classifications of space, time, food, clothes, animals and the universe. In general, these correspond more or less closely with the findings reported for other Romani groups by Ann Sutherland (1975), Judith Okely (1983) and Michael Stewart (1987, 1989) although there are certain notable differences in where the line of acceptability is drawn. Amongst the Rom I studied those lines were often subject to individual interpretation. Thus, for example, my hostess's daughter in Community B allowed her favourite kitten to sleep in the room despite the fact that the grooming habits of dogs and cats render them 'unclean' as a rule. An even more extreme case was a puppy that my hostess in Community B had herself breast-fed and which grew up to be treated as a trustworthy and, so to speak, 'Romanised' member of the family.

Contrary to Stewart's observation among the northern Hungarian Vlach Rom, the Rom in the south-east make distinctions between various classes of non-Gypsies or *gajo*. The term *gajo* [Romani – herafter R] is applied to those with whom they would not mix socially, accept food or clothes from and often referred to as "dirty peasants". Non-Gypsies with whom they can eat, accept clothes from or even marry are considered to be 'genteel', *úri* [Hungarian – herafter H]. This is similar to the findings of Andzrej Mirga (1986) in the Tatra mountains of Poland where non-Gypsies who respect the Rom are accepted as *patjan* [R] or 'good persons' worthy of being invited to sit at the same table, *manus* [R] 'non-Gypsy man' or *raj* [R], 'genteel' non-Gypsies. The converse applies to other Rom. Although in one sense they are always regarded as superior to the non-Rom they are placed within a subtle hierarchical division. Every family or individual will find another who is in some way inferior, either because "their women are whores" or because "they are dirty Rom" whilst those in a higher 'nation' can be belittled for being "mean". This implies that the rules, although in one sense static and rigid as abstractions, are also flexible enough to be expanded to incorporate precisely those aspects which are normally excluded as 'other' and 'outside' or, alternatively, to be narrowed to exclude aspects that would be incorporated in another context.

Some expressions of the public / private dichotomy in folk views
It must be emphasised that 'public' and 'private' should be understood here in the Vlach Rom cultural context. For example, privacy in the western sense does not exist amongst the Vlach Rom. Families often sleep in the same room and visitors can call at any time, even during the night. Everyone knows almost everything about one another. Food and household utensils are often shared and letters opened. The notion of 'between you and me' may involve another half-dozen people who are also present but, being cognate to the speaker, would be regarded as one with her or him. Nevertheless, at times of conflict the knowledge of any past breach of Romani rules may be used to gain advantage over another. Thus Vlach Rom social life underlines the primacy of public and communal values, in contrast to the stress laid on privacy in western life. It is important for the following argument to understand that the continuum of Vlach Rom social contexts could be perceived as one that ranges merely from the widely public to the less public. Nevertheless, certain aspects of life – mainly those associated with pollution such as physical love-making or certain illnesses – must remain private knowledge. These subjects are not talked about in public, especially by women in front of men, although men may occasionally boast about their sexual life in a competitive spirit regardless who is present. (Women would talk about private matters only among reliable kin).

The folk view indicates a difference between public and less formal events either explicitly or implicitly through various instructions as to how one should behave in public. A woman might say, for instance, "I will not argue with my husband in front of strange Rom" whilst a man might tell his son, "You must learn, my little boy, how to make merriment nicely, singing well, using your hands to clap, to click your fingers, to dance and beat up your wife if she misbehaves!" I have even heard a child say, "There are times when children must leave the adults to enjoy their own merry-making."

In most cases the nature of a gathering is indicated by the type of food and drink that is served. On grand occasions, such as weddings and funeral rituals, food is compulsory. At weddings a variety of dishes, including desserts, is prepared whilst at a funeral rite the deceased's favourite dish will be offered along with the traditional Rom stewed lamb with paprika. In some instances a relative's dream will reveal the dead person wishes. For remembrance rituals held six weeks and one year after the funeral the Rom who attend eat a meal cooked by a non-Gypsy woman whilst specially invited non-Gypsy guests have a different meal cooked by a Rom woman. Since the latter meal is held to contain the soul of the deceased, any Rom would be horrified to partake of it, even by accident. Whilst a wide range of drinks is available for both events, for a funeral wake male guests must bring also a bottle of *retjija* [R] or spirit. For calendar festivities like Christmas stuffed cabbage (*sarma* [R]) and various cakes (*kalaco* [R]) are made whilst the men drink beer and the women sweet liqueurs. On less formal occasions the refreshments may consist solely of beer for all.

Repertoire as a model for social boundaries
In their song repertoire the Vlach Rom differentiate between two main genres: 'slow' or 'listening' songs and dance songs. The Rom of both communities where I studied label slow songs as *mulatoso*, meaning revelling or merry-making, or *hallgatoso,* meaning listening to or quiet. (The same label 'listening song' applies to slow songs among the Polish Highlanders and in Romania in areas where the Gypsies had an obvious influence on the local musical culture.) These etymologically Hungarian terms have gradually replaced the formerly used Romani term, *loki djili,* which also means slow song. The *mulatoso-hallgatoso* category compromises both Vlach Rom songs, the *romane djili* [R], and Hungarian ones, called either *magyar nóta* [H] or *ungriko djili* [R]. The latter are mainly nineteenth century compositions in imitation folk style but also include some Hungarian folk songs. Singers make a distinction between Hungarian and Vlach songs but they do not differentiate between Hungarian folk song and *magyar nóta* within their Hungarian repertoire. However, Hungarian songs heard on the radio or television are divided into *magyar nóta* and folk songs (i.e. those that they themselves do not sing).

Stewart (1989) has proposed the crucial insiders' requirement that Vlach slow songs must be performed in Romani. While this is generally true, from an analytical point of view, language cannot be the sole determinant as I have come across many instances where the Vlach Rom use Hungarian in *romanes djili* and, conversely, Romani in Hungarian songs (see also Hajdú 1958:23; Szegö 1977:272). For the Vlach Rom, melody also plays an important part in determining the nature of the songs, despite the fact that their verbal analysis does not seem to extend to discriminating between different musical structures. Whether singers voluntarily choose, or are instructed by other Vlach Rom to choose, *romane djili* as opposed to Hungarian songs or, alternatively, whether they insist on expressing the texts of both genres in Romani wherever possible, will depend greatly on the social context of the performance. The age of the singers and the extent to which Romani is used in everyday life will also influence the language of song texts. The elderly, with their knowledge of an older repertoire, are more likely to sing entirely in Romani or at least use very little Hungarian. Members of Community B who are relatively recent migrants to Hungary (Erdös 1989:66) have a much larger Romani vocabulary and speak Romani more than the Rom of Community A and this carries through into the song texts of each community.

The *mulatoso* songs known to the two communities I worked with included some Vlach Gypsy songs of non-Hungarian origin (e.g. from Romania) but these were not regarded as a separate category as far as I could determine. The one possible exception was a Serbian song which was in the repertoire of a few older Vlach Rom, one of whom lived in Community B. Members of the family with whom I worked, being distant relatives, had heard the song from her but their knowledge of it was mainly passive. On one occasion when one of the younger Community B women tried to perform a variant of this song with a visiting Rom she lost the melody after a time, no doubt because of its relatively strange musical structure.

The dance songs are labelled *khelimaski djili*, to use the Romani term or *pattogoso* (crackling) and *pergetöso* (rolling) – again words that stem from Hungarian. The Romani term given to dance songs derives from the verb *khelel pe* (to play). As with the slow *mulatoso* songs there are many Hungarian songs among the *khelimaski djil* but the Vlach Rom themselves do not generally make such a clear distinction between them. An important criterion for *khelimaski djili* is that they should be danceable in the Vlach Rom way. Many adopted Hungarian folk songs are now perceived as Vlach Rom and danced to in that manner, whereas those from the popular genre are likely to be designated Hungarian. Thus a Hungarian *csárdás* [H] is recognised as a Hungarian tune and will be danced to in the Hungarian style but with Romanised steps and movements which results in the Gypsy *csárdás*. Nevertheless, here too one must take into account the musical occasion, the community and specific individual perceptions. For example, one dance song which, despite its Hungarian song text, was performed in Community A as a Vlach *khelimaski djili* was rejected as being Hungarian by a Vlach Gypsy woman in another community that I briefly visited. I later discovered that she had earlier had contact with a group of Hungarian researchers making field recordings with Japanese musicologists. Since the emphasis during such short-term visits tends to be on recording only what the researchers themselves consider to be 'authentic' (Kovalcsik 1985:28), I suspect that this may have influenced her judgement.

The Vlach Rom I worked with also keep alive an assortment of Hungarian and western popular songs as part of their occasional dance repertoire. They include a group of Hungarian popular songs from the 1950s that deal with familiar Vlach Rom experiences such as falling in love or being jailed – these are called *tangos* and are danced to in a non-Vlach style. Another group comprises more modern songs in the *magyar nóta* or *csárdás* style, whilst the western imports include a small number of 1950s 'hits', such as *Let's Twist Again* and *Rock Around the Clock,* performed as 'party pieces' by middle-aged Rom in a deliberately parodistic style and, for younger Vlach Rom, the current English/American and Hungarian pop-songs, labelled as *disco* songs. Typically, such foreign imports undergo considerable transformation in performance by the overlaying of a characteristic Vlach rhythmic accompaniment played on spoons, water cans, table tops, etc.

The distinction between Romani songs and adopted non-Gypsy songs is one of the most important and explicitly noted musical boundaries. Nevertheless, there is a subtle generational difference in what is regarded as own and adopted material. Contrary to Stewart's suggestion (1989:95) that the Vlach Rom consider all their own songs to be 'old' (*dolmutani*), the Rom I have worked with differentiate between 'old' and 'new' songs. The former are often in the repertoire of the older generation whereas new songs usually enter into the repertoire of the younger generation, although both generations share a large number of songs which form a bridge between past and present. We also find that a few Vlach Gypsy songs are sung only by specific families and often kept alive by a single person.

The adopted repertoire of the Hungarian Vlach Rom is also an immediate, palpable marker of generational, gender and family differences. Thus older people – mostly, but not exclusively, women – sing mainly Hungarian popular songs with some folk songs among them, whilst middle aged men may sing 1950s hit songs and the younger generation adapt modern pop songs that they hear in discotheques, on the radio, etc.

A Vlach Rom analysis of songs distinguishes between the melody, or 'voice' (*glas* [R]), the 'words' (*vorba* [R]), and the particular Romani way of performance including the timbre of the singer's voice. The latter is often regarded as very special, almost as an inherited ethnic characteristic: "You can learn the song but not the way we sing, not our voice," a young Vlach Romani woman told me. However, she also admitted that certain features of performance must be acquired in childhood, suggesting that nurture may matter more than nature. In the Vlach Rom perception there is a stable relationship between melody and text. Every melody has its own words and a good singer should not mix these with other song texts. As one Rom put it, "It is like driving a horse and cart; you must follow a single track instead of moving all over the place," although another person accepted such textual additions, saying, "This was all in this song" or, "In the case of a particular song you can take out verses or add to it." This discourse between the static and flexible verses can lead to debate among singers as to what does and does not constitute a song. Therefore a song, as far as the text is concerned, is perceived both as an externalised and impersonal communal entity and as an individual statement. This supports the analytical observation that a certain degree of flexibility is allowed in text creativity, although not as much freedom as is suggested by some researchers.

The folk analysis accepts individual compositions which 'stem from the life experience of the singers'. When the Vlach Rom talk about a "new song" they are referring both to a new melody with new texts and to an old melody to which a new combination of texts has been fitted. This process, often referred to by the Vlach Rom themselves as "constructing" a new song, is a common enough practice in different parts of the world (e.g. Merriam 1964:181-4; Feld 1982:166). Therefore the western insistence on a 'new song' having a new melody can be misleading when applied cross-culturally.

Whilst one could say that in some instances the Vlach Rom conceptually separate the song from the performance, in practice the two are very much intertwined. Regardless of whether a song is Hungarian or Romani or even a Vlach Romani melody with a Hungarian text, the performance itself must be perceived of as 'Vlach Gypsy' both in style and spirit. A poor performance can lead to a song that is 'Vlach Gypsy' by all other measures being rejected by its Rom audience as 'non-Vlach'.

Performance style as a model for social interaction
All Vlach Rom songs, whether Romani or adopted, have a monophonic
structure which, in slow song performance, transforms into heterophony
although in north-east Hungary, near the border with Ukraine, Vlach
Gypsy songs have shown a recent musical development in which singers
spontaneously harmonise the cadences. Contrary to Michael Stewart's
observation, the songs are not delivered in unison and they carry a quite
different social connotation from that suggested by him. In this, the song
performances of Vlach Gypsies resemble the playing of Romungro Gypsy
bands which follow the line of the *primás* [H], the lead violin player.
One of the Rom I know consciously invokes this analogy by crying out,
"*Banda* [H] – wait" when he wants the group to stop singing. Indeed,
singing in unison is perceived by the Vlach Rom as being "like Hungarian
folk singers on the television" or "priests singing together" which is a *gajo*,
non-Gypsy way of delivery.

In slow songs, a lead singer chooses the song and starts the
performance; as the Vlach Rom say, "Only one can drive the horse-cart."
It is obligatory first to ask permission to say some 'true' words (Stewart
1987, 1989). When permission is granted the performance can commence
and the lead singer is then supported by a group of 'helpers' who join in
slightly behind in each line. Whilst the helping group must never jump
ahead of the lead singer, the lead singer reciprocally has to wait for the
group to finish their part before moving on to the next line or verse.

The most frequently verbalised criteria of good performance are tempo
and delivery. For a slow song these must be realised 'in a refined way'
(*finoman* [H]), 'slowly' (*lokes* [R]) and 'peacefully' (*csendesen* [H]).
This applies mainly to the start of a performance after which the dynamics
between musical lines are more pronounced. In the area where I worked a
basic speed of around 54-60 beats per minute seems to be the desired norm.
However, a singer must also pace each line, taking the tempo somewhat
faster at the beginning (*opre ingrel* [R], 'take up') and slowing it at the end
(*tele ingrel* [R], 'take down'). Marked pauses at the end of the second and
fourth lines of a stanza and before the very last tone also play a great part
in conveying a feeling of tranquillity (Kertész-Wilkinson 1990) although
these pauses may also reflect an internal tension or excitement which is
expressed by short passages of finger-clicking or clapping that first
accelerate in tempo before dying out. The break between the last two tones
of a stanza is referred to as a jump (*xuttjavel* [R]). This term was again
explained to me with the simile of driving a horse and cart: "When you
want to stop the horse, you must pull back the rein which makes the horse
jump a bit." This 'jump' can also be introduced in the middle of a melody
line, albeit sparingly, in order to give special emotional intensity and
individual character to a performance. Incidentally, certain interjections
that are shouted out during singing are the same as commands used for
controlling horses; *Ho, ho, ho,* for instance, can be a warning to singers who
press ahead of the lead performer or a sign of appreciation.

Great importance is attached to 'stretching' (*cirdel* [R]) and to singing
with vibrato or *rezgetösen* as the Vlach Rom often refer to it in Hungarian.
This subtle form of vibrato, which develops into a shake on the longer
durational tones, is one of the first things children imitate when they start
singing. Singing in an affected way, generally by women, is labelled

kényes [H] which is a word applied to horses of a frisky, hard-to-handle tempera-ment. Used in the context of ritual talk between men the same word, however, has a positive connotation as an expression of respect, this time with reference to the noble aspect of a horse's clean 'fussiness'. At the end of a song the lead singer thanks the others for their attention and wishes them good luck and health.

Vlach Romani dance songs also have monophonic melodies but the heterophony of slow song performances is here transformed into a rhythmic polyphony provided by various household utensils; by vocal imitation of instruments, called a mouth-bass; by a technique of rhythmic variation of the tune, called rolling, in stanzas that are without lexical words and by the hand-clapping and foot-stamping of dancers. These different accompaniments variously emphasise the on- and off-beats which go parallel with or against the melody. The dancers imitate these rhythms and step out their own combinations as well; indeed, in a sense they constitute the real focus of the performance.

In the context of large group performances, alongside the requirement to be 'refined', the leader must sing with strong voice (*zurales* [R]) – another term used when driving horse-drawn carts – especially as the performance progresses towards its climax when the accolade of "Now s/he really caught it" may be heard. (This seems to be the same whether one is considering the performance of an individual singer's song or the performance event as a whole during which a number of singers may lead.) As regards voice quality, for women a 'thick' quality of timbre is preferred to a 'thin' one since the latter is associated with children's voices. This 'thickness' accords with the Vlach Rom ideal of the female figure and also has connotations of generosity (as opposed to being 'thin-handed' or mean). The members of Community A favour 'high' male voices whereas in Community B a deeper, coarser timbre is more admired.

In the most public contexts the Vlach Rom generally perform only songs that they regard as their own, and mainly in the Romani language, but there are many instances when Hungarian is employed. Even when the Hungarian language is used, the sentiments of the song texts must still accord with Rom public values. Furthermore, at public events the songs performed are mostly those known to all whereas songs belonging to an individual repertoire will be neglected. Nevertheless, there is scope for variation during the whole event as I witnessed both at a wake and at a baptism when visitors were given the chance to perform quasi solo with only close family members helping whilst others listened.

Wakes, along with funerals, are the most significant public occasions for the Vlach Rom, being "bigger than weddings".

Wakes and funerals are the only rites in which musical performances form an obligatory part and are also among the few events where any Rom is welcome, even without an invitation, and feuding must be set aside. Furthermore, the strictest rules are attached to wakes and funerals when only slow songs may be sung whereas during weddings and baptisms, dance songs predominate.

Within the general form provided by the main social context, however, there is scope for variations according to the degree of kinship between people and the space allocated for the ritual. During a wake, for example, those who are not closely related to the bereaved family may sing slow

Singing at a funeral.
The grandson of the deceased leads the singing. He underlines his feelings with strong physical gestures. His aunt, standing next to him, tries to moderate his movements.

songs with happier, even 'jocular', overtones, especially if a separate room is available. Furthermore, the general rule of limiting the permitted repertoire to slow songs is complemented by a rule demanding the performance of the deceased person's favourite songs which seem invariably to be dance songs. (Since I had opportunity to study only two wakes I am reluctant to state that this is always the case without further evidence. Nevertheless, the possibility of incorporating dance songs during the wake as a polarity to slow songs is already evident. Since the dance songs performed during a wake tend to be Hungarian adoptions, this introduces a further paradox in that the deceased is incorporated into the group as a non-Vlach 'outsider'.)

During weddings too there are alternations between dance and slow song performances. The slow songs, in complementary opposition to the shared happiness conveyed by dance songs, mark the different 'nations' and their position within the marriage ritual. At some point the bride's family perform slow songs as a kind of lament for losing a daughter, whilst within the groom's family the younger men sing slower songs together. Those who are not closely related to either groom or bride also have their own 'sessions' of slow song performances, thereby asserting their distinctness among the others.

Thus the musical repertoire is a public demonstration of how the everyday symbolisms of life and death can be reversed yet simultaneously re-established. During a wake the mourners symbolically take part in death by singing slow songs, wearing black clothes, not washing for three days and other displays of 'pollution', whilst the deceased is recalled through dance songs which are a metaphor of life. (The complementary polarity between life and death is further emphasised by the fact that non-kin often look for marriage partners for their sons during wakes whilst girls are carefully watched and accompanied everywhere to guard against their being abducted. The combination of death, life and love gives the wake a very intense and unpredictable aura until the morning when the gathering is suspended for a while.) The public rule of mourning extends into the private domain of close relatives of the deceased, who are not allowed to sing dance songs or dance, even in private, for a prescribed period of time. At the end of this period a ritual dance is performed to trample red wine into a garment that has been worn during mourning. Even in this, however, there is some scope for individual choice as to whether to abstain for six weeks or a year. This already shows that whilst overall prescriptions exist, they can be stretched in some contexts to incorporate the contradictions or polarities. These contradictions are rationalised as respect for personal needs – all the more so as the Vlach Gypsy kinship system, which reinforces many aspects of musical performance, constantly affirms the right to express and negotiate individual deviations according to rules agreed within each specific community, extended family and nuclear family.

Conflicts, however, remain even in what seem to be clearly private contexts. For example, I once saw a middle-aged Rom man walk angrily out of the room when a young boy began whistling in accompaniment to his performance. Regarding this as an affront both to himself and to the very nature of musical performance, the older man was upholding the public, ritualistic attitude to a musical performance that the boy interpreted as a private event, although the fact that the two were males of different generations and social status undoubtedly also played a part. In this respect, the incident reflected the use of a private performance to assert authority in the sense that Bloch and Stewart applied solely to public performances. Since that episode, however, the same young 'offender' has grown up to become a much appreciated performer; during my last visit to his community, in the summer of 1994, middle-aged singers would not sing without him.

Since the Vlach Rom always consider individuals in relationship to one another, and never as bounded, autonomous entities, the same general rules which govern their everyday actions and feelings in public and private also operate in musical performance. The election of a lead singer is itself governed by a mixture of social rank and musical excellence. At more formal public occasions the leaders of slow songs are normally older men and a few older women, sometimes regardless of musical ability. In this respect they are acting as public representatives of their community and extended family. It is not unusual, however, to have a group of women singing together with a couple of related men joining in softly in the supporting part. The lead is usually passed on according to a hierarchy of social prestige and then community identity. During a wake in Community A no members from Community B took the lead, except one who had lived in Community A for a long time; their low social status put them behind even younger men from other communities. Nevertheless, in most instances those with a reputation for being excellent performers are allowed to escape the social constraints. This may give even a young, unmarried woman the chance to lead if her musical talents are such as to show her family to advantage. In addition, the use of song for consolation can also allow young women to take the lead during singing, especially if they are relatives of the deceased or mourning women. Women may also lead during other sad occasions such as when someone is taken to hospital or prison.

A male leader's peers may voluntarily provide support but close family members, especially wives, are obliged to show respect by joining the accompaniment. This also gives a woman a chance to draw attention to the unique qualities of her voice and ornamentation and thereby augment her husband's pride in her. A wife will usually do this whenever her husband feels a particular need to sing, even at home. This suggests that musical

Singing for an imprisoned relative. *This picture has been taken at the climax of a long evening dedicated to the support of both the imprisoned person and his relatives. The lead singer, a young woman, cries bitterly whilst her father (the second man from the front) disguises his emotion by looking at a book. The second support singer (first man in the front) follows her singing with complete emotional involvement. A non-relative observes the event from the back.*

performance both in a wider public and in a very personal context is always regarded, to some degree, as a ritualistic communication and thus subject to seemingly similar rules. Yet different meaning can be ascribed to performances of man and wife in public and private. Whilst in both instances their relationship is based on mutual respect, which the Rom I worked with intertwine with the feeling of love, its function of showing solidarity in front of others in public is in private transformed into one of giving personal psychological support or consolation. It can be perceived as a concealed way of admitting a man's need for his wife's love.

The wife is permitted a wider latitude of choice when the setting is informal where she may even compete with her husband's performance. Furthermore, at some formal as well as smaller public events we find that women in their forties who, by that age have 'grown up' in social standing along with their children, frequently take the lead – especially since they are no longer regarded as posing a sexual threat to the purity of the group.

In the most private contexts we find both men and women performing very personal songs which they admit they would sing only in front of a few trusted Rom.

The most obvious and immediate influence of context is on the song texts. Since all Vlach Romani song texts are built up from sets of more or less fixed couplets, told in the first person and present tense, the differences between expressions of public and private experience are hard to discern for an outsider whether Gypsy or non-Gypsy (see Appendix 1). In public performances the verses sung by men and women alike concentrate on the general Gypsy experience from a male point of view – feeling lonely in the world or having a good time with the 'brothers' at a horse fair. Here a wife is typically portrayed as a disturbing or unreliable figure, as opposed to the 'good' mother or father. The texts of dance songs, in contrast, concentrate on the physical aspect of love. Dance song texts still regard women as unfaithful; however, success in this, for women as for men, is treated with approval in the dancing itself where the aim is to cheat on the partner by getting behind the barrier presented by the partner's arm movements.

Returning to the song text, we find that in a less formal context the same textual couplets can be used to describe individual situations. Men may then transform the feeling of loneliness in the world to one of being

"You managed to cheat on him"
A series of photographs from a wedding celebration. The last of these illustrates how a young girl has managed to manoeuvre so as to dance briefly behind her partner's back to the delight and applause of the observers.

alone among the brothers. Sometimes men even express very private griefs and secrets, such as their powerlessness against or their strong love for and emotional dependence on their wives – the very opposite of the strong and independent character that they strive to project in public – although the ambiguities of the symbols are such that these connotations would be clear only to those who know the individual well. Women in private transfer the general public image of all woman as being bad to another woman and the condition of general loneliness into one of being alone among strangers, that is non-kin, often implying their husbands. In the absence of their husbands, women may also turn the texts around to make fun of the male-dominated public rules, often by means of adopted Hungarian dance songs which express feelings of jealousy, revenge and the like which the Vlach Rom public consciousness ascribes exclusively to non-Gypsies. During a Christmas celebration, which is a formal event amongst related families, one older woman started singing a Hungarian song with the following text:

"I am going to cut off your pumpkin
And get my corn field ploughed.
I am angry with your pumpkin
Because it has climbed into the garden of the woman next door."

Later I learned that when she was first married her husband started going after another woman and this song referred to her feelings about this. However, the song was still repeated long after the event, accompanied by much joking about its meanings. This kind of remembrance of once painful or shameful events seems to be a common enough practice among elderly couples. It seems that age permits one to show the imperfect side of human relationships by incorporating and transforming remnants of past pains into jokes.

Quarrels between couples also find their way into songs at less formal or private occasions which could not happen in a public context without incurring disapproval. This appears also to be valid for men singing in public when the aim of the song texts, as Stewart noted, is to express their unity. Nevertheless, even here a competitive element is evident in displays of better delivery of song texts or virtuoso dance steps. Such competitions are often seen at weddings and other happy occasions, as well as at less formal private events where women may be allowed to join in or else compete amongst themselves.

Whilst dance song texts can be more explicit in private than in public, the rules regarding dancing between couples are, more often than not, individually applied due to the sexual connotations of dance. The type and intensity of permitted movements depend largely on the partner's feelings. A jealous man would restrict his wife to dancing with him alone or not at all, whatever the circumstances, whereas a jealous wife can only react in a less formal context. Nevertheless, most men with jealous wives tacitly comply with their wishes and would not risk upsetting them by dancing with others or would do so only in a modest manner.

When we examine melodic variations, including temporal ones, these are less affected by context or gender than by family and community traditions (Appendix 2, Example A). From these influences individuals may develop an idiosyncratic style which they may choose to produce in all contexts (Appendix 2, Examples B and C). Public events are nevertheless important occasions for the Vlach Rom at which to encounter a large number of singers from whom they may learn if they wish.

What emerges from the foregoing is that some parameters of Vlach Rom musical performances, such as the choice of text and who sings with whom, may to some extent be regulated by the context, whereas other features, such as musical and temporal variations, are connected more with the people from whom one learns and with whom one regularly performs.

Thus the structure of various social contexts is both fixed and flexible due to its strong link with the kinship system that guides individual actions, including performance. Hence a less formal context may be transformed into a more formal one by the appearance of an outsider, not just a visitor from another community but also by the husband entering whilst his wife is singing or even by turning on a tape-recorder. In contrast, the private may involve a large number of people who, being cognate, still represent a homogeneous 'we'. Furthermore, the relationships between individuals, except those between mothers and children, include elements of co-operation as well as competition with others. The paradoxes of human interrelationships can only be enacted simultaneously within musical performance because it operates and proceeds on various layers, such as text, melody, temporal aspect, timbre and kinetics, and thus is able to accommodate similarities and contrasts which would be impossible in speech.

In addition, the performance practices of the slow and dance songs of the Vlach Rom offer further fields for realising different but complementary relationships between people. The two main parts of the slow songs, the 'lead' and the 'support', can also be interpreted as 'masculine' and 'feminine'. Since each part may be performed by either gender, these two polarities become unified in the individual 'human'. This is complemented by the dance songs and the dance which stress the biologically given differences between humans that struggle with each other in order to grow and be united in love. A public group of one gender will tend to glorify their unity at the expense of the other gender, whereas in mixed groups the unity/division of extended families and communities is emphasised. However, it must be borne in mind that such boundaries are fluid and constantly shifting even within the scope of a single event.

Hence, in contrast to the authors cited at the beginning of this article, I regard public performances as representing the diverse statements of a group of individual performers, the less competent as well as the best, who alternate between private and communal expressions through a set of prescribed yet flexible rules. Hence solo performances may be inserted between communal deliveries and either gender may be co-opted to perform at public events out of respect for their social or musical authority. The song texts are left open to interpretation through their use of non-specific symbolism and their grammatical blurring of the difference between the personal and the communal 'I'. Even when texts and performance practice takes their most general and communal form there is still scope for individual expression through melody, temporal delivery, timbre or a combination of dance steps.

A different picture emerges when one takes account of a full range of contexts. Musical performance encompasses all the socially important rules that divide non-Gypsies and non-Vlach groups from the Rom as well as the internal divisions between genders and generations. In my view, therefore, the social significance of public performances among the Vlach Rom lies partially in the renewal and reinforcement of the ethnic, kinship and gender boundaries of the social structure but also, at the same time, in their transcendence through musical aesthetics and thus in the creation of a model for a more democratic, fuller way of life. The aim in public is to express the *same* idea, or 'truth' in varied ways, whereas in a private context it is to express *different* individual experiences, or 'truths', through the same medium.

Vlach Gypsy musical performance is largely a socially created phenomena. In performance, individual and social identities, personal rivalries and the dialectical oppositions between the various factions are enacted and reconciled through the interaction between the communal and individual creativity within the various parameters. A musical performance, however, also has the attribute of creating different relationships between individuals from those emphasised on the social plane. The striving for equality between men – as expressed in everyday existence in the extra-musical speech forms as well as in song texts – is counterbalanced by the subtle hierarchies that emerge in performance structure. Musical performance produces an implicit leadership that would otherwise be challenged in everyday contexts – a leadership that is open mainly, but not exclusively, to men in public, but to all in private. Musical performance also creates not only a subtle hierarchy among men but embodies the possibility of a complementary equality between genders. The possibility of making a different order from the existing ones lies in the central value that Vlach Rom culture attaches to music and individual's musical creativity. Musical authority, which in theory is available to all, can supersede everyday roles and values whilst still acknowledging those roles and values in some of the aspects of musical performance.

Appendix 1
Text of *Foro* ('Fair') in different social contexts

Example A
During a wake with non-kin participants singing in a side-room to the centre of the ritual. The verses are the ones that singers most generally use in public. Whilst the song is in a "happy" mood, the delivery became sadder towards the end mixing the moods of happiness and melancholy within one performance.

English Translation

1
My colts are in front of me,
My wife is next to me.
I have not sold or swapped [horses],
[yet] I ordered wine with soda water for the Rom.

2
I ordered wine for the Rom,
I beat it up with soda water.
I beat it up with soda water,
I punched my wife in the eye.

3
I hit my crazy one [wife]
Because she did not follow me.
And she let me get lost,
In the great danger.

4
I have a black and a grey [horse],
They have jumped into the ditch.
They have jumped into the ditch,
[Because] The rein was weak.

5
I buy a harness and a rein,
I drive to the fair.
I bought and swapped
I ordered for the Rom wine with soda water.

6
I ordered wine for the Rom,
I beat it up with soda water.
I beat it up with soda water,
I punched the eye of my crazy one.

7
Do not hit me with your hand,
[but] Give me a kiss with your lips.
Give me a kiss with your lips,
With those small, beautiful lips.

8
I place my hat on the bridge,
I throw myself into the Danube.
I throw myself into the Danube.
After my black head.

9
When I die, mother,
Bury me beautifully.
When I die, mother,
Bury me beautifully.

10
Let my headstone be from nothing else,
Let it be from lilac blossoms.
Let it be from lilac blossoms,
But not from my mother's tears.

Original text in Romany and Hungarian [italic]

1
Muŕe khure angla mande j,
Muŕa gaži paša mande j.
Či bikindem, či parudem,
E ŕomenge fröččo manglem.

2
E ŕomenge mol me manglem,
A sodasa opre mardem.
A sodasa opre mardem,
Muŕi gaži sembe mardem.

3
Azer mardem muŕa dila,
Č'a-j-avilas pala mande.
Voj muklas man te xasajvav,
Ando baro vesedelmo.

4
Si m'ek kalo haj ek surno,
Andre xuklas ando šanco.
Azer xuklas ando šanco,
Kovle sas e salivara.

5
Kinav hamo, salavari,
Andre tradav ando foro.
Vi bikindem, vi parudem,
E ŕomenge mol me manglem.

6
E ŕomenge mol me manglem,
A sodasa opre mardem.
A sodasa opre mardem,
Muŕe dila sembe mardem.

7
Na mala ma tje palmasa,
Čumide ma tje mujesa.
Čumide ma tje mujesa,
Kokol cini šukeresa.

8
Kolopom a hídra teszem,
Magam a Dunába vetem.
Magam a Dunába vetem,
Pala muŕo kalo šero.

9
Me te mero, *édesanyám,*
Apol *szépen temessetek.*
Me te mero, *édesanyám.*
De šukares de praxon ma.

10
A fejfám se legyen fából,
Legyen nyíló orgonából.
Legyen nyíló orgonából,
Ne az anyám könnyeiből.

Example B

This is a performance of *'Foro'* at another wake. All participants shared the same room and thus the texts were selected to share in the bereaved family's grief. Only Verse 3 is common with Example A. Despite the obviously sad tone of the text and a resigned tone of delivery, the lead singers also expressed much joy with their beaming, smiling faces, which brought out two important attributes of music making together: the consolation and transformation of grief into joy through performance.

English translation

1
To die, to die, one has to die,
One has to go to the cemetery.
Who has invented this thing
That one has to go to the cemetery?

2
....
One has to go to the cemetery,
Which has no door, no window,
Through which to take my father out.

3
My coffin should not be from anything else,
[than] From flowers of the lilac.
From flowers of the lilac,
But not from my mother's tears.

4
To die, to die, one has to die,
I have to leave my family behind.
Unfortunate as I am,
I must perish this way.

5
It is hard for me to walk,
To separate from you, mother.
I will go away, you will see,
[and] You will hear not a word about me.

6
I live, I live, but for what?
When I do not have a single happy day?
I pay up my debt,
I don't even care if I shall die.

7
Life, life, wretched life!
What do I owe you?
I pay up my debt,
I don't even care if I shall die.

8
The river Tisza flows downstream,
It will never turn back.
How could it turn back,
When it has its own path?

9
I am wandering and cannot find a place,
Where I could put my head down.
I put my head on the soil,
Look how much I am suffering!

10
I live, I live, but for what?
When I do not have a single happy day?
Oh, my God, it is so bad for me,
My life is full of mourning.

11
Dreams are in my eyes,
My mother came to my mind.
My mother came to my mind,
Oh, my God, what could I do?

Original text in Romany [one word] and Hungarian [italic]

1
Halni, halni meg kell halni,
Temetőbe kell már menni.
Vajon ki találta ezt ki,
Temetőbe ki kell menni.

2
....
Temetőbe kell kimenni,
Sem ablaka, sem ajtaja,
Hogy jó atyám, kivehessem.

3
Kopórsom se legyen másból,
Legyen orgona virágból.
Legyen orgona virágból,
Nem az anyám könnyeiből.

4
Halni, halni, meg kell halni,
A családomat itt kell hagyni.
Bárhogy milyen szegény vagyok,
Nékem így kell elpusztulni.

5
Nehezen esik a járás,
Tőled anyám az elválás.
Úgy elmegyek, meglássátok,
Hírem hangom nem halljátok.

6
Élek, élek, minek élek,
Ha egy víg napot nem élek.
Leróvom az adósságom,
He meghalok azt se bánom.

7
Élet, élet, betyár élet,
Mivel vagyok adós néked,
Leróvom az adósságom,
Ha meghalok azt se bánom.

8
Lefele folyik a Tisza,
Nem folyik az többet vissza.
Hogy is folyna az már vissza,
Mikor néki van szállása.

9
Járok nem lelem a helyem,
Hová tegyem a fejemet?
Födre hajtom a fejemet,
Nézzed, hogy szenvedek érted.

10
Élek, élek, minek élek,
Ha egy víg napot nem élek.
Jaj, istenem, jaj már nékem,
Gyászba borult az életem.

11
Álom esett a szemembe,
Anyám jutott az eszembe.
Anyám jutott az eszembe,
Jaj Istenem, mit csináljak.

Example C

This performance took place in a private context, in the home of the singer. From Verse 6 onwards it gradually moved away from the general theme to bring in texts which are usually found in other songs, suggesting a personal meaning to this particular version. The singer's grandmother regarded this version to be 'wrong'.

English translation

1

I have two dapple-grey horses,
Both are four years old.
One I gamble away on the skittles,
The other I gamble away at cards.

2

I gamble at skittles and at cards,
I don't even care if I die.
My coffin should not be from anything else,
Let it be from lilac blossoms.

3

Let it be from lilac blossoms
And from my mother's tears.
Great Lord, how you have struck me!
Nothing is good, you destroyed me.

4

I drive to the fair,
I order wine with soda for the Rom.
I order wine with soda for the Rom,
I beat the soda water out.

5

Order wine, brother, for the Rom,
So they won't be angry with us!
I did not sell or swap [horses]
Yet I had a merry time.

6

Let God smite that hour,
That unlucky hour!
Were she a good woman,
She would have come after me.

7

But because you are not good,
Let the plague take you!
I'll beat you so badly, you whore,
That the skirt will fall off you.

8

Give me my whip, woman,
So I can hit the colts!
Don't hit me with your whip,
Kiss me with your lips.

9

Don't hit me with your whip,
Kiss me with your lips.
Tell me, woman,
Who was here last night?

10

That was your lover,
Your unfortunate lover.
The Rom is totally crazy,
He tied me to the pole.

Original text in Romany and Hungarian [italic]

1

Van két lovam almás deres,
Mind a kettőnégy évesek.
Az egyiket elkuglizom,
A másikat elkártyázom.

2

Elkártyázom, elkuglizom,
Ha meghalok azt se bánom.
Koporsóm se legyen másból,
Legyen nyíló orgonából.

3

Legyen nyíló orgonából,
Az anyámnak könnyeiből,
Bare Devla de mardan ma,
Mišto khanči, xasardan ma.

4

Andre tradam, ando foro,
Fröččo manglom le ŕomenge.
Fröččo manglom le ŕomenge,
Haj i soda avri mardem.

5

Mang mol phrala, le ŕomenge,
Te na xoljajven p'amende.
Či bikindem, či parudem
H'anke voja me de kerdem.

6

Marel o Del kodo časo,
Kodo bibaxtalo časo.
Laši ŕomnji t'avilasas,
Pala mande avilasas.

7

Mivel aba či san laši,
Šilavel tut -j-i pustija.
Úgy megverlek bárcás kurva,
Lepereg a szoknya rólad.

8

Ante gaži muŕi čunji,
Mek te šinav ande khure.
Na mala ma tja čunjasa,
Čumide ma tje mujesa.

9

Na malama tja čunjesa,
Čumide ma tje mujesa.
Phenta mange muŕi gaži,
Kon sas tute kade ratji.

10

Haj sas kodo tjo kurvari,
Kodo čoro lubinari.
Ke o ŕom si čupa dilo,
Haj phandel ma kaj o kilo.

Appendix 2:
Melodic Variations in Performances of *Foro*

Example A
The table shows some possible variations that singers make in the first motive of the second musical line of *Foro*. The contexts of the performances ranged from public (I, II, III, VI, V) through less formal (VI, VII. VIII) to private (IX, X). In most cases the singers follow the general pattern of Variation No.1. However, Peter (Variation No.4) developed a slightly different version which he stuck to more or less regardless of context. His version also influenced Ibolj (Variation No.5), who explicitly confirmed that she regarded Peter's version to be the right 'voice'.

Melody of 'Foro'

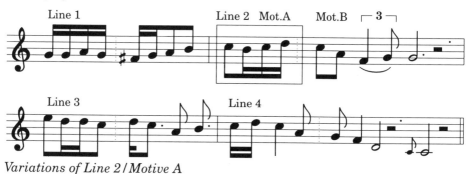

Variations of Line 2 / Motive A

Variation No. 1

Performance	Verse	Singer	Locality
I	1-4, 9	Bišar	B
	5, 7, 8, 10	Tonči	B/A
	11-13	Šonka/Eva	A
II	7	Peter	X
	11-21	Dilo	X
III	1-4	Peter	X
IV	2, 4, 8	Gomboš	A
	11, 15	Bači	A
V	1-3, 7	Gabor	X
	4-6, 9	Gomboš	A
VII	1, 3	Jaga	B
	4	Ibolj	B/A
VIII	2, 11	Popa	B
	9, 10	Terka	B
IX	1-10	Tonči	B/A
X	1-10	Gomboš	A

Variation No. 2

Performance	Verse	Singer	Locality
IV	3, 5-7, 9, 12	Gomboš	A
	14, 16, 17		
	10, 18	Bači	A
V	8, 10, 11	Gomboš	A

Variation No. 3

Performance	Verse	Singer	Locality
I	6	Lajoš	X
VII	13, 14, 16	Kořo	B

Variation No. 4

Performance	Verse	Singer	Locality
II	1-3, 5-10	Peter	X
III	2, 3, 5	Peter	X
VI	1-8	Peter	X

Variation No. 5

Performance	Verse	Singer	Locality
VII	5-9, 11	Ibolj	A/B
VIII	1, 3, 5-7	Ibolj	A/B
	4	Popa	B

Example B
In other cases singers may develop a characteristic temporal delivery, such as the following, in which the two motives of the first musical line are subdivided by a pause:

Example C
In this case the singer's idiosyncratic style comprises more or less fixed ornamentations of certain tones:

Acknowledgements
This fieldwork was carried out with financial assistance from The British Council and the University of London Central Research Fund. My Ph.D. studies during 1988-91 were supported by a grant from The British Academy. I would also like to express my gratitude to the Institute of Musicology of the Hungarian Academy of Sciences, and especially to Mrs. Katalin Kovalcsik of the Folk Dance Department, for the help they have given at all stages of my work.

This chapter is a revised and enlarged version of a paper delivered at the IX European Seminar of Ethnomusicology 1993 in Barcelona as well as at the ESRC seminar in 1994. I have drawn much benefit from several long and useful discussions with Dr. Suzel Riely who kindly drew my attention to a number of links that were missing from the original paper. I am also grateful to my partner, Tim Wilkinson, for his editing comments.

References
BAUMANN R 1978 *Verbal Art as Performance* Newbury House, Rowley, Massachusetts

BAILY J 1994 "Learning to Perform as a Research Technique in Ethnomusicology" in Niemöller K W, Pätzold U and Chung Kyo-Chul eds. *Lux Oriente – Begegnungen der Kulturen in der Musikforschung. Festschrift-Robert Günther zum 65. Geburstag* Gustav Bosse Verlag, Köln, pp.331-45

BLACKING J 1985 "Universal Validity in Musical Analysis" *ICTM UK Chapter Bulletin* 12 pp.13-22

BLACKING J 1986 *Agenda for the Arts* NAEA University of London, Institute of Education, London

BLACKING J 1990 "Towards a Reintegration of Musicology" in Buckley A ed. *Proceedings of the Second British-Swedish Conference on Musicology: Ethnomusicology* privately published, pp.61-9

BLOCH M 1974 "Symbol, Song, Dance and Features of Articulation: Is Religion an Extreme Form of Traditional Authority?" *Archives Éuropéennes de Sociologie* XV/1, pp 55-81

COHEN A P.1985 T*he Symbolic Construction of Community* Routledge, London

ERDÖS K 1989 *Erdös Kamill cigánytanulmányai* [Collected Gypsy studies of Kamill Erdös] Erkel Ferenc Muzeum, Gyula, Békéscsaba

FELD S 1982 *Sound and Sentiment* University of Pennsylvania Press, Philadelphia

FINNEGAN R 1992 *Oral Traditions and Verbal Arts: a Guide to Research Practice* Routledge, London and New York

HAJDÚ A 1958 "Les Tsiganes de Hongrois et leur musique" *Études Tsiganes* IV (1) pp.4-28

HOOD M 1960 "The Challenge of Bi-Musicality" *Ethnomusicology* 4 pp.55-9

HOWARD K 1991 "John Blacking: An Interview"*Ethnomusicology* 35 (1) pp.55-76

KERTÉSZ-WILKINSON I 1990 " '*Lokes Phen!*' An investigation into the musical tempo feeling of a Hungarian Vlach Gypsy community based on their own evaluation" in M Salo ed. *100 Years of Gypsy Studies* Gypsy Lore Society, Cheverly, Maryland pp.193-202

KERTÉSZ-WILKINSON I 1994 "Bi-Musicality and the Hungarian Vlach Gypsies: Learning to Sing and Dance as Ethnomusicological Research Tools" Paper at Interdisciplinary Symposium on Music, Language and Literature of the Romani and Sinti, International Institute for Traditional Music, Berlin (Proceedings in press)

KOVALCSIK K 1985 *Szlovákiai oláhcigány népdalok* [Vlach Gypsy folk songs in Slovakia] MTA Zenetudományi Intézet, Budapest

MEAD H G 1934 *Mind, Self, and Society* University of Chicago Press, Chicago and London

MERRIAM A P 1964 *The Anthropology of Music* Northwestern University Press, Evanston, Illinois

MIRGA A 1986 "Stereotype as a Model of 'One's Own' and a 'Stranger': Theoretical Remarks on Ethnic Stereotype" *Ethnologia Polona* 12 pp.95-108

OKELY J 1983 *The Traveller Gypsies* Cambridge University Press, Cambridge

STEWART M 1987 *Brothers in Song: The Persistence of (Vlach) Gypsy Identity and Comunity in Socialist Hungary* Ph.D. dissertation, London School of Economic and Political Science

STEWART M 1989 " 'True Speech': Songs and Moral Order of a Hungarian Vlach Gypsy Community" *Man* 24 (1) pp.79-101

SZEGO L 1977 *Csíkóink kényesek: Magyarországi cigány népköltészet* [Our foals are fussy: Hungarian Gypsy folk poetry] Europa Könyvkiadó, Budapest

SUTHERLAND A 1975 *Gypsies: The Hidden Americans* Tavistock Publications, London

TURNBULL C 1990 "Liminality: a synthesis of subjective and objective experience" in Schechner R and Appel W eds. *By means of performance* Cambridge University Press, Cambridge

WILLIAMS P 1984 *Marriage Tsigane: une cérémonie de fiancailles chez les Rom de Paris* L'Harmattan Selaf, Paris

Chapter 8 "I want more than green leaves for my children". Some developments in Gypsy/Traveller education 1970-96

Mary Waterson, Teacher and writer, formerly fieldworker for the Advisory Council for the Education of Romany and other Travellers

Twenty-five years in Traveller education? Impossible to pinpoint a year for starting such a story. There have always been some schools where Gypsies were welcome and others where they were turned away.

'Gypsy schools' existed in the 1830s but Surrey County Council's Hurtwood School, established in 1926, was the first one provided by a local authority (Camm 1934). I remember, in the summer of 1929, wandering round the wooden-hutted winter site, set in woodland, and looking in through the windows of the deserted schoolroom. It remained there until 1934 when it was re-erected at East Walton beside the Council school. "Only four of the forty pupils could read or write. In addition to the ordinary rudiments of education, the children (were) instructed in various handicrafts such as basketry, woodwork ... rugmaking ... and gardening" (op. cit.). What was meant by "reading and writing"? Does anyone know whether any of the Hurtwood children went to other schools during their travelling time, or whether any of them transferred to mainstream schools?

Reviewing Gypsy education raises many questions. Did this segregated education provide a philosophical as well as a physical model for many similar ventures over the next fifty years? Or were all those separate establishments merely an extension of the general educational compartmentalism that existed, and persisted, into the 1960s, whereby children were categorised by age and by performance in literacy and numeracy? Separate education for Travellers is still considered in some places when a child of eleven is found to need practice in counting to twenty and is able to write only one or two words. But Gypsies and Travellers need mainstream education for the same reasons as all children do – so that they have access to the opportunities on offer at schools and so that they can get to know, and be known by, their peers.

Many Traveller families considered school a potential danger. Some considered that allowing those in authority to know you had children was to run the risk of their being taken away. How many children *were* taken away from their parents and placed in boarding education? Some who were whisked off suffered greatly from the separation; some say they would never have learned to read and write if that had not happened. Has there been any research into this? And along with such factual research has anyone recorded the fears families experienced that their children would be taken from them and how those fears led to their keeping children out of school altogether? Many hid their children rather than have it discovered how little time they had been able to send them to school – a discovery which could lead to children being taken into care. When did those fears begin to die away? Or are they still present?

Community grapevines kept alive such concerns, not only in the families who actually experienced children being taken but also through later generations, among those living at a time when the likelihood of children being taken into care was no greater for Travellers than for any other families.

The 1960s

Government Reports and Circulars relating to Travellers appeared throughout the 1960s. Life for many Gypsy/Traveller families became more and more difficult and often more dangerous. School was not an option for many (Dodds 1966). Norman Dodds MP and Eric Lubbock were among those who campaigned in the House of Commons for local authority caravan sites. Jocelyn Aldous, who later became a founder member of the Advisory Committee for the Education of Romany and other Travellers (ACERT), worked closely with Dodds. The Caravan Sites and Control of Development Act 1960 had led to the closure of sites not fulfilling new government requirements. This had two opposite effects: some families accepted housing and were then expected to send their children to school regularly, others went back on the roadsides where possibilities for schooling became even more difficult.

The Ministry of Housing and Local Government Circular 6/1962 (HMSO 1962) provided guidance on the implementation of the Ministry of Housing and Local Government Act 1962. The Circular acknowledged that Gypsies had the right to follow their traditional mode of life but limited that right to "true gypsies or romanies" and it was assumed that they were more ready to settle down. It was emphasised that "Moving people off one unauthorised site and leaving them to find another is no solution and no answer to the human and social problems involved" (op. cit.). "But the exhortation of the 1962 Circular was however almost entirely ineffective" (Adams 1975). No governmental circular has the force of law; its dicta have to be tested in the courts.

The Plowden Report, *Children and their Primary Schools* (HMSO 1967), and the Ministry of Housing and Local Government's Report, *Gypsies and other Travellers* (HMSO 1967), appeared in the same year. The latter described what life was like for thousands of Gypsy families. Lady Plowden, in her report, stated that Gypsy children were probably the most deprived children in England and Wales. They were deprived in three ways: because of the living conditions experienced by so many (Dodds

1966), because of relentless harassment and because, almost everywhere, the school system ignored their existence.

The Gypsy Council (founded in 1966) established the Gypsy Council Education Trust in 1969. It was members of the Trust who formed the National Gypsy Education Council in 1970. Lady Plowden and many others began their involvement in Gypsy education at that time. A split in the NGEC in 1973 led to the formation of the Advisory Committee for the Education of Romany and other Travellers (ACERT). (From 1986 ACERT has been the Advisory Council for the Education of Romany and other Travellers and in 1993 the NGEC took the title Gypsy Council for Education, Culture, Welfare and Civil Rights (GCECWCR)).

A year after the publication of the reports of the Plowden Committee and the Ministry of Housing and Local Government, Parliament passed the Caravan Sites Act 1968, placing a duty on local authorities to provide accommodation for Gypsies residing in or resorting to their area.

The Caravan Sites and Development Act in one Hertfordshire borough
The Caravan Sites Act and Control of Development Act 1960 (op. cit.) resulted in the closure of *The Willows*, an unlicensed site on the borders of Hertfordshire and Essex. Travellers had been living on it for some sixty years. In 1974 a Traveller teenager whose family had lived there described it as having been an awful, rat-ridden place. When it was closed families living there had the choice of either accepting council accommodation or going back on the road. His family chose to be housed. There was no support available in acclimatisating to house-dwelling. For some who became council house tenants the trauma of suddenly losing the support of their extended family was disastrous.

Families who managed to find temporary stopping places within the borough, moving or being moved from one patch of waste ground to another, were often subject to dangerous practices by police and bailiffs. At one 1961 eviction from a roadside verge in the borough, the fire was kicked over the legs of an expectant mother. Her baby lived for three and a half months.

For children whose families accepted houses, school attendance became the expected norm, although making it a good experience for children, parents and schools was not easy. Travellers in that borough were enrolled in mainstream schools but the extra information and support that could have made school a more positive experience for all was not available.

It was the period of 'remedial groups' and many Travellers, together with others who had missed a good deal of school and children whose first language was not English, were allocated to remedial groups and/or found themselves in the 'lowest sets' in secondary school.

There were Traveller families in houses who still travelled for three or four months of the year. No one thought then of providing school work that the children could do while away. The summer-long absences just reinforced the low expectations of both teachers and learners, particularly in secondary school.

It was 1977 before a local authority site was opened. That summer, among families due to be evicted from the 'closed' authorised temporary site were three pregnant women. One of them wrote to Derek Walker Smith, the local MP. Through his intervention the local authority had to give way and the three families were able to stay until the babies were well established.

Between 1960 and 1978 hundreds of Traveller families stopped for a time in the borough. As more land was taken for London overspill housing it became more difficult to find somewhere to stop and the Designation Order granted in 1986 compounded the difficulties. Families continued to stop where they could in the mid-1990s. There were also, of course, hundreds of Traveller families living in houses and flats.

Before 1977 Traveller children were attending primary schools on six school sites but by 1982 there were Travellers in primary schools on thirteen locations in the borough.

Into the 1970s
From the end of the 1960s an increasing number of summer schools began to be organised for Traveller children by voluntary organisations. They were staffed by volunteer students and teachers although some secured local authority backing. Enthusiastic take-up by the children and job satisfaction for many teachers kept the schools going summer after summer (Tinker 1975). In some areas the success of the summer schools appeared to prompt LEAs to take on their statutory responsibilities for the education of Gypsies and Travellers.

Then, at the beginning of the 1970s, a number of developments coincided:
■ the Caravan Sites Act 1968 became law
■ Norman Thomas HMI, in 1970, was given a watching brief in relation to Traveller education
■ the first DES (Department of Education and Science) Traveller Education Short Course was organised, attracting twenty participants; the DES Short Courses made an important contribution to the spread of LEA action on Traveller education
■ Don Byrne, who had been Environmental Health Officer in Hemel Hempstead, joined Hertfordshire's County Environmental Health staff, concentrating on Gypsy matters which, for him, included Gypsy education – not then a concern of the County Education Department; by 1974 he was the Department of the Environment's National Gypsy Liaison Officer
■ Kit Sampson, in 1971, drew the attention of Save the Children Fund to the situation in Hertfordshire of young Gypsy children and SCF began to organise playgroup activities on Travellers' stopping places
■ Penny Vinson's *Roadside Families* (SCF Playgroup Department 1973) was perhaps the first public involvement in Traveller welfare by Save the Children Fund
■ a year later Ann Bagehot became Playgroup Adviser to the SCF Hertfordshire Travellers' Playgroup Project and in 1976 was made SCF National Gypsy Liaison Officer
■ co-ordination began in 1978 in Hertfordshire between SCF playgroup workers and teachers. This developed into the multi-disciplinary Hertfordshire Traveller Education Group (HERTEG) eventually winning recognition and participation by county education officers
■ also in 1978 the Cambridge Institute of Education set up a Regional Consultative Group for Traveller Education (Waterson 1993:134).

The No-Area Pool

The No-Area Pool provided extra funding to support the education of children of parents with 'no fixed abode': children whose parents were employed in the forces, on the roads, in circus or fairground, who were bargees or who were Gypsies or Travellers. All LEAs contributed to the Pool on a per capita basis, whether or not they drew funding from it themselves.

The origins of the No-Area Pool are difficult to discover. I had wondered if its use in relation to Gypsies and Travellers had been given some impetus by the passing of the Caravan Sites Act 1968 which perhaps alerted some local authorities to the need to give greater attention to the education of Gypsies and Travellers.

However, in 1972-3, a time of local government re-organisation, budgeting was becoming tighter and LEAs were looking for additional possibilities of financing specific aspects of their educational provision. Previously, extra support for Travellers in school had, for the most part, been on an ad hoc basis, funded entirely by LEAs. A letter to Avon from the DES in April 1976 stated:

> "It has been agreed that the children of Travellers can be regarded as not belonging to the area of any authority, and that those authorities who provide services to meet the educational needs of such children should have their costs fully reimbursed under the 'no-area' pooling arrangements." (Perez 1995)

Full reimbursement was always available and unlimited as long as the claim was for "special and additional provision". The greater part of expenditure was at the rate of 75 per cent with LEAs having to provide 25 per cent of the cost – a requirement found to be an anathema to some councillors who did not wish to be seen to agree to any outlay benefiting members of communities so unpopular with their constituents.

To claim on the Pool, a retrospective operation, detailed records were necessary. LEAs which decided to claim began to extend their records. However, some LEAs continued to ignore the Pool, frequently a political decision although in some instances a pragmatic one based on inability to gather appropriate detailed records. More productive use was made of the Pool by an increasing numbers of authorities as councillors came to realise that the extra funding benefited all the children in their area. LEAs which developed carefully considered policies in relation to the education of Traveller children and activated those policies by employing more teachers, non-teaching aides and sometimes nursery nurses and education welfare officers, were able to provide a service much valued by their schools.

Variation in approaches

Traveller participation in widely varying educational provision was unevenly spread. Often the level and quality of provision was closely related to the degree of persistence exercised by individuals in particular areas.

The West Midlands Travellers' School (WMTS 1972) was funded by the Van Leer Foundation and functioned during term time and through summer schools during the early 1970s. A Travelling People's Education Project based on Walsall operated in the mid-1970s (Worrall 1977).

"The West Midlands Education Service for Travelling Children (WMESTC) was established in 1973 following a joint application by five county boroughs, under Urban Programme Number 7, for the appointment of a regional co-ordinator for Gypsy education. Subsequent grants, under Urban Programme Number 11, led to the establishment of a full regional scheme which became fully operational in January 1976" (DES 1983). At the time of their inspection by HMI in 1983 there were eleven participating LEAs.

Some LEAs established 'schools' on sites, in for example, Newham, Hemel Hempstead and Peterborough. The Gypsy Council Education Trust set up a school on Redbridge site (Manley 1971). A number of LEAs, including Avon, Essex, Hertfordshire, Oxfordshire and Somerset, operated mobile schools for varying lengths of time.

There appears to have been no serious national consideration of the random nature of Traveller education: Gypsies and Travellers were allowed to be kept out of mainstream schooling for no reason other than that they were Gypsies or Travellers. Many LEAs turned a blind eye towards schools which said, "No Gypsies here." The Education Act 1944 decreed that all children should be educated according to their age, ability and aptitude: that law was flouted in many places and over many years.

Many teachers, although committed to establishing a welcoming and effective learning environment, had to work on sites in buildings, some of which would not have been given approval as school buildings. Uninsulated roofs made buildings miserably cold in winter and like ovens in summer. Teachers worked with sub-standard facilities and insufficient resources, isolated from professional colleagues, often working without any adult helper of any kind and where many – sometimes most – of the children had little or no experience of school. Those who tackled such assignments term after term, sometimes year after year, deserved accolades from their LEAs. With hindsight, those LEAs which operated such schools were irresponsible.

There was no specific national policy and what happened within LEAs could vary from district to district, from school to school. Avon (Perez 1995) and West Glamorgan (Waterson 1989) provide examples of diversity in policy and practice in two LEAs.

Segregated education was not limited to site schools. Many mainstream schools arranged for Gypsies to be taught separately, often on an all-age basis, sometimes in separate buildings set up on the school playground. Separate provision, once established, was exceedingly difficult to unscramble: opposition came from Gypsy and non-Gypsy parents, from Gypsy and non-Gypsy children, from teachers and what were then school managers and are now governors.

Opposition to enrolling Gypsies continued. One head teacher of an infant school, having in 1979 reluctantly agreed to enrol a Gypsy child, said, "Don't think this is the thin end of the wedge," but as one Traveller child after another joined her school her attitude changed completely. Another primary head who, with the support of parents and governors, worked hard to keep Gypsy children out of her school when a site was built in the area, eventually worked equally hard to allow children to stay in the school until the age of thirteen if she felt they were not ready for transfer at eleven.

Sometimes opposition took the form of delaying tactics. Querying whether families were "really within our catchment area" was one ploy. And if the school concerned 'knew' someone in their local education office, obtaining an answer to this query could take an unconscionable time. In one case, once the catchment entitlement had been incontrovertibly established, the children were admitted on a half-time, segregated, all-age teaching group basis, they and their teacher the continuing focus for prejudice. Heads of voluntary-aided schools had the edge on local authority established schools when they wished to avoid enrolling Traveller children. One head, in 1979, with the support of his governing body, maintained his refusal despite receiving, during a visit from the divisional education officer, an offer of a 0.5 teacher to work with six Gypsies. This was at the time when he received an MBE for services to education. A school bus passed the children's stopping place on its way to his school. Instead of going to that school, the nearest, the children had to be picked up by taxi and taken to school across the county boundary, an extra charge on the No-Area Pool. Eleven years later one of the families moved into a house and their primary aged children naturally attended the nearest school, the one where their older sisters had been refused places.

The 1970s and into the 1980s

The *Cripps Report* (1977) and the subsequent DoE Circular 57/78 (Welsh Office 98/78) laid the basis for the Local Government Planning and Land Act 1980 which enabled local authorities to apply for grants from the DoE to cover the cost of site construction once the Department had approved the plans submitted. Although the expenditure was subject to rate capping this legislation led to a considerable improvement in the rate of site provision which made it easier for some families to send their children to school. But the 1980 Act also gave local authority districts power to apply for Designation Orders (Caravan Sites Act 1968) which made schooling more of a problem for families without authorised accommodation. Previously, 'no-go areas' for Gypsies could be created only within entire shire counties and in London and metropolitan boroughs; after the 1980 Act they could cover county districts.

The Education Act 1980 unequivocally placed a duty on LEAs to ensure that appropriate full-time education be provided for all children residing in their area, whether permanently or temporarily and regardless of the status of the camp site where they lived. Clause 5 of DES Circular 1/81, *Education Act 1980: Admission to Schools, Appeals, Publication of Information and School Attendance Orders*, specifically related this duty to Gypsies and Travellers:

> "The reference to children 'in the area' of the authority means that each authority's duty extends to all children residing in their area, whether permanently or temporarily. The duty thus embraces in particular travelling children, including gypsies, and subject to what is said in the Annex to this Circular, children from overseas."

This was the first clear direction on the subject to be issued by the Department. A footnote stated: "A Circular cannot be regarded as providing an authoritative legal interpretation of any of the provisions of an Act as this is exclusively a function of the Courts." It was March 1981 before DES Circular 1/81 came into force.

The need for DES Circular 1/81 was illustrated by the experiences of a group of Travellers who, through the autumn term of 1980, had stopped in a Hertfordshire borough. Evicted from their first stopping place at half term they had found a second stopping place where the children could continue at the same schools. Evicted again on 6 January 1981 they stopped on railway land in the adjoining borough of Enfield. When I contacted Enfield Education Department concerning the continued education of the children I was told, "Housing would not like it" if those children were placed in school. Had DES Circular 1/81 already come into effect, would it have affected the issue?

Developments in Traveller Education in the 1970s and 1980s were strongly influenced by a number of factors additional to those outlined in the section *Into the 1970s* above:

■ the allocation, in 1973, of responsibilities for an overview of Traveller Education to a single member of Her Majesty's Inspectorate, Don Buckland. From 1976 to 1986 Don Buckland HMI and Arthur Ivatts HMI shared these responsibilities. Since 1986 Arthur Ivatts has been the only HMI with Traveller Education as part of his brief; in September 1993 he became a member of OFSTED (Office for Standards in Education).

■ DES Traveller Education five-day courses held regularly. These multi-disciplinary courses promoted networking, enabled the spread of good practice and a greater awareness of issues affecting Travellers among those whose work involved them in education, health and social services. The course reports provided not only a record of the work carried out but they also included names and addresses of participants – a most important contribution to networking. The last of these, *Planning and Providing Education for Travellers including Gypsy, Fairground, Circus and other Traveller Communities,* took place in Winchester in 1990 with 251 participants; the Short Course Programme was then terminated.

■ more information on the No-Area Pool led to its more effective use by growing numbers of LEAs. A letter in 1979 from DES to all LEAs clarified, as its title suggested, *Pooling of expenditure on the provision of educational services for Travelling children.*

■ the development of regional courses and conferences dealing with Traveller education led to the involvement of an increasing number of universities and polytechnics and the extension of networking made possible through the DES courses.

■ a growth of action in relation to the education of fairground and circus Travellers (for fairground case studies see Pullin 1982).

■ the work of the voluntary organisations (ACERT, NGEC, SCF) augmented in 1980 by the formation of the National Association of Teachers of Travellers (NATT).

■ distance learning packs, produced by a number of Traveller Education Services, used particularly with fairground and circus families

■ DES documents/publications.

■ HMI Surveys on Traveller education.

■ European seminars, publications, resolutions, recommendations.

In some schools segregation continued into the mid-1980s e.g. in Avon, Bedfordshire, Buckinghamshire, Manchester, South Glamorgan and West

Glamorgan. Although by then the general expectation was that primary aged children would go into mainstream school, there continued to be schools where overt antagonism to the presence of Travellers made their integration very difficult. Some separate provision at secondary stage still continued.

Throughout this period a small, but ever-growing, number of teachers and others working in education at all levels were becoming experienced in matters affecting the education of Traveller children. This experience, together with networking, gave many of them, particularly teachers, the confidence to make known to their LEAs the educational situation of Travellers. Very slowly the situation began to change, in an uneven fashion, as more people became aware of the serious neglect of the educational needs of the Gypsy/Traveller communities. Parallel with the commitment of increasing numbers of educational workers, more Traveller children had positive experiences, for the most part in primary schools, leading to a slowly growing commitment among some Traveller parents to school education. The interaction of these last two factors has been all important.

Malpractice by an LEA
In 1977 Croydon LEA decided it had no responsibility to educate children whose parents were not ratepayers, in other words, children of Gypsies/Travellers whose families had no place on an authorised site. The NGEC-led lobbying of the DES highlighted the illegality of Croydon's stance. Could this have influenced the wording of the subsequent Education Act 1980 and the DES Circular 1/81 which followed?

The 1980s
From 1970 those involved in Traveller education had called for/hoped that the DES would produce a Circular on Traveller education. Year after year those hopes were dashed. In 1983 the Department for Education and Science produced not the long-awaited Circular but *The Education of Travellers' Children: an HMI Discussion Paper* (DES 1983), the first government publication focusing entirely on Traveller education. The Discussion Paper acknowledged that only a minority of Traveller children attended school; it also referred to the "disparity between local education authorities in the provision they make for the education of traveller children." In spite of its perpetuation of a sheaf of stereotypical views about Traveller children the paper was a useful tool for teachers and officers.

The Swann Report (1985)
The Committee of Inquiry into the Education of Children from Ethnic Minority Groups was established in 1979. "The origins of this committee (chaired first by Rampton and later by Swann) can be traced back to the concern expressed by the West Indian Community during the late 60's and 70's about the academic performance of their children" (Swann 1985:vii). The interim report dealt with children from that community but the committee's brief, which covered only England, was extended to include other ethnic minority groups.

Did the Committee originally envisage including consideration of Gypsies/Travellers? Paragraph 2 of the introduction to their report states:

"we were also led – by the sheer volume of evidence which we received on their needs – to consider the situation of children from *The Travelling Community,* whose needs have often previously been almost entirely passed over in any consideration of ethnic minority communities. From our consideration of the plight of this community (sic), many of us were led to believe that their needs were if anything even more deserving of attention than the other groups we had considered. In many respects indeed, their situation appears to embody very strikingly many of the issues raised by the education experiences of other ethnic minorities."

This volume of evidence enabled the group dealing with Traveller education to produce Chapter 16, The Educational Needs of Travellers' Children, ahead of other chapters of *Education for All* (1985), more generally known as the Swann Report.

Tess Richards (ACERT 1981), in the conclusion to ACERT's submission to the Committee, wrote: "the time for action by charitable bodies has passed and the statutory services must accept the responsibility to take the steps which are necessary to end the isolation of Gypsy children so that they may receive the same benefits of education as other children in this country."

The Swann Report, an authoritative government publication, continued to give the impression that individual views/experiences cited could be typical of all children from the many and varied Traveller communities. Chapter 16, 18 (:749) informs the reader "Teachers have said to us that travellers' children "dont [yes, they omitted the apostrophe] know how to play"! It is amazing that this myth continued to be around for so long (Waterson 1987).

But Chapter 16 made some telling observations: it records (:746) that:

"The DES acknowledged in evidence to us that some LEAs might not be fulfilling their responsibilities in seeking to ensure that travellers' children attended school."

A flagrant disregard of their responsibilities for the education of Traveller children continued to be demonstrated by numbers of LEAs without effective censure from DES. The Report also dealt summarily with the 'open door' policy (:747).

A new departure for an education document was the acknowledgement that the provision of education and accommodation were inextricably linked:

"Whereas, with the other groups of children whom we have considered, we have been chiefly concerned with their needs *within* schools, many of the particular educational needs of travellers' children arise because of difficulties in gaining access to the education system at all. In many respects the situation in which travellers' children find themselves also illustrates to an extreme degree the experience of prejudice and alienation which faces many other ethnic minority children" (:740).

The Swann Committee owed its establishment to the concerns of the 1970s. The evidence on Traveller education was submitted on an ad hoc basis, there was no attempt at systematic research and by the time of publication much of it was four or five years old. It is still the most authoritative review available in published form and remains a source of reference for students and others.

The Courts and the 1968 Caravan Sites Act
Until 1985 Section 9 of the Caravan Sites Act 1968 had never been invoked. Under this section directions could be issued against local authorities not complying with the requirements of the Act. It was Diana Allen who instigated the first consideration of a judicial review. Mr Justice Mann found Hertfordshire in neglect of its duty and the county was directed to provide accommodation for a further 110 caravans. Other cases followed including West Glamorgan, Avon, Surrey, and Hereford and Worcester. From 1985 a series of judicial reviews took place, creating a situation where legislation was, in fact, court led. The resulting extra accommodation on authorised sites made more continuity in education possible for many more children.

The Public Order Act 1986
According to Douglas Hurd,

> "Section 39 of the Public Order Act 1986 was introduced into the Public Order Bill as it was going through Parliament in response to the depredations suffered by landowners by members of the so-called peace convoy during the summer of 1986." (Hansard Vol.158 c.620W).

However, it was obvious it would be used wherever authorities, police and others decided and where it was used any chance of schooling melted away.

> "In some areas Travellers were being moved several times within one day. One family moved twenty five times in the space of a fortnight and, although their case is extreme, it is by no means isolated" (ACERT 1990).

ACERT contributed evidence from eleven local authority areas to the Home Office survey on the way the Act was working (op. cit.). Eventual guidance to the police on the Public Order Act made clear Home Office reservations on its use.

The 1986 DES Short Course on Traveller Education in Chester
Thirty-five education personnel participated in this Future Professional Needs/Action Seminar. Their deliberations formed the basis for *Traveller Education – Post-Chester Proposals: Planning and Providing Education for Gypsy, Fairground and Circus Children* (ACERT 1986) which was produced by a joint NATT/ACERT Working Party, set up at NATT's 1986 Annual General Meeting. Ten years later this paper retains its relevance.

In September 1986 it was sent to all Chief Education Officers and to those who chaired Education Committees, as well as to government departments, political parties, teaching unions, church bodies and concerned voluntary organisations. In January 1987 it was followed up with a questionnaire to facilitate responses to the document. Thirty-nine of the 105 education authorities completed the questionnaires, providing evidence that the education of Traveller children was indeed administered through a wide variety of educational umbrellas with an even wider variety in the levels of commitment.

However, the evidence contained in the paper and the analysis of the questionnaire was ignored by most of the recipients, politely acknowledged by some and completely 'mis-read' by one political party. The only positive response came from the National Union of Teachers which, in April 1987, issued a press release to accompany their policy statement *The Education of Travellers' Children* (NUT 1987).

Malpractice repeated

Eleven years after Croydon's 1977 refusal of school places to Traveller children because they were stopping on an unauthorised site, the same LEA again transgressed. In 1988 when one of their schools agreed to take children from an unauthorised site the LEA countermanded the head's agreement. The family contacted a teacher from the authority where they had last been in school who put them in touch with ACERT which agreed to take up the case. The LEA confirmed its position to ACERT which then alerted HMI. The LEA was shown its error and school places were made available for the children but by then the family had been forced to move on. The LEA's stonewalling had once again kept children out of school. Children who had been in school in one area were refused school places in a neighbouring authority, another instance of the chancy character of Traveller children's education and a blatant example of an LEA ignoring a DES Circular.

Media coverage

Press reports, particularly in local newspapers, have often revealed prejudice at many levels.

The National Union of Journalists' *Guidelines on Race Reporting* (NUJ 1987) stated: "If you are a member, these are your guidelines. " The guidelines are clear and include specific ones on Travellers, the last of which begins:

> "Strive to promote the realisation that the travellers' community is comprised of full citizens of Great Britain and Ireland whose civil rights are seldom adequately vindicated ..."

Swann revisited

Worlds Apart? A Review of Research into the Education of Pupils of Cypriot, Italian, Ukrainian and Vietnamese Origin, Liverpool Blacks and Gypsies (1988), the fourth and final report in a series of reviews of research commissioned by the Swann Committee, appeared three years after the Swann Report. The editor wrote: "The review was originally undertaken in three months during 1983 and has been revised and updated in 1986" (Taylor 1988). Inevitably, much of the material was pre-1980. The chapter on Gypsy children (Hegarty 1988) is not helpful. Although he counselled against drawing on minor studies for evidence he described at great length investigations which purported to show Gypsy children as "poor communicators"! Student teachers could be tempted to quote such descriptions, without having access to very different evidence. Hegarty did acknowledge that: "Research literature on the education of Gypsy children is sparse" and: "It is clear that educational provision for Gypsy children is a political matter." Both statements remain true in the mid-1990s.

Travellers and the Race Relations Act
A test case by the Commission for Race Equality was to some extent won in the Court of Appeal in July 1988. In the leading judgment Lord Justice Nicholls concluded that, "Gypsies are an identifiable group of persons defined by reference to ethnic origins within the meaning of the [Race Relations] Act." The court found that the term 'Traveller' encompassed both Gypsies and other caravan dwellers and that a 'No Travellers' notice in a public house was, therefore, indirectly discriminatory. Indirect discrimination is illegal under the Race Relations Act 1976.

The Education Reform Act 1988
The Education Reform Act 1988 heralded years of continual change in schools and LEAs. The funding arrangements set out in Section 210 replaced the No-Area Pool. Instead of claiming retrospectively, LEAs were required to submit plans, initially covering three years, to claim 75 per cent of the estimated necessary expenditure for specific provision supporting the education of Travellers and Displaced Persons. Consultation was carried out around a DES Draft Circular based on Section 210 of the 1988 Act. The definitive DES Circular 10/90, *Education Reform Act 1988: Specific Grant for the Education of Travellers and Displaced Persons: Section 210* included guidelines on the type of provision which could be covered by the new funding.

There were still LEAs which did not bid for a grant, some which received grants too small to cover the cost of an extra teacher and some whose bids were found unacceptable. By 1994, however, 83 per cent of English LEAs were using Section 210 funding. That year the level of funding was reduced to 65 per cent. The annual reports sent to DES/DfE/DfEE provide a clearer picture of Traveller education than was previously available. An admittedly simplified assessment by DfEE was that, in the mid-1990s, 80 per cent of primary aged Travellers and 20 per cent of secondary age are registered with schools.

From April 1996 the global sum available through Section 210 was reduced and this at a time when some LEAs had bid for funding for the first time. Although Section 210 funding has led to more careful consideration by many LEAs, the whole fabric of Traveller education remains fragile, subject, perhaps more than any other specific education provision, to the fortunes of local authorities and the financial policies evolved by them to deal with other responsibilities. Section 210 monies constitute a minute proportion of education expenditure nationally. To whittle it down, first through the lowering of the percentage given and then to reduce the global sum available with no allowance for inflation, is to undermine the recommendations of the European Resolutions of 22 May 1989 (see below in the section *Europe and Travellers*). The uncertainties affecting the employment of teachers working specifically with the schools attended by Travellers lead to the loss of experienced staff and put at risk strategies devised by the Traveller Education Services to support schools.

The root of the trouble is that there are no votes to be gained by making effective education truly accessible to Travellers. The numbers in the different Traveller communities are so small and the lobbying power of the organisations concerned with their rights is infinitesimal. The continuing contraction of the Save the Children Fund's work with Travellers has further reduced the possibilities of positively influencing the situation. The Specific Grant has indeed led to overall improvement in the level and extent of Traveller education in England and provided the DES/DfE/DfEE with more accurate statistics from the eighty-three authorities which use Section 210. There is no information from the twenty-four which do not and there are still disparities in returns of those who do making analysis very complicated.

The Education of Traveller Children (OFSTED 1996), a survey of educational provision for Travelling children, summarises the evidence from a series of visits made by Her Majesty's Inspectors in England to thirty-one named LEAs and three self-governing grant maintained schools over a period of three years from September 1992. One of the main findings was that the "administration of Section 210 and other additional funding [was] efficient and effective". The report emphasises the importance of outreach work, stating: "There appears to be a direct link between the level of positive community liaison and the levels of registrations and patterns of attendance." The Report also points out how it is "unacceptable that access (to education) for some Travelling children should be further hampered by open or hidden prejudice within the wider community or among Travellers themselves." Advances made in take-up of primary education are considerable but unmet need at secondary level is widespread. The Report makes clear there are no grounds for complacency.

Education Otherwise
There is, mid-1990s, increasing disquiet about the growing numbers of secondary aged children whose families are opting for teaching by parents at home as advocated by *Education Otherwise* (Meighan, 1984). Minimal hours of tutoring, with no statutory requirements for close monitoring, cannot offer the opportunities available in schools. Whatever the shortcomings of state education at secondary level, using the state system is a political right for all families. Don Buckland often said, when he was a member of Her Majesty's Inspectorate, "If they get it right for Travellers they will get it right for all children."

Wales, Scotland and Northern Ireland
Scotland and Northern Ireland have their own Education Acts in line with the Education Reform Act 1988. The Department of Education Northern Ireland (DENI) Circular No 1993/37 *Policy and guidelines for the education of Children from Traveller Families* is an exceedingly encouraging document. It should be possible to assess the situation in Scotland and Northern Ireland after the publication of the Traveller Education Reports submitted to Brussels at the end of 1994 in accordance with the 1989 Resolutions.

Wales is covered by the same Education Act as England yet the amount made available under the *Specific Grant for the Education of Travellers and Displaced Persons* in the whole of Wales has been less than that allocated to a number of individual county education authorities in England. Whereas the English education authorities are informed of their allocations before the commencement of the spring term it has often been the last week in that term before that information is given to the Welsh education authorities. In some areas overt prejudice, at all levels, has led to the erosion of the small advances that had been made. Waterson (1993:136-9) documents how the clock has since been turned back in one Welsh county. In another Welsh county, however, considerable progress has been and continues to be made. More information should be available in the European Reports on member states' performance in relation to the Resolutions of May 1989.

The Children Act 1989
Carole Shaw, Senior Field Welfare Officer WMESTC, prepared a statement on the Act which was presented by Pat Holmes to the NATT Conference in May 1991. This was welcomed by those working with Travellers. If the requirements of the Act could be met it could safeguard the welfare of innumerable children and their families, Traveller children and children from the more settled population, but the finances have not been made available to allow it to be effective. It is, however, an act which can be cited by families under threat of eviction under the terms of the Criminal Justice and Public Order Act 1994. DoE Circular 18/95 specifically refers to the need for evicting authorities to take into account the requirements of the Children Act 1989.

The Criminal Justice and Public Order Act 1994
The Criminal Justice and Public Order Act (CJPO) 1994 had been foreshadowed in the Conservative Party's 1992 Election Manifesto. Two years of consultation led ineluctably to a parliamentary majority passing the Act in spite of opposition from a hearteningly wide spectrum of organisations, august bodies, and many individual members of the House of Lords, led by Lord Avebury (Eric Lubbock). Detailed assessment of the proposals can be found in the ACERT Briefing (1994).

The CJPO included the repeal of the Caravan Sites Act 1968 and the introduction of draconian measures which, when operated, deny all possibility of conforming with the *UN Convention on the Rights of the Child* which came into force in September 1990 and was ratified by the UK government in 1991. In January 1994 the government was examined by the UN Committee on the Rights of the Child on its record to date in implementing the Convention. It found

> "more pro-active measures are needed to protect the rights of children in Gypsy and traveller communities including the right to education and to adequate numbers of adequately appointed sites"

and that

> "careful monitoring of the Criminal Justice and Public Order Act

1994 is needed to ensure its compatibility with the principles and provisions of the Convention" (Children's Rights Office 1995).

The UK government is also a signatory of the Council of Europe's Convention for the Protection of Human Rights and Fundamental Freedoms which is in accordance with the Universal Declaration of Human Rights proclaimed by the General Assembly of the United Nations on 10 December 1948. Have children's rights and welfare organisations examined the CJPO Act in relation to these conventions and in relation to the UK's Children Act 1989? If guidance in DoE Circular 18/95 is followed there can be some mitigation of CJPO powers.

Europe and Travellers

For some years documents concerning Gypsies and other Travellers in Europe were being published unbeknownst to most of those in the UK whose work touched Traveller communities.

For example, both the Committee of Ministers *Resolution 75 (13) on the social situation of nomads in Europe*, adopted on 22 May 1975 and the Standing Conference of Local and Regional Authorities of Europe *Resolution 125 (1981) on the role and responsibility of local and regional authorities in regard to the cultural and social problems of populations of nomadic origin* were potentially important.

The understatement of the 1990s is contained in paragraph 5 of *Resolution 249* of the same standing conference, meeting in Strasbourg in 1993:

"Regretting that the afore-mentioned texts have as yet been followed up with little concrete action".

Paragraph 8 "Invites local and regional authorities ... to take necessary measures as part of an overall strategy to facilitate the integration of Rom/Gypsies into the local community, in the area of housing, caravan sites, education, health and support for the expression and development of these people's identity and culture ... ".

It surely would be preferable to alter the last few words so that they read: "these peoples' identities and cultures". Who receives copies of these documents?

The Synthesis Report

In 1984 Thomas Acton and Donald Kenrick were invited by Jean-Pierre Liégeois to carry out a survey of Traveller education in the UK. They sent copies of the grid they were to work from to NATT, ACERT and SCF as well as to what was then the NGEC, the organisation in which they were themselves active. ACERT, NATT and SCF's Gypsy Section found the methodology unacceptable and in detailed responses explained why they could not be associated with the survey. Nonetheless, Acton and Kenrick produced a report and a draft became available to the organisations concerned. Foreseeably, it drew hard hitting criticisms.

So far as England was concerned the controversy detracted considerably from any potential impact of *School Provision for Gypsy and Traveller Children: A Synthesis Report* (1987), a document which drew on, and quoted from, monographs from nationals of nine European States, including the report by Acton and Kenrick on the UK. An index enabling reference to be made to all the information on particular states would have been an advantage. The *Synthesis Report* gives no idea of what Traveller education was like across the UK at that period: the most useful information is found in the few case studies. The editing team must accept responsibility for the statement that "very precise statistics are available". No precise statistics existed then, nor do they in the mid-1990s.

The episode of the *Synthesis Report* was not a productive one. Considerable disquiet was engendered by the impression that reports were being requested only from 'experts' and not from practitioners. That the experts in question had for some years advocated that Gypsies/Travellers be allowed to leave school two years before their peers did not foster confidence in their stance on equal opportunities. (See editorial note at the end of this chapter.) A new *Interface* edition of the *Synthesis Report* is in preparation (1996).

Seminars in Continental Europe
In June 1983 a European seminar took place in Germany: *The training of Teachers of Gypsy children*. Don Buckland HMI, then responsible for the overview of Gypsy Education in England, knew nothing about it until after it had taken place!

A seminar in Germany in 1987 became known to UK teachers of Travellers through an educationist not involved with Gypsies. *Schooling for Gypsies' and Travellers' Children: evaluating innovation* had three UK participants from ACERT, NATT and SCF.

In 1989 a seminar in France, *The education of Gypsy and Traveller children: action research and co-ordination* (ACERT 1993) drew four UK participants from ACERT, NATT, NGEC and WMESTC and a measure of co-ordination and joint preparation was achieved. The seminar occasionally experienced a very slight feeling of euphoria, meeting as it did within two months of the adoption of the *Resolutions on School Provision for children of Occupational Travellers* and *School Provision for Gypsy and Traveller Children* (Council of Ministers, 1989). It was at the 1989 seminar that we learned of the 1988 seminar in France – apparently for French nationals – *Gypsy Children in school: training for teachers and other personnel* where Donald Kenrick was a lecturer.

Other European Seminars followed:
■ in France in 1990 – the Education of Gypsy and Traveller Children: distance learning
■ in the UK in 1991 – Models of Access, organised by the DES and the EC (DfE 1992)
■ in Slovakia in 1994 and 1995 – Gypsies and Local History: analysis of the question of minorities and of the possible responses of history teaching and history textbooks
■ and in the UK in 1995 – Educational Provision for Travellers and Refugee Pupils: promoting achievement, organised by the Council of Europe.

Publications
Interface (the newsletter published by the Centre for Gypsy Research, Paris) was launched in February 1991 and *Newsline* (the newsletter of EFECOT – the European Federation for the Education of the Children of Occupational Travellers) first appeared in March 1991. Both publications are distributed free on request and both are supported by the Commission of the European Community in implementation of the Council of Ministers Resolutions of 22 May 1989.

    Interface makes known the opportunities for funding particular innovations, action-research, publications and exchanges between students and teachers of different states: in most cases projects have had to involve co-operation between two or more member states. Useful work has been achieved through these channels which would not have occurred without such funding. *Newsline* carries equivalent information on developments in fairground, circus and bargee children's education, as well as on seminars, other events and funding possibilities.

Resolutions on school provision
One outcome of the Council of Ministers of the European Community Resolutions of 22 May 1989 on *School Provision for children of Occupational Travellers* and *School Provision for Gypsy and Traveller Children* (Council of Ministers, 1989) was the establishment of the Ad Hoc Group, which in 1989 took over from a 'panel of experts'. This allowed an exchange of information on Traveller education between Euro States at the level of civil servants with specific responsibilities, some with specialist knowledge. The Ad Hoc Group also covered migrant workers. It is to be regretted that the UK, which in effect comprises four countries – England, Scotland, Wales and Northern Ireland – has been represented solely by two representatives from England.

    The Ad Hoc Group had its last meeting in 1995 and has been superseded by the Socrates Committee and its education sub-committee. Representation from the UK will be through both the International Relations Branch and the Pupils, Parents and Youth Group at DfEE.

    There are serious difficulties, however, in obtaining financial support from the EC. Long delays take place before monies are actually deposited in the bank accounts of those whose bids are successful. Also the time between the arrival of the finance and the date on which a report has to be in the hands of the fund-givers has often been so short that the proposed work is placed in jeopardy, perhaps at risk of being abandoned altogether. This is a matter which needs urgent attention in Brussels.

    A requirement of the Resolutions of 22 May 1989 was that in December 1993 member states should submit reports demonstrating the progress (or otherwise?) made towards implementing the improvements in Traveller education which were advocated in the Resolutions of 1989. ACERT from the beginning was concerned that the reports would indicate only what had been achieved without setting out what remained to be tackled. Accordingly, their committee suggested to DES Schools Branch II, that a draft report be circulated to co-ordinators of Traveller Education Services and concerned organisations for comment before finally being forwarded to Brussels. This suggestion was not accepted.

    The long awaited composite report based on the national reports was finally published on the 22 October 1996 (Commission of the European Communities) and is available from the Office for Official Publications of the European Communities, L-2985 Luxembourg (ISSN 0254-1475, ISBN 92 78 09937 6, Catalogue No. CB-CO-96-503-EN-C).

It has not been widely distributed, and concentrates more on the actions carried by the Commission itself, than the actions carried out by individual countries, which it found hard to quantify in any comparative form. We are still a long way from having a league table for European countries regarding achievements in Traveller education.

Domestic reports from each state have also been promised by the Commission.

The mid-1990s position – a summary

During the last twenty-five years there has been:
- the acknowledgement of the inadequacy of the 'open door' policy
- a move away from segregation in education
- a move away from Traveller Education Services supporting individual children into whole school support
- DfEE Circulars providing firmer guidelines to LEAs and demanding greater accountability
- the development of distance learning packs, used in particular by fairground families but now benefiting circus and Gypsy/Traveller children
- gradually increasing involvement with the rest of Europe, not only by DfEE and HMI but by LEA teachers
- research, in particular action-research, being carried out by practitioners
- the production of publications by those working with Travellers using duplicating, then photocopying and eventually desktop publishing to achieve commercial print quality
- the Caravan Sites Act becoming law in 1970 and being repealed under the Criminal Justice and Public Order Act 1994
- a continuing lack of unity among Gypsy organisations
- the taking to task of the UK in relation to its performance under the UN Convention on the Rights of the Child particularly in regard to Travellers
- an ever-increasing understanding and awareness of Traveller issues extending to a steadily growing number of people
- a steadily growing number of schools where Gypsies are welcome.

Conclusion

During these twenty-five years there have been far-reaching changes in education generally. The education of Travellers needs to be acknowledged as integral to the whole, being considered within policies on anti-racism, bullying and equal opportunities, in addition to policies and strategies promoted by the Swann Report and the Elton Report. The education of Travellers' children who have special needs must, as with all children with special educational needs, be considered in accordance with *The Code of Practice on the Identification and Assessment of Special Educational Needs* (DfE 1994) and, in particular, when the integration of special education needs into mainstream education is being planned.

Much has been achieved in Gypsy/Traveller education but while 80-85 five per cent of Traveller children of secondary age do not appear on any school roll (OFSTED 1996) much remains to be done. Prejudice continues to afflict many at all levels in national and local government. Prejudiced views are endemic in our society. Prejudice leads to fear and to rejection of Travellers. People who devise policies affecting Gypsies and Travellers, and those who put such policies into practice, need continually reminding that they are responsible for the lives and needs of men, women and children.

We all are responsible for the future.

References

ACERT/NATT 1986 *Traveller Education – Post-Chester Proposals: planning and providing Education for Gypsy, Fairground and Circus children* ACERT, Harlow

ACERT 1990 *Section 39 Public Order Act 1986: ACERT response to Home Office Review 1990* ACERT, Harlow

ACERT 1994 *Briefing on Part V of the Criminal Justice and Public Order Bill (provisions affecting Gypsies and other Travellers)* ACERT Harlow

ACERT 1993 *The education of Gypsy and Traveller Children: action-research and co-ordination* University of Hertfordshire Press, Hatfield

ADAMS B, OKELY J, MORGAN D and SMITH D 1975 *Gypsies and Government Policy in England* Heinemann, London

CAMM E 1934 "Hurtwood School", *Journal of the Gypsy Lore Society: Third Series, Vol.XIII, 4.*

CHILDREN'S RIGHTS OFFICE 1995 *Making the Convention work for Children* Children's Rights Office, London

COMMISSION OF THE EUROPEAN COMMUNITIES 1996 *School Provision for Children of Occupational Travellers; Report on the implemenation of measures planned by the Council and the Ministers of Education 22 May 1989; COM(96)494 Final. (89/C 153/01)*

COMMISSION OF THE EUROPEAN COMMUNITIES 1996 *School Provision for Gypsy and Traveller Children; Report on the implemenation of measures planned by the Council and the Ministers of Education 22 May 1989; COM(96)495 Final. (89/C 153/02)*

CONFERENCE OF LOCAL AND REGIONAL AUTHORITIES OF EUROPE 1981 *Resolution 125 (1981) on the role and responsibility of local and regional authorities in regard to the cultural and social problems of populations of nomadic origin*

CONFERENCE (STANDING CONFERENCE) OF LOCAL AND REGIONAL AUTHORITIES OF EUROPE 1993 *Resolution 249 (13) on Gypsies in Europe: the role and responsibility of local and regional authorities, 2,* paras. 5 and 8

COUNCIL OF EUROPE 1975 *Committee of Ministers Resolution 75 (13) on the social situation of nomads in Europe,* adopted 22 May 1975

COUNCIL OF MINISTERS OF THE EUROPEAN COMMUNITY 1989 *Resolution of the Council and the Ministers of Education meeting within the Council of 22 May 1989 on School Provision for children of Occupational Travellers (Fairground, Circus and Bargee) (89C 153/01)* Official Journal of the European Communities C.153. 21 June 1989:1-2

COUNCIL OF MINISTERS OF THE EUROPEAN COMMUNITY 1989 *Resolution of the Council and the Ministers of Education meeting within the Council of 22 May 1989 on School Provision for Gypsy and Traveller Children (89/C.153/02)* Official Journal of the European Communities C.153. 21 June 1989:3

CRIPPS John 1977 *Accommodation for Gypsies: a report on the working of the Caravan Sites Act 1968* HMSO, London

DEPARTMENT OF EDUCATION NORTHERN IRELAND 1993 *DENI Circular 1993/3 Policy and guidelines for the education of Children from Traveller Families* DENI, Belfast

DEPARTMENT OF EDUCATION AND SCIENCE 1981 *DES Circular 1/81. The Education Act 1980: Admission to schools, appeals, publication of information and school attendance orders (Sections 6-11 Schedule 2)* DES, London

DEPARTMENT OF EDUCATION AND SCIENCE 1983 *The Education of Travellers' Children: An HMI discussion paper* DES, London

DEPARTMENT OF EDUCATION AND SCIENCE 1983 *A survey of the West Midlands Education Service for Travelling Children: carried out February/March 1983* DES, London

DEPARTMENT OF EDUCATION AND SCIENCE 1990 *DES Circular 10/90 Education Reform Act 1988: Specific Grant for the Education of Travellers and Displaced Persons. Section 210* DES, London

DEPARTMENT OF EDUCATION AND SCIENCE 1992 *The education of Traveller children: Report of a seminar organised by the UK DES and the Commission of the European Communities 1991* DfE, London

DEPARTMENT FOR EDUCATION 1994 *The code of practice on the identification and assessment of special educational needs* DfE, London

DEPARTMENT OF THE ENVIRONMENT 1978 *DoE Circular 57/78 Accommodation for Gypsies: Report by Sir John Cripps* HMSO, London

DEPARTMENT OF THE ENVIRONMENT 1995 *DoE Circular 18/95 Gypsy sites policy and unauthorised camping* DoE, London

DODDS Norman 1966 *Gypsies, Didikois and other Travellers* Johnson, London

ELTON Lord 1989 *Discipline in Schools (The Elton Report)* HMSO, London

EUROPEAN CONVENTION FOR THE PROTECTION OF HUMAN RIGHTS AND FUNDAMENTAL FREEDOMS: signed 1950 and came into force 1953

HAWES D and PEREZ B 1995 *The Gypsy and the State* SAUS, Bristol

HEGARTY S 1988 "Gypsy Children" in Taylor M ed. 1988 *Worlds Apart?* pp.363-4 NFER/Nelson, Windsor

HURD D 1989 written answer dated 26 October 1989 Hansard Vol. 158, c. 620W

LIÉGEOIS J-P 1984 *The training of teachers of Gypsy children* Seminar 1983 CCC, Strasbourg

LIÉGEOIS J-P 1987 *School Provision for Gypsy and Traveller Children: a Synthesis Report:* EC Brussels/Luxembourg

LIÉGEOIS J-P 1988 *Schooling for Gypsies' and Travellers' children: evaluating innovation* Seminar 1987 CCC, Strasbourg

LIÉGEOIS J-P. 1989 *Gypsy children in school: training for teachers and other personnel* Seminar 1988 CCC, Strasbourg

MANLEY V 1971 "The work of the Gypsy Council Education Trust" in Acton T ed. *Current Changes Amongst British Gypsies* NGEC, London

MEIGHAN, Roland 1984 "Political consciousness and home-based education" *Educational Review* Vol.36 (2)

MINISTRY OF HOUSING AND LOCAL GOVERNMENT 1962 *Circular 6/ 1962* HMSO, London

MINISTRY OF HOUSING AND LOCAL GOVERNMENT 1967 *Gypsies and other Travellers* HMSO, London

NATIONAL UNION OF TEACHERS 1987 *The education of Travellers' Children: a policy statement* NUT, London

NATIONAL UNION OF TEACHERS 1987 "NUT says Travellers' children need extra support to boost educational opportunities" press release 6 April NUT, London

NATIONAL UNION OF JOURNALISTS 1987 *Guidelines on Race Reporting* includes "Guidelines on Travellers" NUJ, London.

OFSTED 1996 *The Education of Travelling Children* OFSTED, London

PLOWDEN Lady 1967 *Children and their Primary Schools* p.59 para.155, p.60 para. 157 and Appendix 12 HMSO, London

PULLIN R T 1982 *Swings and Roundabouts – The Education of Travelling Fairground Children – a Survey* Division of Education Sheffield University

RICHARDS T 1981 *Evidence submitted by ACERT to the Committee of Inquiry into the education of children of ethnic minority groups* ACERT, London

SHAW C 1991 *Contents of the Children Act 1989, a paper given by P Holmes* NATT, Bradford

SWANN Lord 1985 *Education for All* pp.649-51 and 739-59 HMSO, London

TAYLOR M 1988 Preface in Taylor M ed. *Worlds Apart?* NFER/Nelson, Windsor

TINKER M and F 1975 "Report of the Potton Trailer School: Summer 1973" *Traveller Education* 4

UNITED NATIONS 1990 *United Nations Convention on the Rights of the Child* Children's Rights Office, London

UNITED NATIONS COMMITTEE ON THE RIGHTS OF THE CHILD 1994 criticisms and recommendations – full text in *Making the Convention Work for Children* p.6. Children's Rights Office, London.

VINSON P 1973 *Roadside Families* SCF Playgroup Department, London

WATERSON M 1987 "Here they expect you to learn" *Nursery World* 22 October, pp.20-1

WATERSON M 1993 "United Kingdom: Co-ordination" in *The Education of Gypsy and Traveller children: action-research and co-ordination* pp.136-9 University of Hertfordshire Press, Hatfield

WORRALL D and JONES I 1972 *West Midlands Travellers School Van Leer Project* WMTS, Walsall

WORRALL D 1977 *Walsall Travellers' School Second Report: Easter 1977* Travelling People's Education Project, Walsall

Editorial Note

Some of the opinions expressed in this paper are rather different from those of the editors. Further information may be found in:

ACTON T 1988 *The Anatomy of a Furore* paper given to the Centennial Conference of the Gypsy Lore Society, Wagner College, New York

ACTON T and KENRICK D, with the assistance of HOME G D 1986 *The Education of Gypsy / Traveller Children in Great Britain and Northern Ireland* Unpublished report to the EC Commission

ACTON T and KENRICK D 1991 "From Summer Voluntary Schemes to European Community Bureaucracy: The Development of Special Provision for Traveller Education in the United Kingdom since 1967" *European Journal of Intercultural Studies* Vol.I No.3

Chapter 9 Opening our eyes:
some observations on the attendance of primary
aged Traveller pupils registered at schools in a
county area of South Wales

*G Sandra Clay, Teacher, South Glamorgan, and Researcher,
University of Wales, Cardiff*

What does a school really mean to Travelling children who are registered to attend it? This chapter, drawing on the author's interviews for her doctoral research with children, parents and teachers, tries to get behind the registration and attendance figures to reveal the diversity of individual Travellers' experiences and the consequent difficulties in drawing conclusions from official schooling statistics. In 1983 a report from Her Majesty's Inspectorate of Schools stated "that as few as 40 per cent to 50 per cent of primary aged children from travelling families attend school and those attending regularly are but a small proportion of the total" (DES 1983:7). Over a decade later, this chapter examines a record of Traveller pupils' attendance in primary schools to look at what the increase of attendance actually means in one area.

It is apparent that to some extent in past discussions the terms 'registered' and 'attended' were frequently used interchangeably. In this chapter we shall be more precise. If a child's name is added to the school's roll or record of students of a school then that child is 'registered' and when the child is actually present at that school he/she is in 'attendance' and so a child can not attend if not registered but can continue to be registered whilst not in attendance. Any consideration of Traveller pupil attendance must be mindful, therefore, that across the European Community, possibly half the number of eligible Traveller children are not registered for school, despite legal obligations, in almost every member state, for them to be so (Liégeois, 1987).

The area of the author's local education authority in South Wales has approximately 300 Traveller children (0-16 years) "residing and resorting" (as the wording of the 1968 Caravan Sites Act has it) within its boundaries (South Glamorgan Traveller Education Service, 1995). The provision of

Traveller education in this area has illustrated a possibly typical development. The local authority originally adopted an 'open door/eyes closed' approach with needs subsequently being responded to by a variety of initiatives from voluntary bodies. With the establishment of the two official sites, unit provision within two primary schools was developed and then abandoned in 1991 with the establishment of a small County Traveller Education Service enabled by the receipt of Section 210 grant.

Over the academic year 1992-3 the attendance of fifty Traveller pupils in this local education authority area was analysed. This sample was 'purposefully selected' from the total of 147 known Traveller pupils enrolled within this local authority at some point in this year, in order to reflect a typical sample for the area. These pupils attended seven different primary schools and all fell within the normal age range for these schools. Secondary school pupils and over-11s were excluded as they pose rather different problems. Several schools were represented to avoid bias from any one exceptionally good or poor attendance record. All of the selected pupils were English or Welsh Gypsies (Romanichals) or Irish Travellers (Minceir). Other groups, such as the circus and fairground folk given the rather misleading title by the European Communities of "Occupational Travellers" (as if they were the only such!) were not included as they are not significantly represented in the area considered and may have distinct seasonal patterns of travelling and aspirations and expectations of schooling that might have produced a different emphasis. In the sample there were twenty-two females and twenty-eight males. As was true of the area as a whole, the majority of the selected pupils were living on official sites.

Table 1.
Percentage attendance of fifty non-Traveller pupils and fifty Traveller pupils in a county area of South Wales (Winter term 1992)

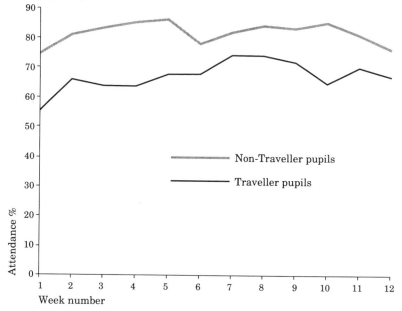

Table 2.
Percentage attendance of fifty non-Traveller pupils and fifty Traveller pupils in a county area of South Wales (Spring term 1993)

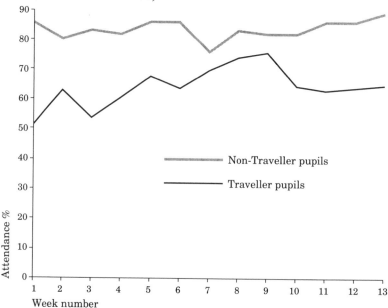

Table 3.
Percentage attendance of fifty non-Traveller pupils and fifty Traveller pupils in a county area of South Wales (Summer term 1993)

Table 4.
Percentage attendance of fifty non-Traveller pupils and fifty Traveller pupils in a county area of South Wales (academic year 1992/3)

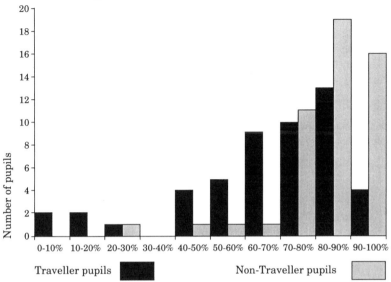

As a control group, to allow comparisons, the attendance records of fifty non-Traveller pupils were also collected and analysed, these pupils being, wherever possible, those listed on school registers next to each of the individual Traveller pupils.

It is apparent that, for the three terms considered, Tables 1, 2 and 3 show that the patterns of attendance were broadly similar. Both samples, for instance, had a relatively poor attendance in the first half of the spring term (January/February) and increased attendance during the second half of the winter term (November/December). There is, however, a consistent and distinct difference between the two in levels of attendance. Table 6 shows the average attendance of non-Travellers (83 per cent) exceeds that of Travellers (67 per cent) by 16 per cent. These fifty Traveller pupils were, therefore, on average, present only for approximately two-thirds of that academic year and lost twice as many days as the non-Travellers. Clearly this may be detrimental to their educational progress

On the other hand, Table 4 shows that over half of these Traveller pupils did attend to a reasonable level, twenty-seven achieving levels of 70 per cent or above. This is a distinct overall improvement in comparison with previous studies. For example, Ivatts (1975) reported that in general the average Gypsy pupil absences were almost four times greater than other pupils, although his study focused on a secondary school at a time when any secondary age attendance by Travellers was very uncommon. Reiss (1975) suggested that in England and Wales approximately one third of Traveller pupils attended regularly, one third were present about half the time and the remainder attended sporadically. Mackay (1981) considered the attendance of 287 pupils in the South Wales area generally and found sixty-four attending regularly, 107 occasionally and 120 intermittently.

As well as a change in overall levels, however, this sample indicates differences in the pattern of Traveller pupils' attendance. If both sets of pupils' attendance are viewed not as actual days attended but as a presence made at some point in a week as equalling an attendance, the overall level of Traveller pupils' attendance rises more significantly than that of non-Travellers (Table 5). This illustrates that much of the Traveller pupils' absence was likely to have been intermittent and cumulative rather than continuous and lengthy. Ivatts (1975) noted this instability of Traveller pupils attendance within the parameters of a week, noting Traveller pupils absences rose approximately 50 to 80 per cent Monday to Friday.

Table 5.
Whole week attendance of fifty non-Traveller pupils and fifty Traveller pupils in a county area of South Wales (academic year 1992-3)

	Whole week presence	
Terms	**Non Travellers**	**Travellers**
Winter	95%	84%
Spring	94%	81%
Summer	92%	82%
Whole year	**94%**	**83%**

Note that part week attendance is included in the above figures

This objectively measurable improvement evident in the Traveller pupil attendance record, was matched by subjective perceptions. Teachers, pupils and parents also said they thought that attendance had improved. Nineteen out of twenty county teaching staff with Traveller pupils and eighteen out of twenty-six local Traveller adults interviewed expressed the view that Traveller pupils' attendance was average or above, although twenty-three Traveller pupils in the sample were still failing to reach a 70 per cent attendance level. Previous studies have recorded generally positive views from Travellers and less positive ones from teachers although there may have been less apparent correspondence with actual performance (Reiss 1975:22, Karpati and Massano cited in Liégeois 1987:80, Shine 1987:87). Both teachers' and Travellers' views, of course, can be coloured by their social and cultural mores and other influences such as the professional role of teachers and the possibility that many Travellers may lack any tradition of regular attendance. It is difficult to generalise as even within the same family there may be contrasting levels such as one Traveller pupil achieving only 50 per cent attendance whilst her sister recorded 79 per cent.

Liégeois (1987:83) has asserted that "equally and doubtless in all states, there are seasonal variations in attendance" and suggests there is an observable increase in Traveller pupil attendance at the period when least travelling was believed to occur – November to April. This is corroborated by Reiss (1975) who stated there was an increase in Traveller pupil absences from May to October. The Traveller pupil attendance record here, however, shows only a slight seasonal variation when a comparison is made of levels achieved by both samples over the summer term (Table 6). A comparative review of the behaviour of the week-by-week record (Table 1, 2, 3,) also only indicates a slight seasonal difference. Given the short term intermittency of the Traveller pupil absence in this study, travelling is a likely significant cause of absence.

Table 6.
Attendance of fifty non-Traveller pupils and fifty Traveller pupils in a county area of South Wales (academic year 1992-3)

Terms	Average % attendance	
	Non Travellers	**Travellers**
Winter	84%	68%
Spring	82%	67%
Summer	84%	65%
Whole year	**83%**	**67%**

Despite the view of HM Inspectorate (1983:8) about the increased feasibility of regular attendance by children located on official sites, it would appear that neither the magnitude nor the length of seasonal variations previously suggested by Liégeois are exhibited by this sample. This change could be postulated as evidence that some Travellers are choosing to undertake less seasonal travel perhaps, in part, because of their increased commitment to the uninterrupted attendance of their children at school as illustrated by the mother who commented: "Well, it's no different here on the site now than being in a *kher* (house) nowadays. Your kids has to go to school, wherever you is. Mine likes school, they never misses. We only goes away once a year now – up country to see our relatives, 'cos we wants them to learn to read and write."

A teacher of Traveller children in this area since 1988 remarked that previously most Traveller pupils would be absent, travelling with their families throughout the summer but recently this phenomena had all but disappeared. Additional supportive evidence is afforded by Shoring's (1991:9) record of unofficially sited Traveller families resorting to the area 1989-91 which shows the greatest incidence in August in the middle of the school vacation.

Both Liégeois (1987:83) and Reiss (1975) had linked seasonal variations in Traveller pupil attendance with the socio-economic activities of the Traveller family such as seasonal migrations to harvest fruit, attendance at traditional gatherings such as horse fairs and the coming together of extended families to celebrate Christmas, etc. The effects of recent change have influenced and reduced the impact of such causations. For example, with the increased use of modern technology and transport systems there is less demand for agricultural labour and less necessity for dispersed extended families to travel just to maintain contact. Some traditional gatherings have been discouraged (such as Stow Fair) and free movement is inhibited by the continuous loss of halting spots and the pernicious effects of the Criminal Justice Act, 1994. The lack of any temporary site provision in the county aggravates the effects of a policy of non-toleration of unauthorised encampment and the shortage of permanent sites. The average waiting time for a plot is approximately three years. In the light of the repeal of the sections of the 1968 Caravan Sites Act requiring local authority site provision there is unlikely to be any short term improvement. Moreover, residents of the official sites are restricted by their licence agreement to a total of thirteen weeks absence or their licence rights are forfeit.

These observations were supported by local Traveller adults and children's responses at interviews with 38 out of 47 stating that travelling away to work at any time of the year was not an important factor in Traveller pupils absence. Rather, they indicated a greater propensity to suggest that social occasions were more likely causes of absence. For example, 24 out of 47 said attendance had been interrupted by family holidays, 26 out of 47 mentioned travelling to visit relatives and three out of 47 identified their involvement in a wedding or funeral or similar occasions, as a significant factor. Most of these instances, however, serve both social and economic functions to differing degrees, for example, a Traveller family visiting relations would not usually discontinue their economic activities. Additionally, many such family or social events also lead to non-Traveller pupils' absence although the majority of these instances are capable of being managed, if desired, so as not to conflict with school attendance. It is apparent that Travellers are indicating, despite the demand for continuous attendance at a non-Traveller institution, the paramountcy for them of the recognition of the importance of the celebration of such occasions. The causes of absence identified by the Traveller sample interviewed serve to reinforce self-identity and demarcate them from majority society. Their cohesion and survival as a people is, therefore, promoted by their children's immersion in such observances. Perhaps this is what the Traveller parent meant by saying, "We don't need to travel to make a living. We are Travellers, we have our own ways, we're not Gaujos!"

Significantly the only question that evoked a differing emphasis in replies of the Traveller children as contrasted with the Traveller adults was asking if absence from school had been caused by remaining at home to care for younger children. This was reported by 15 out of 21 children but only admitted by 11 out of 26 adults. We must be mindful that no matter how warm the established mutual rapport, these interviews were undertaken by a teacher and a symbol of authority and perhaps Traveller adults may have been aware of such considerations when responding to this particular enquiry. This instance also illustrates the ambivalence of whether a factor is primarily attributed to economic or social considerations as responsible Traveller parents might see that opportunities arose for children to practise relevant life skills, such as child care, even if this was not directly linked to an opportunity to undertake greater economic activity. Very few families were observed to undertake this practice just from considerations of economic necessity but, nonetheless, it would be inappropriate to refer to such absences as 'trivial' or 'casual'.

Over a relatively short period of time, Travellers have had to accommodate a series of tremendous inter-related changes including, for many, the possibility of regular schooling for their children. Considerations of Traveller pupil attendance involve a number of complex factors in differing combinations that impact to different degrees. It would be mistaken simplistically to identify travelling as a lone or even major consideration as it is not unique to Travellers, nor is it a significant feature of all Travellers' life and, where it is, it is not necessarily detrimental to attendance. For example, an unofficially sited pupil in this sample achieved 66 per cent over the year considered, compared with the 49 per cent of one officially sited pupil, vindicating the Swann Report's (1985:743) observation that "by no means all the educational problems of Traveller children would be solved, were all Travellers to be accommodated on sites".

When we recall that the 1980 Welsh Report of the National Gypsy Council (p.22) referred to this county area as having "the worst record for harassment and eviction in the country to date" and Mackay (1981:61) felt justified in stating that the prevalent attitudes and practice locally regarding Traveller school attendance were 'dishonesty and evasion', the current situation presents a great contrast. Policies promoting assimilation and coercion have come to be seen as inappropriate. Support offered via the operation of the county specialist service has proved effective. Essentially, progress has been made only with the co-operative partnership of Traveller families and schools. Where Traveller identity and culture is respected it is self-evident that attendance will continue to improve.

References

DEPARTMENT OF EDUCATION AND SCIENCE 1983 *An HMI Discussion Paper – The Education of Traveller Children* HMSO, London

IVATTS A 1975 *Catch 22 Gypsies, a Report on Secondary Education* ACERT, London

LIÉGEOIS J-P 1987 *School Provision for Gypsy and Traveller children – A Synthesis Report* Commission of the European Communities, Brussels

MACKAY A H 1981 "Social Structure and Political Process: A Study of Travellers in South Wales" PhD thesis University of Wales, Cardiff

THE NATIONAL GYPSY COUNCIL 1980 *Welsh Report* NGC, Leeds

REISS C 1975 *The Education of Travelling Children* Schools Council Research Studies/Macmillan Education, London

SHINE P 1987 "Traveller Education – How is it seen by Teachers and Travellers" B.Ed thesis, Didsbury School of Education, Manchester

SHORING A 1991 *The Roadside Project* Second Annual Report, Cardiff Gypsy Sites Group, Cardiff

SOUTH GLAMORGAN TRAVELLER EDUCATION SERVICE 1995 "Annual Report to the Welsh Office 1994/95" unpublished report, Cardiff

SWANN M 1985 *Education for All: The Report of the European Committee of Inquiry into the Education of Children from Ethnic Minority Groups (The Swann Report)* HMSO, London

Chapter 10 Researching the religious affiliations of Travellers and their beliefs

Bernard Mends, Secretary, Stepping Stones School, London

There can be no doubt that the Gypsies have undergone many religious adaptations, during their migrations. The fact that in the past, like non-Gypsies, they tend to belong to religions within the country they are residing has been used by Gypsylorists to assert that the Gypsies have no firm religious convictions or perhaps no religious beliefs at all. The variety of alleged superstition and belief in this unreliable literature has been somewhat credulously documented by Trigg (1973). Before we can begin to think how to investigate the current sutuation, however, we have to take note of the fact that it is impossible to give a clear and concise definition of the word 'religion'. The word religion has even been used to refer to whatever one does with one's own leisure time. Any questionnaire has to explore not only belief in certain propositions, such as the existence of God, but what those propositions are taken to mean by those who assent or dissent from them.

What, in effect, do the words 'God' or 'religion' mean to the Gypsies? To find the answer to these a survey was carried out during the Christmas period 1983/4, as part of preparation for a student dissertation on Gypsies. At that time the international growth of Gypsy pentecostalism (Acton 1979) had already taken root in England (Ridholls 1986). In the light of the considerable growth in religious revival amongst the Gypsy people in this country since then (Boston 1996), however, there is now ample scope for further studies in this field to be undertaken.

In conducting the survey 110 Gypsies were interviewed. These interviews took place on Traveller sites in Kilgetty and Merthyr Tydfil in Pembrokeshire, in Wandsworth, Southwark, Hammersmith and Lambeth within Greater London and in the Guildford area of Surrey. Sites in England and Wales were selected in order to get responses from both

English and Welsh Gypsies. The Irish Traveller views were also obtained from official and unofficial sites in the London area.

The interviewees were interviewer-selected on an adhoc 'snowball' basis either by talking to Gypsies that were outside of their caravans on the site or by knocking on caravan doors. Although I knew a few, I did not know the majority of them personally nor did I know their religious beliefs previously. Whilst none of the Gypsies refused to take part in the survey, there were two people on the site at Merthyr Tydfil who made it quite clear that they were upset that God's existence should be in doubt.

The make-up of the sample

Table 1.
An overview of the sample by age, gender and geographical location

Age	10 - 20		20 - 30		30 - 40		40 - 50		Total
Gender	*M*	*F*	*M*	*F*	*M*	*F*	*M*	*F*	
London	3	6	3	13	4	5	4	8	46
South East	0	6	2	4	4	2	5	4	27
Wales	0	3	6	8	3	0	8	9	37
Male	*3*	-	*11*	-	*11*	-	*17*	-	*42*
Female	-	*15*	-	*25*	-	*7*	-	*21*	*68*
Total	**18**		**36**		**18**		**38**		**110**

There was no noticeable correlation between these independent variables of age, gender and location and the attitudinal variables examined below.

Questions on religious attitudes
The attitudinal interview schedule is reproduced in Appendix A. It was found necessary to give additional explanations for some questions as the interview proceeded.

God's existence
93.64 per cent believed that there was some kind of spiritual being, or power that existed. It is difficult to generalise about what this means, however. My impression from my discussions was that around half of them were expressing either a belief based on superstition or they had a pantheistic idea of God. A pantheistic approach can be seen when Clifford Lee, the father of the Ken Lee who contributed to this volume, was quoted by McDowell (1970, p.15) as answering a question about Gypsy religion with:

> "I was baptised a Roman Catholic in Ireland, as a boy I went to church often, but only to other baptisms! The priest, used to give a baptised child a bit of money, I recall when I was a boy, that we went to eight churches one Sunday and got the same infant baptised each time; different names in every church. A borrowed baby! But here in England, most Gypsies are Church of England,

in Scotland Presbyterians and in Turkey, Muslims. We're what the country is!"

Of the seven atheists or agnostics who did not believe or were not sure of God's existence, 2 each opined it was a form of escapism or that there was too much suffering, two were not sure, and one ascribed his non-belief to a personal tragedy, the recently suffered loss of a relative.

The usefulness of the church
80-90 per cent saw some use or need for the church within the context of their daily lives. Of the 6.36 per cent who doubted God's existence, 3.63% believed that there was both a need and use for the church within their daily lives.

The purposes of the church were seen as follows:
- in preaching Christ 41.81%;
- point of contact with the local community 12.72%;
- upholding moral standards (both local and national) 2.72%;
- a building to worship God 17.27%;
- involved in social issues 4.54%;
- unsure of the use or need 1.81%.

Church attendance
- weekly 19.41%
- occasionally 25.88%
- weddings and funerals only 21.84%

On a weekly basis, from the 19.41 per cent who went to church once a week, 23.52 per cent would not go to an organised church service but preferred to attend a church where no service was in progress. The reason for this was due to illiteracy. One lady in particular was prepared to spend one hour per day in quiet meditation, but would have been highly embarrassed to have attended a formal service because of her inability to read.

Of the 25.88 per cent who attended church occasionally, 13.63 per cent said they would go more often if they could read; they felt humiliated when given books they could not read. Of the 21.84 per cent who only attended church for weddings and funerals 5.5per cent said they would go more if they could understand the service.

The total number of Gypsies who professed definite experience of the new birth, that is, declared themselves born-again Christians, and who could give a clear account of what this meant was 11.81 per cent, but of this figure, only 53.84 per cent went on a regular basis (i.e. at least once a week) to church services as illiteracy kept the remaining 46.15 per cent away.

Possible changes in church services
Of the 110 Gypsies interviewed 59.4 per cent wanted progressive changes such as modern hymns (12.47 per cent), dramatised or shorter sermons (7.27 per cent), congregational involvement (8.31 per cent) and visual aids (3.56 per cent). Of the remainder, 42.9 per cent were traditionalists and 11 per cent were not interested.

Question 8 was a back-up to question 4, in that it asked for the importance of the church's role in society:

- More political activities would have been welcomed by 26.4%;
- more outreach to non-Christians by 58.3%;
- the importance of providing a meeting place for the neighborhood was emphasised by 15.4%;
- better use of resources and other issues were emphasised by 24.2%.

As one lady stated: "People coming to evangelise the Gypsies should come with the attitude of being servants of the Gypsy and not try to enforce their culture upon them."

Conclusion

In hindsight, much could have been done better and explored in more detail in this survey. But however naive it may appear in retrospect, it was undertaken at a time when most social scientists were suggesting that Gypsies' thought processes and hostility to interviewers from the outside were too great for questionnaire or interview methodology to be used with them. I hope this chapter shows Gypsies are as willing to share their opinions and feelings with an interviewer for the sake of knowledge as any other group in society, and I cannot see there is any reason to believe they would do so less sincerely than anyone else. Further research would be more than advisable.

Secondly we can read from these results a portent of what has become abundantly clear in the last ten years: that the absence of Gypsies from organised religion was caused far more by the racist rejection of Gypsies by the organised religious than the rejection of organised religion by the Gypsies.

Many of the Gypsies felt that they were too isolated and inadequate to take part in a regular church service due to literacy problems; most of them felt ashamed and inferior by this and felt that they stood out from the rest of the congregation. But a prime difficulty at the time was that some churches resented their presence. The spiritual revival amongst the Gypsies, however, and the publicity and interest this has awakened has perhaps changed attitudes amongst many non-Gypsy church members. What must not be forgotten, is that, if it is to be true to itself, the message of the church is to all. The church must never become just another élitist social club but has a commission and a duty to reach the whole community.

Appendix:
The interview schedule

Survey of religious attitudes amongst Gypsies

1. Do you believe that there is a God? Yes/No/Do not know/Refuse.

2. If 'No' Why?
a) because there is too much suffering in the world?
b) because this is a form of escapism?
c) because of some personal tragedy?
d) because of some other reason?

3. Do you believe that the church serves a useful purpose? Yes/No/Do not know/Refuse.

4. If 'yes' which of the following do you think most important?
a) gives a lead on social issues?
b) preaches the Gospel of Christ?
c) upholds moral standards?
d) provides a meeting place where we can worship God?
e) other

5. How often do you go to church? Weekly/Monthly/Occasionally/Weddings/Funerals/or Never?

6. Can you say there was a particular time when you became a Christian? If so, what differences have occurred since then?

7. Given the opportunity, what changes would you make in the church services?
a) shorter sermons (15 mins.) or dramatised ones?
b) more modern hymns?
c) more use of visual aids?
d) more congregational involvement?
e) other ...?

8. What do you think is the most important thing that the church should be doing?
a) engaged in political activities, e.g. unemployment defence and racial issues?
b) reaching those who never, or hardly attend, with the Christian message?
c) provides a meeting place for the neighborhood?
d) makes the most efficient use of its resources?
e) other

9. Age Group (10 - 20) (20 - 30) (30 - 40) (40 - 60+)
Gender
No. of children
Roadside or Site location
Group

References

ACTON T 1979 (ed. S Cranford) "The Gypsy Evangelical Church" *The Ecumenical Review* (Journal of the World Council of Churches) Vol.31 (3) pp 289-95

BOSTON I 1996 "Gypsies swept into God's Kingdom" *Renewal Magazine* No.238, March, pp. 40-3

McDOWELL B 1970 *Gypsies, Wanderers of the World* National Geographic Society, Washington DC

RIDHOLLS J 1986 *Travelling Home* Marshall Pickering, Basingstoke

TRIGG E B 1973 *Gypsy Demons and Divinities* Citadel Press, Secaucus, N.J.

Chapter 11 Gender issues in accounts of Gypsy health and hygiene as discourses of social control

Thomas Acton, Reader in Romani Studies and
Susan Caffrey, Lecturer in Sociology, University of Greenwich
Sylvia Dunn, Founder-chair, National Association of
Gypsy Women, Essex
Penny Vinson, Social worker, Suffolk, formerly adviser with
East Anglia Regional Health Authority

Nobody is more concerned with the health of Gypsies than Gypsies themselves. We shall presume that, like members of any other ethnic group, most will have a tender concern for their bodily well-being, and that this is part of their human condition. Nonetheless, much of the limited scientific, epidemiological and policy literature on Gypsy health in the United Kingdom tends to assume rather the opposite: that as well as conventional knowledge about particular diseases and symptoms, health education for Gypsies must also teach a new and previously lacking general concern for health. Existing UK Gypsy society is often presented as lacking such concern on account of Gypsy life being particularly stressful, especially for women, not only because of discrimination by non-Gypsies, but also because of the possibly oppressive dominance of Gypsy men. British Gypsy women have been presented in non-Gypsy scientific health discourse as peculiarly disadvantaged and, therefore, appropriately the prime target of intervention.

Gypsy women do, of course, share in the general disadvantages of women in the countries within which they reside and conflict between men and women takes on the cultural forms of the community within which it takes place. It is wrong, however, to identify a culture as a whole with one side of that conflict: to suggest that Gypsy culture *per se* is oppressive to women. This is not to say there are no sexist Gypsy men nor that there are not plenty of Gypsy women who collaborate in the repression of their sisters and daughters. Even when we regard certain power relations as unjust in society, it is hard for any of us to avoid all compromise or collaboration. Nonetheless, those who resist oppression are as validly members of a cultural group as those who oppress.

From the 1880s to the 1960s non-Gypsy students of Gypsies reacted to the marginalisation of their topic by defining it as a discipline in its own right, "Gypsy Lore" or "tsiganologie" in French. It was an ill-defined mish-mash of folklorism (often amateur) and linguistics, which also drew heavily upon the racist anthropology of the era. Its conservatism on gender issues can be perhaps be ascribed to that source. Because classical anthropologists usually entered other cultural groups under the protection of the powerful, they tended to buy into the self-conception of the powerful; so powerful elderly men are presented as traditional, (and, for male anthropologists in particular, with women as mere appendages). Those who are less exploit-ative are presented as liberal and those who reject authority as rebels or modernisers, as though rebellion was impossible without the importation of foreign ideas (Acton 1974:31). The identification of innovation with 'foreign ideas' has been the cry of those who have sought to subvert the community to seize personal power down the centuries but, in fact, those who rebel find their resources in culture as much as those who oppress. The independent solidarity of Gypsy women is sometimes hard to trace in the older literature on Gypsies, largely written by men for men (such as the early issues of the *Journal of the Gypsy Lore Society*). Nonetheless, the one substantial early text on a Gypsy woman's life written by a woman observer makes clear the sense held by some north Welsh Gypsy women of the deep historical roots of their special knowledge of sexuality, the management of men and, indeed health (Lyster 1926:115ff).

The ultimate focus of this chapter will be upon the way in which, Gypsies, and in particular Gypsy women, have begun to see the policy interest in Gypsy health as a real potential resource for their community. This has both stimulated the growth of Gypsy women's movements and altered the nature of the presentation of gender issues, as Gypsy women begin to appear as active agents rather than passive victims. The new approach, although still emphatically gendered, takes a holistic rather than a fragmented approach to Gypsy health needs with a distinctive approach to the need for effective communication in health education for both men and women.

Sources of innovation in discourses on Gypsy health

Any new approach within discourses on Gypsy health in Britain, however, has to be seen as the outcome of a dialectical interaction between Gypsy health practices and changing mainstream concepts of public health and adjustments within the medical model. Public health itself is a product of the last 150 years, a shift from older ideas of quarantine (Armstrong, 1993) to those of sanitation.

The concept of a general improvement in health is a projection back of epidemiological discourse onto individual concepts of well-being. In practice, for most of humanity, health behaviour consists of two parts: first, everyday ordinary actions for the conscious avoidance of discomfort, pain and death and second, extraordinary actions (the so-called 'sick role') taken to end or moderate painful or uncomfortable symptoms seen as potentially temporary. From the perspective of British society, the move towards a managed collective responsibility for health matters, through social and environmental measures which are beyond the individual's responsibility for their own health began with the Medical Officers of Health and nineteenth century public health. The influence of these declined in the twentieth century under the impact of the technological advances in curative medicine but their ideas have re-emerged in the 'New Public Health' (Acton, 1984; Acton and Chambers 1986, 1990; Ashton and Seymour, 1988; Kelly, 1990) and have been to some extent reincorporated into the basic ideas of public policy through *The Health of the Nation Consultation* (1991) and *Strategy* (1992) papers. Health is becoming an object of collective consumption; a public good which can hardly be ignored by any ethnic group strategy for collective advancement. Any such strategy, however, to be successful, has to bridge the cognitive gap between the concepts of individual health, and the proper ordering of the environment held within the group and the overlapping 'scientific' discourses of the medical model and public health.

This Western medical model has often carried with it overtones of that other discourse systematised by Europeans in the nineteenth century, the missionary model. Health was among the values to be brought to the primitives who were often at first presumed to lack the very concept of it. When it became obvious that this was not so, study of non-European thought was segregated into mixed disciplines like ethno-botany, in which cultural relatavism was permitted, without being allowed to reflect upon the master discourse of European science itself. More recently such boundaries have broken down in the "new sociology of science" associated with Michael Mulkay and others, reflecting not only a new understanding of how scientists work (Mulkay and Gilbert 1984) but also of how culture affects science policy as it affects the family and health (Mulkay 1994). We are not sure, however, how far this has penetrated the thinking of practising scientists, teaching sociologists or health care professionals. Before we can look at what is happening now, therefore, we have to examine two 'scientific' discourses which existed without apparent interaction (at least at a scientific level): that which discussed Gypsy hygienic practices and that which discussed epidemiological investigations. A third, non-scientific genre of literature may also be considered relevant: that which seeks to use Gypsy stereotypes to add authority to various herbal prescriptions.

Hygiene, propriety and social control in Gypsy thought

One of the most notable features both of Gypsy groups across Europe and those occasional groups like Irish Travellers which commence their account of their own ethnic identification by asserting they are *not* Gypsies, (cf Acton 1994; Kenrick 1994) is their practice of a system of washing taboos. In practically all groups (except for the occasional generational group in flight from authoritarian elders, where taboos may be deliberately reversed) there is a hierarchy of cleanliness reflected in keeping various levels of washing apart: bowls for washing crockery must not be contaminated by bowls for washing one's face and hands and these, in turn, must not be contaminated by bowls for washing clothes. We suggest that this sense of cleanliness or propriety is the foundation of Gypsy health practices.

The details of how these taboos are elaborated or simplified, however, are as various as the dialects of the Romani language (of which, by Bible Society criteria, there are more than eighty) and the terminology to describe the taboos varies with the dialect. We shall concern ourselves here primarily with the English Romanichal Gypsies, the largest of the Traveller groups in the British Isles, at least 60,000 out of the 110,000 estimated total ethnic Traveller population; there are also 200,000 or so Romanichals in North America and maybe 20,000 in Australasia (Acton and Gallant 1997). The key word in English Romani is *mochadi* which means filthy or polluting. Parallel words in other Romani dialects are *marime* (Miller, 1975; Sutherland, 1975) and *magerdi* (Ficowski 1951). In English Romani *mochadi* can be contrasted with *chikli* (from *chik* = dust), which generally refers to good honest non-polluting dirt (*chikli mui* = unshaven); although confusingly, because the word *mochadi* is itself slightly mochadi in mixed company, *chikli* can be used as a euphemism for *mochadi*.

There exists a Romani word for clean, '*uzhi*', which in some sense is the opposite of *mochadi* (as well as '*chikli*') but it does not possess the defining power of a term like *kosher* or *halal*. Romani cleanliness tends to be negatively defined by the avoidance of what is mochadi.

The modern non-Gypsy literature bangs on at considerable length about the role of these taboos as a mechanism of boundary-maintenance between Gypsies and Gaujos; what is more certain, however, is that knowledge of mochadi avoidance serves, and is perceived to serve, as a *pons asinorum* which must be crossed if one is to lay claim to the status of being a Gaujo who knows about Gypsies. Thus a Gypsy Liaison Officer (Jones 1994) starts a poem in a support group newsletter attacking the Criminal Justice Bill with the words: "Stand firm, ye ancient sons of Mokhadi " which may slightly invert the thrust of the taboo but, nonetheless, serves as a firm assertion of the possession of esoteric knowledge. To have discussed this personally with Gypsies is a mark of authenticity for the aspiring social researcher; one of the perils that Gypsies encounter when they start going to conferences is to be cornered by post-graduate students and less mature members of the caring professions and badgered with embarassing questions about their washing habits.

The great majority of the literature on various Romani groups makes gender differentiation fundamental to the understanding of Gypsy uncleanliness taboos. Indeed, the classic Gypsylorist description (Thompson, 1922, 1929) of pollution taboos refers to the taboos generically as "the uncleanness *of women*" (our italics.) In contrast to this literature, Acton (1971) suggests that amongst one group of English Gypsies at least, in South Essex where he carried out fieldwork, "the most remarkable fact about the mochadi taboos... is that sexual differentiation in them is vestigial, and not on the whole seen by the Gypsies as very important. The Gypsies from whom I collected information did not see women as a 'threat' to men... If there was a threat it came from 'dirty Gaujos', who are all moxhadi". Acton asserted "the highest priority of the taboos...seemed... to prevent anything unclean being eaten". Contrasting his data with Thompson's, Acton claimed "what I have presented here, however, are not the memories of a dying race of fifty years ago; they are the current practices of a thriving community, that have developed and are developing in accordance with the social and economic needs of that community." In short, Acton suggests that the primary conscious rationale of this group of informants for their cleanliness practices was a hygienic approach, seen as rational, without acknowledgment of its social rationale. Gypsies on the roadside had, and often continue to have, difficulty in obtaining clean water. In these circumstances anyone may develop rules about the use of water. It has been noted that some New Age Travellers facing the same difficulties have adopted similar practices (Lowe and Shaw, 1993:61-2; Stangroome, 1993:13).

Okely (1975, 1983), from a mixture of her own and Thompson's observations, reasserts the classical position that gender differentiation is at the heart of mochadi avoidance:

> "Acton (1971) claims that the emphasis on the uncleanliness of women has virtually disappeared. However, his own material sometimes contradicts this. Moreover, he does not discuss the pollution associated with childbirth. If, indeed, female pollution taboos have become less important, this coincides with the relative decline in the women's external economic role; and thus my case that the two are interconnected is strengthened" (Okely, 1983:207).

Okely was to some extent right to redress the balance; virtually all of Acton's data was gathered from men, many of them young unmarried men who appeared genuinely ignorant of female biology. Indeed, Acton (1971:115) had already suggested that the "decline in the element of sexual differentiation in the sexual taboo 'fits' well also the changes in the role of women." Okely's differentiation of her work from Acton's goes beyond, however, a mere enrichment of the database. Okely (1983:80) positions herself in the theoretical canon thus:

> "Usually taboos among English Gypsies are presented merely as evidence of 'Eastern Origins' (Seymour 1970:187). Undue emphasis on a theory of origins or 'survivals' risks the loss of the current coherence and meaning of the system. The observance of these taboos among English Gypsies has been explained more meaningfully but vaguely by Acton as a 'commitment to a culture which will remain Gypsy' (1971:109), but, he does not escape mentioning a 'hygienic function' (1971:120) in addition to a symbolic interpretation. The anthropologists Miller (1975:46) and Sutherland (1975:8) in their studies of American Rom have recognised the role of pollution taboos in maintaining an ethnic boundary, and have found greater emphasis on the Gypsies' distinction between the upper and lower parts of the body (Sutherland 1975:264) with the waistline emphasised as the symbolic boundary."

Okely sees the cleanliness taboos as an essentially coherent functional system to preserve the boundaries between men and women and then between Gypsies and non-Gypsies. This essential system exists in various versions which, for Okely, are all clues to that one essential symbolic-functional system, even if they come from different ethnic groups with different languages and religions, or indeed if the data comes from different historical periods. In common with many anthropologists, she sometimes appears to regard historical explanation *per se* as a derogation from, an unnecessary competitor to, functional explanation. But although she rejects historical origins as a valid explanation of anything, nonetheless change and variation are all seen in terms of decline from the original system. It must be admitted, however, that Acton (1971), writing before he had developed a critique of modernisation theory, also tended to present the system he recorded in terms of change from an original. In fact, instead of a unilineal modernisation theory, there is no reason why we should not see the more complex taboo-sets as symbolic elaborations of an originally simpler hygienic system to meet new social threats, such as changes in the balance of cash income earned by men and women in a new country (cf Acton 1979:237). Social changes occur all the time. Since the 1970s, when Acton and Okely carried out their separate doctoral fieldworks, the proportion of Gypsy caravans legally sited has risen from under 10 per cent to over 60 per cent (Department of the Environment, 1978-), television reception has become universal in those trailers, adult literacy has risen from under 10 percent to possibly around 25 percent (Acton and Kenrick, 1991) and, since the mid 1980s, there has been a great wave of conversion to Pentecostal Christianity. Do these changes affect attitudes to cleanliness and health? It is noticeable to us that whereas in the 1970s the wearing of aprons by English Gypsy women as a regular part of their dress throughout the day was common, this is very much rarer at the present. But in the 1970s the apron could more easily be seen as a badge of propriety rather than of domestic subjection. We must not fall into the trap of seeing all change as coherent, linked and uni-directional.

Okely (1983:81) sees Gypsy cleanliness as in conflict with "Gorgio concepts of hygiene" and any real function it may have to avoid discomfort, pain and death is discounted. This dichotomy, between 'primitive' thought and 'scientific' thought is hard to sustain in the world after Foucault, especially after the reading which Turner (1987, 1992) has given of him. What do any of us, however many doctorates we have, do to explain the world but check around on the data of our environment and make sense of them using whatever tools we may find to hand, like a village handyman, or *bricoleur* as in the famous analogy of Lévi-Strauss (1966). After Mulkay has looked in more detail at what scientists actually do, we can see that *bricolage is* the scientific method; there is no other. The badge of scientist is no prophylactic against false logic, empirical error or lack of integrity. There is no magic bullet, no general protective against these things. We have to watch in detail for each, all the time. Integrity is no guarantee of logic and logic is no guarantee of accuracy and previous success is no guard against future error.

In the same way that our explanations of the world are all socially constructed, so are our cleanliness practices. They are, for all of us, a way of ordering the world. As Mary Douglas (1966), quoting Chesterfield's Letters, has taught us, "Dirt is matter out of place." And place is a social concept. But most of us still order the world, in part, at least, so as to avoid personal discomfort, pain and death. It is that hygienic practice which gives our boundary-maintaining uses of cleanliness discourse their symbolic power. When we call someone filthy, or a book dirty, we are likening them to that which really has the power to threaten pain and death.

Symbolic force may blind the observer to hygienic rationales which may transcend cultural boundaries. Acton (1971) was sure that, in the particular group of Gypsies with whom he had been living, the first function of avoiding mochadi kovels was to keep themselves healthy but when he recorded a Traveller who told him that while a lick from a horse might be unpleasant, a lick from a mochadi dog might send him blind, he still did not take it literally. The subsequent *toxicara canis* scare, however, made him realise that he should take Gypsy warnings seriously. Equally, within a given social system, boundary-maintenance, and even gender-differentiation, may be important for the sick individual, in that by conforming to the rules s/he reinforces the duty of kin and, failing kin, any nearby member of the ethnic group, to care for them. It is important to acknowledge that cleanliness practices may serve a variety of functions, some of which may not be immediately apparent to the health researcher.

The presumed dichotomy between medical science and mochadi avoidance can lead those less relativistic than Okely to rather judgmental conclusions. Perhaps already under a degree of coercion from official Polish government policy, Ficowski (1951) concluded: "on the whole, mageripen is a retrograde factor, a curb which retards the cultural emancipation of the Gypsies and effectively helps to keep the women in a state of degradation and slavish subjection to the men." This has been echoed more recently in Reisman's critique of a defence by Weyrauch and Bell (1993) of Gypsy "autonomous lawmaking". Reisman (1993:416-7) asserts bluntly "Romani practices that effectively subordinate women and train them to believe that for most of their lives they are 'polluted' and sources of pollution for others are not compatible with the international human rights code. The con-tention that suppressing marime practices that subordinate women will weaken Romani cohesion is about as compelling as the argument that prohibiting female mutilation in East Africa will undermine the indigenous cultures of the peoples who practice it."

Acton and Caffrey (1994) have criticised both Weyrauch and Bell, and Reisman. They assert that these American academic lawyers have reified what they start off by describing as "autonomous law-making" into a set of rules, as though one could take the practice of a certain section of American Rom as if it was the only authentic version of Gypsy law, without looking either at the ways in which this is systematically contested from within and without this particular group, or without looking at the particular historical strains which led to these abuses.

It is possible to use cleanliness discourse to define someone else as unclean but it is equally possible to use cleanliness practices as a way of including the stranger, even the ignorant but willing non-Gypsy who is open to gentle instruction. The offer of food and drink carries with it (even if, for a while, a special cup may secretly be used for the outsider) a formal welcome into the companionship of propriety. This is why one should always accept the offered cup of tea; not to do so is tantamount to suggesting one's host may not be clean enough.

We believe that for most English Gypsy women, the gender-specific aspects of mochadi avoidance into which they have been socialised are a practical way of coping with menstruation and childbirth. Whether these aspects are intrinsically part of male dominance, or whether they are only incidentally affected by the overall nature of gender relations in society (both Gypsy society and the ambient Western society) is a matter for dispute even among the authors of this chapter. Nonetheless, they are open to modification and innovation provided this can be achieved within an atmosphere of trust, decency and order. It is the way in which Gypsy notions of propriety can reconcile and reintegrate the interests of the sexes, can bring them together, can provide the platform and the vocabulary within which differences of knowledge and need can be bridged, which ultimately interests us in this chapter, rather than the ways they have been abused to oppress women or perpetuate dysfunctional family relationships.

The contribution from medicine and epidemiology

The most comprehensive review of epidemiological literature relating to Gypsies occurs in an Med.D. thesis by Feder (1993:53) who nonetheless remarks on its sparseness: "The most surprising aspect is how rarely Traveller health and health care was studied."

What impact, if any, has the literature on Gypsy cleanliness beliefs had on non-Gypsy epidemiological and medical discussion of health? We suggest that it is relatively little, partly because any positive contribution has been overshadowed by the major implication that epidemiologists have drawn, somewhat perfunctorily, from the anthropologists, that its prime role is to enforce a rigid gender differentiation. The most influential survey, by Pahl and Vaile, (1986:9) sums this up as

> "Gypsy culture imposes strict rules relating to hygiene (Okely 1975). For this reason Travellers do not have all-purpose kitchen sinks but keep separate bowls for washing clothes and for washing food, and typical Gypsy trailers do not contain toilets. Changing customs are responsible, however, for the gradual introduction of built-in sinks and toilets, which can now be found in some vans on some sites. The Traveller culture also imposes a strict separation between the worlds of men and women, a separation which in part reflects the idea of the private nature of female sexuality."

Practically every stereotypical element of the sympathetic scientific approach is present in this account:

Gypsy cleanliness practices are a survival of the past;
    being eroded by modernisation;
        and therefore to be reported in carefully non-judgmental ways;
            but, oh dear, they are tough on women
                who must be persuaded to be more upfront
                    about having babies and all that.

Their survey data deal only with women and children.

Another factor that may have overshadowed real everyday Gypsy attempts to lead healthy lives is the very substantial quack literature which attempts to attach the mystique of the Gypsy stereotype to various herbal remedies or 'magical' practices (cf G Petulengro, 1935; L Petulengro 1968; X and P Petulengro,1990; Bowness, 1970; Henwood, 1974; Leek 1970 (the latter a particular betrayal, since in 1964 she wrote a half sensible book on Gypsies), Buckland 1990, etc.). These writers plagiarise one another mercilessly. Their major original source, along with slightly more honest Gypsylorist accounts which probably include some original fieldwork (Vesey-Fitzgerald 1944; de Bairacli-Levi 1951) is a single paper (Thompson 1925), which certainly indicates that one Gypsy family, at least in the 1920s, had a substantial range of remedies at its disposal. But what is also clear is that this family, like most families, were prepared to try anything that worked but kept only the knowledge which made use of materials which could be still obtained. Maybe neglected folk herbal remedies should be examined to see if they should be added to the battery of therapeutic tools. Sutherland's (1992) examination of the *materia medica* of Vlach Rom in California suggests this is worthwhile. Nonetheless, neither the quack, nor the Gypsylorist authors claiming to give clues to special Gypsy health knowledge have made much impact on health professionals whose studies seem to indicate serious health disadvantages for Gypsies rather than the possession of miraculous secrets, although there is continuing controversy over the extent to which the differences in health statistics between Travellers as a group and the rest of the population is real or just a statistical artefact (Feder 1989, 1993), and then again, how much of recorded health outcomes are the result of lifestyle and how much might be genetic (Thomas, Doucette, Thomas and Stoeckle, 1987).

These epidemiological or quasi-epidemiological studies have often been criticised for exaggeration by Gypsies who have read them. This criticism has some basis, since the samples are always drawn from poorer Travellers, from among those known to health visitors and social workers, i.e. from among those most likely to suffer high rates of morbidity and mortality. Even the 1966 census of Gypsies (Ministry of Housing and Local Government, 1967) in England and Wales which showed an age distribution of Travellers similar to that of the total population in 1841, with the proportion of over sixty-fives being only just over a quarter of that in the general 1966 population, can be challenged on the basis that elderly Travellers are much more likely to have settled, either in houses or in little private yards away from the eyes of the census-takers. The 1969 Scottish Census of Travellers (Scottish Development Department, 1971) found a very similar distribution.

A survey by Linthwaite et al. (1983) of 265 mothers showed a stillbirth rate nineteen times greater than in the population as a whole and much higher rates of morbidity (i.e. illness) in under-fives than in the general population. This report was criticised by Gypsies, in particular, for having an unrepresentative sample and for appearing to suggest that Travellers in general were irresponsible about health. Nevertheless, its findings were not too far out of line with observations from either the more rigorous and influential study in Kent by Pahl and Vaile (1986) of 263 mothers with 814 children, or with data reported periodically from the Sheffield area in the magazine *Travelling Life* which was started in 1987 from the Mobile Health Clinic and continued for several years although it has now lapsed.

It would appear that death in the first year of a baby's life is more common among nomadic Travellers than in the population at large, but not so great, according to government surveys (MHLG 1967; SDD 1971) as to prevent the average number of living children in British Traveller households with children being around 50 percent higher than in the population as a whole – just under three, as opposed to just under two. How far these characteristics are present among housed Gypsies must be a matter for speculation, however. The weight of this evidence has left Gypsies uneasily aware that there are real health gains possible for members of their community but unhappy about the implication that Gypsy life is in itself a health disadvantage. To express that unease in terms of epidemiological theory, one would say that outcome measures in these studies identify real and unnecessary pathology but the independent (i.e. the lifestyle) variables are so crudely defined, because of a lack of cultural sensitivity, that only the broadest brush strategy conclusions can be drawn, and there is scarcely any empowerment of the individual in terms of greater understanding or informed lifestyle choice. To say this is not to attack these studies, which carried our invaluable path-breaking work but to try to make explicit the questions they beg.

One specialised study *Susceptibility of itinerants ("travelling people") in Scotland to poliomyelitis* (Bell et al. 1983) concluded that Travelling people in Scotland who live on well-equipped sites do not pose a poliomyelitis "hazard to nearby settled populations and, indeed, are no more vulnerable to infection than members of those communities." It is not immediately clear why, apart from local newspaper scares, they chose to test this hypothesis, but apparently its salience was sufficient to warrant its confirmation two years later in a Glasgow MSc. thesis (Rider M. cited in Feder 1989:426).

Teachers often report that at the time of eviction Traveller children exhibit disturbed or withdrawn behaviour but whether one should consider this a medical problem to be treated by a doctor rather than by political action, seems dubious. Suggestions that lower Traveller school attendance may be caused by health problems seem generally to be based on anecdotal more than serious evidence; the data seem to show the most important differences are amongst the under-fives and the elderly rather than among those of school age, although scares about Traveller health, from polio infection to nits infestation, are among the manifestation of prejudice against admitting Traveller children to school. Strehlow (1980) suggested that high lead content on one site was a severe health hazard and may have caused disturbed child behavioural patterns and that this may have been parallelled on other sites.

However one interprets the statistics, though, the fact remains that Travellers are often forced to live in unhealthy conditions. At a conference in June 1984 workers from three special health projects for Travellers and others around the country spoke of encampments without running water, rubbish collection or any sanitation (Cornwall 1984). They spoke of discrimination by health service agencies, doctors simply refusing Travellers and the lengths Travellers will go to cultivate a friendly doctor or hospital when they find one, driving miles to come to them. It was suggested illiteracy might make attaining good health care difficult. Finally, there was added "the social and psychological stress of living in a hostile society where they frequently come into conflict with police and other authorities."

An uneven growth of provision followed. Hussey (1988) gained survey responses from 168 of the 191 health districts in England and found that ninety had "staff with designated responsibility towards Travellers". Of these districts, eighty-one appointed health visitors with special responsibility for Travellers but only twenty-two "offered them training about Travellers."

This burgeoning core of interested professionals began in the 1980s to contribute accounts of their work to professional magazines and *Traveller Life*, which have been reviewed by Feder (1989, 1993). A growing concern for Travellers in health education was reported by McCann (1987). Much of this work was focused on women's needs; a report *Traveller Mothers and their Babies* (Durward 1988) led to a specific *Campaign for Safe Childbirth for Travellers* backed by the Maternity Alliance, Save the Children Fund and several Gypsy organisations. Despite their misgivings about reports which often appeared to put Travellers in a bad light, Gypsy organisations began to see these appointments and the resources that went with them as a potential source of real benefits for Travelling people. In 1993 one Gypsy organisation, the Northern Gypsy Council carried out its own survey, albeit with the help of health visitors. This survey side-stepped the question of gender differentiation by the rather suspect methodological device of taking a sample of sixty-three *families* rather than specific men or women, and recorded high levels of satisfaction with GPs and other NHS provision, including a massive 100 per cent of families who "were very satisfied with health visitors"! More to the point, the families' responses were used to back up demands that Travellers should be allowed to carry a health record with them, to facilitate continuity of medical care; that safe play areas and improved sanitation be provided on sites; that specialist health visitors should continue to be appointed and that health impacts be taken into account before evictions are authorised. A similar emphasis on Traveller women's satisfaction with health visitors is recorded in Oxfordshire by McIntyre (1994).

This growth of interest in health coincided with (and perhaps even encouraged) a remarkable growth of the women's movement among Gypsies in the late 1980s. Whereas in the 1970s it was a platitude that Gypsy politics was a men-only business, the 1990 World Romani Congress (although attended by probably the last all-male English Gypsy international delegation), saw a number of forceful female personalities including from neighbouring Ireland. Even at that time two of the authors of this chapter were members of the committee of the Essex Romani Association which included five Gypsy women and only two men, one of whom was Gypsy Council Chairman, Charlie Smith who, unlike some older male Gypsy civil rights workers, has encouraged women to participate and organise. Four English Gypsy women attended the 1994 European Union consultative Romani Congress in Seville which was opened by the Queen of Spain and concluded by the Spanish Prime Minister. There they were able to network into a number of international associations of Gypsy women. Most recently, Sylvia Dunn, formerly Vice-President of the Gypsy Council for Education, Culture, Welfare and Civil Rights, has founded the growing National Association of Gypsy Women (NAGW).

In April 1993 the Gypsy Council appointed a working party on health which made its first report a year later. This lists a series of meetings in Cambridge and elsewhere in the East Anglian Health Region with many "fruitful discussions" but also records frustration at being tipped the wink by a research and development officer that "there is no interest at executive level to implement any of the suggestions made" (Carman, Dunn and Spiller, 1994:1).

These suggestions covered a wide range of issues, such as the request for records that could be carried by patients, and the seeking of acknowledgment that continual evictions and poor site conditions are major threats to health, need for clear advice on immunisation, and concern that GPs should not be deterred from taking Travellers because they might prove expensive. One of the most prominent issues was the problem of creating health education materials which will fit in with Gypsy culture. Non-Gypsy professionals sometimes seemed to see this in terms of how to get Gypsies to take notice of leaflets they have produced. The Gypsy Council working party eventually felt it had to tell one official "unequivocally that written leaflets with drawings of pinmen are unsuitable when advising people about such serious diseases like hepatitis and meningitis" (Carman, Dunn and Spiller, 1994:2). They argued that, in any case, leaflets may not be the right medium for those who cannot read and write. Videos, they suggested would be a better bet. The case against "written health education materials" is endorsed by Feder (1994, p.141) but he goes on to say that the Travellers in his survey were not very interested in videos either and would prefer "personal health education on Traveller sites."

It is true that when a case is made out clearly and explained well, then health education on matters which a few years ago might be considered too embarassing even to mention, can work very well. A case in point is the smear test for cervical cancer. Once the avoidability of a death which had overtaken at least one person within most adult Gypsies' acquaintance was understood, the women, who had actually had treatment after a smear test showed positive, become the most effective health educators possible. A further consequence is that in a suitably formal setting, such as the committee of a Gypsy organisation, discussion of cervical cancer became possible even in groups including men and women.

Let us mark the importance of this. The work of Lyster, Acton and Okely all show that there are different standards of propriety in conversation among English Gypsies in all-female, all-male and mixed company, with the standards for mixed company clearly being the most restrictive. The success of the smear test has ultimately enlarged the vocabulary of discourse proper in mixed company, and has in a small detail, changed the nature of gender relations. This, in turn, creates a possible precedent for other health matters. We suggest that this is a preferable model to say, trying to sneak sex education into a youth group before the parents notice.

It is a highly misleading commonplace that Gypsies oppose sex education for their children. Etiquette compels a public opposition to mochadi discourse. In a statement prepared for the ESRC seminars which preceded this book, the National Association of Gypsy Women (NAGW) said "The NAGW does not see sex education for Gypsy children as very important in the Gypsy community. Sex education for Gypsy children is a very personal family matter, so we do not see the NAGW giving any support to sex education." The problem of incorporating a generalised form of sex education for Gypsy children is that it denies Gypsy parents the possibility of socialising their children as they think appropriate. This does not mean for one minute that Gypsy parents wish to see their children act irresponsibly or dangerously through ignorance.

The NAGW is moving towards the idea that what are needed are not leaflets which help professionals with little deep knowledge of Gypsy culture to preach to Gypsies, but materials, specifically videos, which will help Gypsy community workers to reach small groups. Obviously these groups may need to be gendered but if there are women working with women and girls there must also be men working with men and boys. The workers of each gender need to have some common discourse. These videos need to be prepared by Gypsy community workers and health professionals working together and many of them may need to be targeted not merely by gender but also for different ethnic groups of Gypsies, for different age groups, even perhaps with a sensitivity to different religious groups, such as Catholics and Pentecostals. They need to be short, and deal with particular problems. Obviously a project to prepare such videos would be a long-term and expensive undertaking but in the long term such work may also contribute to our general understanding of what makes health education work.

An effective health education policy for Gypsies requires us to move right away from the image of Gypsy women as victims, to the reality of Gypsy women as effective change agents. This is not to say there are no victimised women but there are also victimised men; victimisation is not a concomitant of one's gender. Safer childbirth is a fine rallying call to try to prick the Gaujo conscience against the Criminal Justice Bill but a real health policy must be for the whole community, old men and maidens too. Effective health education is not a matter of simply translating instructions without concern for whether they touch upon the problems perceived by the target population. Travellers must prepare themselves, and be helped, to intervene in epidemiological debates. There is no way to shift the actions of the powerful without learning their discourse. This should not frighten Travellers too much; in so far as they have in their own lives treated the avoidance of mochadi kovels thoughtfully as a set of principles, rather than rigidly as a set of externally imposed rules; they have been doing practical epidemiology all their lives. The point is to translate, to map different thought systems onto one another, so that there can be a real meeting of minds.

We would suggest that future research will need to bring concerned Travellers fully into the work. Through fieldwork and discussions the variables to be measured and the hypotheses to be tested must be developed and refined before any rush to to gather survey data. We should seek to identify elements in Travelling life which promote health, rather than treat a Travelling lifestyle as though it was a single monolithic variable. Such a period of preliminary fieldwork could very usefully be combined with the task of developing health education videos with specific target audiences. The growth of the Gypsy women's movement has brought into focus that the point of sensitivity to gender, age and ethnicity is to serve the whole community, not to lock particular sections into a victim mode.

References

ACTON T A 1971 "The Functions of the avoidance of Moxadi Kovels" *Journal of the Gypsy Lore Society* Series III, Vol.L (3- 4), pp. 108-36

ACTON T A 1974 *Gypsy Politics and Social Change* Routledge and Kegan Paul, London,

ACTON T A 1979 "Academic Success and Political Failure: a review of modern social science writing in English on Gypsies" *Ethnic and Racial Studies* Vol.2(2), pp. 231-41

ACTON, T A 1984 "From Public Health to National Health: The Escape of Environmental Health Officers and the Fragmentation of Nineteenth Century Concepts of Health" *Radical Community Medicine*, No. 19, pp. 12-23

ACTON T A 1994 "Categorising Irish Travellers" in McCann M, Siochain S O and Ruane J eds. *Irish Travellers – Culture and Ethnicity*, Institute of Irish Studies, Queen's University of Belfast, Belfast

ACTON T A and CHAMBERS D 1986 "The Decline of Public Health" *Nursing Times*, 13 August

ACTON T A and CHAMBERS D 1990 "Where was Sociology in the struggle to re-establish Public Health?" in P Abbott and G Payne eds. *New Directions in the Sociology of Health*, Falmer, Basingstoke pp. 165- 174

ACTON T A and CAFFREY S 1994 "Theorising Gypsy Law" Paper given to the Economic and Social Research Council Seminar on Romani Studies, University of Greenwich, April

ACTON T A and GALLANT D 1997 *Romanichal Gypsies* Wayland, Brighton

ACTON T A and KENRICK D 1991 "From Summer Voluntary Schemes to European Community Bureaucracy: The Development of Special Provision for Traveller Education in the United Kingdom since 1967" *European Journal of Intercultural Studies* Vol. 1(3) pp. 47-62

ARMSTRONG D 1993 "Public Health Spaces and the Fabrication of Identity" *Sociology* Vol.27(3), pp. 393-410

ASHTON J and SEYMOUR H 1988 *The New Public Health* Open University Press, Milton Keynes

BAIRACLI-LEVY J de 1951 "Gypsy Herbalists in France and England" *Journal of the Gypsy Lore Society* Series III, Vol. XXX (1-2)

BELL E J, RIDING M H, COLLIER P W, WILSON N C and REID D 1983, "Suceptibility of itinerants ("travelling people") in Scotland to poliomyelitis" *Bulletin of the World Health Organisation* Vol.61(5), pp. 839-43

BOWNESS C 1970 *The Romany way to Health* Thorsons, London

BUCKLAND R 1990 *Gypsy Dream Reading* Llewellyn Publications, St.Paul, Minnesota

CARMAN J, DUNN S and SPILLER H 1994 Health Spokespersons' Report Report to the Annual General Meeting of the Gypsy Council for Education, Culture, Welfare and Civil Rights, April, mimeo

CORNWALL J ed. 1984 *Improving Health Care for Travellers* Save the Children Fund/King's Fund Centre, mimeo, London

DEPARTMENT OF THE ENVIRONMENT 1978- (continuing) *Biannual Gypsy Counts* Department of the Environment, London

DEPARTMENT OF HEALTH 1991 *The Health of the Nation – A Consultative Document for Health in England* HMSO, London

DEPARTMENT OF HEALTH 1992 *The Health of the Nation – A Strategy for Health in England* HMSO, London

DOUGLAS M 1966 *Purity and Danger* Routledge and Kegan Paul, London

DURWARD L 1988, 1990 *Traveller Mothers and their Babies* The Maternity Alliance, London

FEDER G 1989 "Traveller gypsies [sic] and primary care" *Journal of the Royal College of General Practitioners* Vol.39, October, pp. 425-9

FEDER G 1990 "The Politics of Traveller Health Research" *Critical Public Health* No.3, pp. 10-14

FICOWSKI J 1951 "Supplementary notes on the Mageripen Code amongst Polish Gypsies" *Journal of the Gypsy Lore Society* Series III, Vol.XXX (3-4)

HENWOOD K 1974 *Secrets of the Gypsies* Pan/Piccolo, London

HUSSEY R M 1988 "Travellers and Preventive Health Care: what are health authorities doing?" *British Medical Journal* Vol.296, April 16, p.1098

JONES G 1994 "The Sons of Mokhadi" *Traveller* (Newsletter of the Derbyshire Gypsy Liaison Group), Summer issue, p.10

KENRICK D S 1994, "Irish Travellers A Unique Phenomenon in Europe?" in McCann M, Siochain S O and Ruane J eds. *Irish Travellers- Culture and Ethnicity* Institute of Irish Studies, Queen's University of Belfast, Belfast

LEEK S 1964 *A Fool and a Tree* Lambarde Press, Sidcup

LEEK S 1970 *The Sybil Leek Book of Fortune-Telling* W H Allen, London

LÉVI-STRAUSS C 1966 *The Savage Mind* Weidenfeld and Nicholson, London

LINTHWAITE P, SAMPSON K, LONGFIELD A and TARLING R 1983 *The Health of Traveller Mothers and Children in East Anglia* Save the Children Fund, London

LOWE R and SHAW S eds. 1993 *Travellers – Voices of the New Age Nomads* Fourth Estate, London

LYSTER E M 1926 *The Gypsy Life of Betsy Wood* J M Dent, London

McCANN V K 1987 "Health Education for a Travelling Community" *The Health Visitor* Vol.60, June, pp. 293-5

MILLER C 1975 "American Rom and the Ideology of Defilement" in Rehfisch F ed. *Gypsies, Tinkers and Other Travellers*, Academic Press, London, pp. 41-54

MINISTRY OF HOUSING AND LOCAL GOVERNMENT 1967 *Gypsies and other Travellers* HMSO, London

MULKAY M and GILBERT G N 1984 *Opening Pandora's Box: A Sociological analysis of Scientists' Discourse*, Cambridge University Press, Cambridge

MULKAY M 1994 "Science and Family in the Great Embryo Debate" *Sociology* Vol.28 (3), pp. 699-715

NORTHERN GYPSY COUNCIL 1993 *The Gypsy Survey 1993 From Myth to Reality*, Tyne and Wear Racial Equality Council, Newcastle

OKELY J 1975 "Gypsy Women: Models in Conflict" in S Ardener ed. *Perceiving Women* Malaby Press, London, pp. 55-86

OKELY J 1983 *The Traveller-Gypsies* CUP, Cambridge

PAHL J and M VAILE 1986 *Health and Health Care among Travellers* Maidstone Health Authority, Maidstone

PETULENGRO G 1935 *Romany Remedies and Recipes* Methuen, London

PETULENGRO L 1968 *The Roots of Health* Souvenir (also Pan, 1971), London

PETULENGRO X and P 1990 *The Open Road to Health* P G Enterprises, Barnsley

REISMAN W M 1993 "Autonomy, Interdependence and Responsibility" *Yale Law Journal* Vol.103(2) pp. 401-17

SEYMOUR J 1970 note in S G Boswell *The Book of Boswell* (ed. J Seymour) Gollancz, London

STANGROOME V 1993 *Investigation into Policies, Priorities and Resources available to New Age Travellers (The Hippy Convoy)* privately published, London

STREHLOW C D 1980 *The Westway Gypsy Caravan Site* Westminster and St Mary's Medical Schools, mimeo, London

SUTHERLAND A 1975 *Gypsies, the hidden Americans* Tavistock, London

THOMPSON T W 1922 "The Uncleanness of Women among English Gypsies" *Journal of the Gypsy Lore Society* Series III, Vol.I(1-2), pp. 15-43

THOMPSON T W 1925 "English Gypsy Medicine" *Journal of the Gypsy Lore Society* Series III, Vol.IV(4)

THOMPSON T W 1929 "Additional notes on English Gypsy taboos" *Journal of the Gypsy Lore Society* Series III, Vol. VII(1), pp. 33-9

TURNER B 1987 *Medical Power and Social Knowledge* Sage, London

TURNER B 1992 *Regulating Bodies* Routledge, London

WEYRAUCH W O and BELL A "Autonomous Lawmaking: The Case of the 'Gypsies" *Yale Law Journal* Vol.103(2) pp. 323-99

Chapter 12 Duty and beauty, possession and truth: lexical impoverishment as control

Ian Hancock, Professor of Linguistics, University of Texas at Austin and UN Representative of the International Romani Union

The manipulation by societies in power of the identities of subordinate groups is achieved in many ways. One such way is through discriminatory legislation, such as that enacted against the Romani people in almost every land where they live. Another is through media representation, both factual and fictional. This last category, the portrayal of Gypsies in poetry, film and novels, is the most effective in establishing such negative feelings because they are absorbed subliminally, even by children at a time when they are most susceptible to acquiring society's attitudes.

Apart from descriptions of Romani people and their life, which are legion, the Romani language has also been the target of comment, always worded as fact rather than supposition. In his *Tales of the Real Gypsy,* Paul Kester (1897:305) gives his readers those 'real' facts about it :

"The Gypsies, like the birds and all wild things, have a language of their own, which is apart from the language of those among whom they dwell ... the Gypsy['s] ... language is deep and warm and full of the charm of the out-of-doors world, the scent of the clover and the ripple of streams and the rush of the wind and the storm. For the Rommany speech is full of all this, and though the Gypsy has few traditions, his rich mother tongue must embalm in each word a thousand associations that thrill in the soul."

Kester was not a linguist and it is easy to see how he was able to allow his fantasies about the Romani people to shape his preconceptions of the language. Doris Duncan, however, presumably is a linguist and can claim no such excuse. Writing seventy years later about Romani in a journal of popular linguistics, she made the following observations (1969:42):

"All authentic gypsy (sic) communication is, and must be, oral. As they settle for a time in a new country, they acquire some of that country's words and incorporate them into *Roum,* more popularly called Romany. It is believed that the *Roum* language began as a very small one, concerned with the family, the tribe, the horses and herd, words required for a simple existence. It must be very old, for *Roum* is highly idiomatic, and the complications of verbs and genders is endless. There is no way to write it except phonetically, and some sounds of the gypsy tongue simply defy our twenty-six letter alphabet ... *Roum* is a disorderly language, and must be learned phrase by phrase. Even the syntax differs from one occasion to another. Verbs are very difficult ... no one can explain why the verb changes so radically. A major problem is that no gypsy really knows what a verb is, and it wouldn't matter anyway if he did, because this is the way it must be said. The idiom is paramount in *Roum* and cannot be changed."

Duncan is right in maintaining that Romani has adopted words from those with whom its speakers have come in contact – this is a natural process affecting all languages and one which has caused English, for example, to retain only 28 per cent of its original Anglo-Saxon lexicon by dictionary count. But Bayle St. John could not simply discuss this phenomenon as lexical adoption when referring to Romani (1853:141) which, he said:

"... contains traces of an original character, [but which] is encrusted, as it were, with words borrowed – it might be more appropriate to say stolen – from a dozen different dialects."

A number of authors have claimed that, because of our character as a people, Roma lack certain virtues, and that this is reflected in the Romani language which cannot even express them. Those which have been discussed by different writers include *duty, possession, truth, beautiful, read, write, time, danger, warmth* and *quiet.* How negatively must the non-Gypsy world regard our people, to think that we cannot even express such basic human concepts and skills!

Over a century ago, Adriano Colocci first introduced a notion which has since become a part of gypsilorist folk wisdom. In his extensive discussion of the Romani people in his 421-page book, *The Gypsies,* he maintained that Roma:

"... have no more conception of property than of duty; 'I have' is as foreign to them as 'I ought' " (Colocci 1889:156).

Citing Colocci as his source, Italian criminologist Cesare Lombroso (1918:41) elaborated upon the statement in his widely-used book and made the jump from concept to actual language by saying that:

"The word *ought* does not exist in the Gypsy language. The verb to *have is* almost forgotten by the European Gypsies, and is unknown to the Gypsies of Asia."

In 1928, Konrad Bercovici, (1928) probably also using Colocci but not acknowledging any source, repeated this notion on the first page (and again on the third page) of his book *The Story of the Gypsies* and also interpreted the original observation linguistically, saying:

"I am attempting to unravel the story of a people whose vocabulary lacks two words – 'duty' and 'possession'.

He goes on to rationalise this by explaining that "what we own possesses us, jails us." This was then picked up from Bercovici shortly afterwards by Erich von Stroheim (1935:12) who, in his racist Gypsy novel, *Paprika,* told his readers that:

"The Gypsy mind is timeless. The Gypsy tongue has no words to signify duty or possession, qualities that are like roots, holding civilised people fast in the soil."

Fifteen years later the anonymous author of an article in *Coronet Magazine* plagiarised and reworded the same statement:

"Even today, there are two important English words for which the Gypsy vocabulary has no known equivalent, and for which the Gypsy people have never exhibited any desire or need. One of them is the word 'duty', the other is 'possession'" *(Anon.* 1950:126).

In a 1962 reissue of Leland's *Gypsy Sorcery and Fortune Telling,* Margery Silver wrote in her introduction to that edition:

"[In Germany], where they had been chronically subjected to the most relentless and brutal oppression of their European experience since their first appearance in 1417, five hundred thousand 'sons of Egypt' – whose vocabulary a recent writer has described as 'lacking two words: duty and possession' – died in the Nazi ovens beside six million sons of Jacob, whose history was founded on just those concepts, duty to God and possession of his law" (Leland 1962:xx).

Five years after that, in perhaps the most invidious way of all, since the plagiarism has been recast in such a way as to suggest an actual verbatim interview, the statement turns up again in an article by Marie Wynn Clarke (1967:210) predictably entitled "Vanishing vagabonds":

"A young Gypsy wife said, "There is no word in our language for 'duty' or 'possession', but I'm afraid there will be soon."

In her introduction to the 1983 edition of Bercovici's *Gypsies: Their life, lore and legends,* Elizabeth Congdon Kovanen repeats this yet again, although adding the suggestion that, because of this, Gypsies themselves are responsible for the discrimination against them:

"The Gypsy vocabulary lacks the words 'duty' and 'possession'. This reflects their unwillingness to settle down, live in houses, obey the

law, educate their children, be employed by others – and helps to
explain their almost universal persecution" (Bercovici 1983:viii).

The eighth repetition of this strange idea is found in a novel by Piers
Anthony (1988), *Being a Green Mother.* The fact that the words "Gypsies! ...
Beware – they steal children!" appear at the very first mention of the
Romani characters when they are introduced on page 18 is an indication of
the overall depiction of Roma throughout the rest of the book. The author
describes someone's attempt to learn Romani, who:

> "... discovered that the Gypsy language had no words for what in
> her own were rendered as 'duty' and 'possession.' This was
> because these concepts were foreign to the Gypsy nature"
> (Anthony 1988:39).

The most recent, although no doubt not the last, is found in Roger
Moreau's *The Rom:*

> "One thing the Romani *chib* never acquired, though, was a future
> tense. Maybe this was a reflection of their attitude to life? ... Neither
> is there the verb 'to have' or a word for 'possession' in Romanes,
> which I suppose makes sense if you don't happen to own anything"
> (Moreau 1995:127-8).

As noted above, other words which Romani has been said not to have
include: *truth, beautiful, read, write, time, danger, warmth and quiet.*
The first was maintained by Jim Phelan, author of several books about
Romanichals in which he describes his intimate life with British Travellers
and in which he claims to have been "long ago admitted to the brotherhood". In his book *Wagon Wheels* (1951:81) he says:

> "There is no word for 'truth' in the romani (sic) language. There is
> the crux of the matter."

The concept 'beautiful' is denied in the language in Virginia Woolf's
novel *Orlando* (1956:142):

> "One evening, when they were all sitting around the camp fire
> and the sunset was blazing over the Thessalian hills, Orlando
> exclaimed, 'How good to eat!' The gipsies have no word for
> 'beautiful'. This is the nearest."

The latest claim to a lack of certain basic human responses or skills is
found in Isabel Fonseca's *Bury Me Standing: The Gypsies and their Journey*
(1995:98) where she maintains that there are no words in Romani for 'read'
and 'write'. Elsewhere in the same book she states that there are no words
for 'time', 'danger', warmth' and 'quiet' either because these are foreign
concepts for Roma. Even before the book reached the bookstores, reviewers
were accepting and repeating these false assumptions:

> "[the Gypsy's] is a world ... where there are no words for 'time'

(or for 'danger', 'warmth' or 'quiet') … where no day is different from any other" (Kobak 1995:14).

Like Bayle St. John, who saw lexical *thefts* as a more appropriate label than lexical *adoptions* in his discussion of the non-native element in the Romani vocabulary, none of the above writers sufficiently overcame their stereotypical preconceptions of Gypsies or of what they *expected* of the language, to ask a Gypsy himself whether these words existed or even to consult a Romani dictionary, of which dozens exist. For a people who were enslaved in the Romanian principalities for five and a half centuries, a people whose lives were an interminable succession of duties and obligations, and for whom possessions were a precious thing, it should not be surprising that there are in fact many words for these two concepts. For 'duty' there are, in the various dialects, the words *musajipe, vója, vuzhulimos, udzhilutno, udzhilipe, kandipe, slúzhba, kandimós, thoximós* and *vudzhlipe;* for 'possession' there are *májtko, arachimáta, sersámo, trjábo, butji, aparáti, kola, prámi, dzhéla, dzhélica, joságo, istarimáta, icharimos, astarimos,* and *theripé.* The words for 'truth' include *tachipen, chachimos, vortimo, siguripe* and others, while 'beautiful' is *shukar, múndro, rinkeno, orchiri, pakváro,* etc., in the various dialects. 'Read' is *dzhin-* or *gin-* or *chit-* or *gilab-*or *drab-;* 'write' is *ram-* or *jazd-* or *lekh-* or *pishu-* or *pishat-* or *chet-* or *shkur-* or *skrij-* or *chin-;* 'time' is variously translated by *vaxt, vakti, vrjámja* or *cheros;* 'danger' by *strázhn;* 'warmth' by *tatichosimos* or *tablipen* and 'quiet' by *míro* or *mirnimos,* although in truth, the fallacy of such a belief, i.e. that such words do not exist in the language, should scarcely need refuting. Many of these words come from the ancient Sanskrit stock of the language while others, like *prámi* or *miro,* have been adopted from Greek and Slavic. Isabel Fonseca concedes in her book that Romani had to adopt the words for 'read' and 'write' from other languages but apparently does not recognise that English, too, has had to borrow most of its lexicon from other languages (incidentally, the word for 'read' is of native Sanskrit origin in Romani). If, as noted above, a dictionary count of English word origins indicates that only 28 per cent of that language is traceable to its original Anglo-Saxon stock; should we assume from that, therefore, that the concepts of *duty, possession, beauty, quiet, danger,* etc., were foreign to the English, since all of these words have been 'stolen' from French? Furthermore, English also 'lacks' a future tense, in the sense meant by Moreau, but constructs it, just as Romani does, with a word which expresses the intention or desire to undertake the action ('will' or 'shall'; in Romani, *kam).* There is clearly a double standard operating in the minds of these writers.

The blind repetition of someone's statement without checking the original source for oneself is the mark of shoddy scholarship; perhaps it is felt that less rigor is needed in Romani studies than in other areas of research. A list of writers who, one after the other, have quoted the Romani proverb about not being able to sit on two horses with one backside, could also be assembled – all traceable without acknowledgement to Jan Yoors' book, *The Gypsies,* or the story about the Gypsy in jail who weeps for his jailer who must stay there; or the story of the nails used to crucify Jesus. Victorian writers unashamedly lifted material from each other too. These descriptions of the Gypsy children on the Romanian slave estates are far too similar to be coincidental and appeared in the British and American press at the time that the fictionalised image of the Gypsy was taking shape, although its inspiration seems to be traceable to a German source dating from 1841:

"The children are seldom provided with clothing before they are ten years old. This is especially true of the wandering Gypsies ... they find every kind of meat good: dogs, cats, rats, mice and even sick farm animals are eaten by them" (Brockhaus 1841:801).

Thus in British literature just a few years later we find:

"The children wear no clothes until the age of ten or twelve years; and resemble imps rather than human beings as they run beside the carriage of the traveller shrieking for alms, with their long matted hair flying in the wind, and their black limbs shining in the light" (Pardoe 1848(I):168).

"The children go naked up to the age of ten or twelve, and whole swarms of girls and boys may sometimes be seen rolling about together in the dust or mud in summer, in the water or snow in winter, like so many black worms" (St. John, 1853:140).

"The children to the age of ten or twelve, are in a complete state of nudity, but the men and women, the latter offering frequently the most symmetrical form and feminine beauty, have a rude clothing" (Gardner, 1857:58).

Another area in which writers have shamelessly appropriated from each other's work, even to the extent copying each other's mistakes, is in Romani lexicography. We find, for example, the English Romani word for 'hedgehog' – *hochiwichi* – turning up in Romanian Romani word lists such as that by de Kogalnitchan (1837:60) who lists *hotschauitscha* or Vaillant (1861:108) who has *hoc'awiça* – although the original word exists only in Britain having been recorded by Roberts in 1836, Vaillant's and de Kogalnitchan's unacknowledged source. There is scarcely a dictionary of Caló (Spanish Romani) that is original, each one copying freely from the one preceding it, mistakes and all, usually without a word of acknowledgement. Grant (1995:53) has addressed the particular issue of plagiarism in Romani Studies, calling it the researcher's "biggest problem".

The *New York Times* (8 January 1992) published the results of a public opinion poll surveying national negative attitudes to fifty-eight different racial and ethnic populations in the USA over a twenty-five year period. For the entire quarter-century, Gypsies were ranked at the very bottom of the list, the most discriminated-against minority in the eyes of the general population. Since most *gadzhé* in the USA have no personal or social contact with the Romani American community, such attitudes can only be based upon how we are presented in literature. The persistent, relentless portrayal of Roma as rootless, lawless, immoral, childlike thieves, as a people for whom the basic human concepts of truth and beauty, obligation and ownership do not exist, and who are ignorant of danger and never seek warmth or peace or quiet, is attributable to such individuals as Colocci, Lombroso, Bercovici, von Stroheim, Silver, Clarke, Kovanen, Anthony, Woolf, Phelan, Fonseca, Moreau and others whose investment in defining our character will ensure that anti-Gypsy prejudice will remain firmly a part of Euro-American racist attitudes.

References

ANON. 1950 "Caravans of mystery" *Coronet Magazine*, August

ANTHONY P 1988 *Being a Green Mother* Del Rey Books, New York

BERCOVICI K 1929 *The Story of the Gypsies* Cape, London

BERCOVICI K 1983 *Gypsies: Their Life, Lore and Legends* Crown Publishers, New York

BROCKHAUS FA 1841 *Bilder-Conversations-Lexicon für das Deutsche Volk* private, Leipzig

DUNCAN D 1969 "The rocky Romany road" *Quinto Lingo*, December, pp. 42-3

CLARKE M W 1967 "Vanishing vagabonds: The American Gypsies" *Texas Quarterly* Vol.10(2), pp. 204-10

COLOCCI A 1889 *Gli Zingari* Herman Loescher, Turin

FONSECA I 1995 *Bury Me Standing: The Gypsies and their Journey* Alfred A. Knopf, New York

GARDNER S 1857 "Notes on the condition of the Gypsy population of Moldavia" *Proceedings of the Royal Geographical Society* Vol.1, pp. 37-9

GRANT A 1995 "Plagiarism and lexical orphans in the European Romani lexicon" in Matras (1995), pp. 53-68

KESTER P 1897 *Tales of the Real Gypsy* Doubleday, New York

KOBAK A 1995 "The Gypsy in our souls" review of Fonseca (1995) *The New York Times* Sunday, 22 October p. 14

KOGALNITCHAN M de 1837 *Esquisse sur l'Histoire, les Moeurs et la Langue des Cigains* Behr, Berlin

KOVANEN E C 1983 Introduction to Bercovici (1983), pp.i-xi

LELAND C G 1962 [originally 1900] *Gypsy Sorcery and fortune Telling* Citadel Press, New York, Reissued in 1995 by Castle Books

LOMBROSO C 1910 *Crime: Its Causes and Remedies* Little, Brown and Co, The Modern Criminal Science Series, Boston

MATRAS Y ed. 1995 *Romani in Contact: The History, Structure and Sociology of a Language* Benjamins, Amsterdam and New York

MOREAU R 1995 *The Rom: Walking in the Paths of the Gypsies* Key Porter, Toronto

PARDOE M 1848 *The City of the Magyar, or, Hungary and her Institutions* Two vols. private, London

PHELAN J 1951 *Wagon Wheels* Harrap, London

ROBERTS S 1836 *The Gypsies* Longman, London

ST. JOHN B 1853 "The Gypsy slaves of Wallachia" *Household Words* 185, pp. 139-42

STROHEIM E von 1935 *Paprika, the Gypsy Trollop* Universal Publishing, New York

VAILLANT J-A 1861 *Grammaire, Dialogues et Vocabulaire de la Langue Rommanes des Cigains* Pilloy, Paris

WOOLF V 1956 *Orlando* Harcourt Brace Jovanovich, New York

YOORS Jan 1967 *The Gypsies* Allen and Unwin, London

Afterword Cultural ingenuity and travelling autonomy:
not copying, just choosing
Judith Okely, Professor of Social Anthropology,
University of Hull

The fixed link between geographical place and culture is being increasingly questioned even for sedentarised peoples (Fog Olwig and Hastrup 1996). It should follow that this is even more relevant to the discussion of Travelling peoples without a permanent national territory which could be called their own. Regrettably, Gypsy studies by non-Gypsies have been dominated by this traditional, increasingly discredited, notion of a fixed geographically located and bounded culture. This reflects what McVeigh (1997) has aptly named the dominant ideology of sedentarism which privileges a fixed abode and denigrates a nomadic way of life. With the unexpected rise of nationalism in recent years such themes have been revived:

> "The idea of nationality has, for example acquired a new appeal to
> some peoples who have had limited experience of the nation-state
> as a democratic political structure. They want their own national
> units but they want them to be pure and culturally homogenous."
> (Gilroy 1993:49)

Gypsies throughout Eastern Europe are increasingly vulnerable to the assumption that a peoples' identity, indeed the entire political legal system, has invariably been associated with neatly demarcated land ownership and settlement. It follows that a sedentarised people or nation may link cultural identity with that land and geographical space. Favoured songs and anthems may reiterate this with themes of 'my own land' or 'the green, green grass of home'. Such images and metaphors are unlikely to be ass- ociated with travelling peoples such as Gypsies (cf. Stewart this volume). This does not exclude land having its markers and favoured sites while being without political and state borders for identity. For example, pastoral nomads who travel seasonally identify and map out locations en route. Former hunters and gatherers, such as the Australian Aborigines, return to sacred sites at key moments. The Romanies have favoured sites and locations steeped in their remembered histories.

Neither peoples with geographically movable traditions nor dispossessed indigenous peoples, such as the American Indians, Maoris and Aborigines, now deprived of sufficient territory, are in a position to link culture to autonomous and bounded political territory as nation. They are enmeshed with other peoples in the same geographical and governmental place. They are subject to others' dominant structures and their cultures cannot be regarded as hermetically sealed although, in contrast to Gypsies, there are politically powerful reasons as to why indigenous peoples, who once inhabited entire continents before European immigrations and predations, should look back to and attempt to reconstruct their pre-contact cultures. At the same time, these peoples are being recognised as having created vibrant, changing cultures on their own terms ever since. In another case, the Afro-Americans and the Afro-Caribbeans who can point to an original 'homeland' before transportation into slavery, are now recognised as having created cultures in new locations and ones which cannot be reduced to Afrocentricism:

> "I am excited, for example, by Rakim's repeated suggestion that 'it ain't where you're from, it's where you're at'. It grants a priority to the present, emphasising a view of identity as an ongoing process of self-making at a time when myths of origins are so appealing." (Gilroy 1993:201-2)

The reconstruction of culture in terms of some grounded, original location is even less plausible with the Gypsies. Yet gajé scholars have been obsessed with legitimating Gypsies in the light of a primordial, self-sufficient and geographically bounded whole. This not only inappropriately fixes Gypsies in a single sedentarist territory but also freezes them in a mythical past. The implication is that everything afterwards is a dilution, weakening and near 'contamination' of a lost purity of culture and people.

Instead, we should look at Gypsy, Traveller or Rom cultures as a complex and pioneering form which refugees, expatriates, migrants and emergent minorities might admire and themselves seek to devise. Gypsy culture inhabits and constructs its internal coherence alongside or in opposition to other dominating cultures in the same geographical and political space. Gypsies have created their own semi-autonomous cultural space rather than legally politically defined territory. There may be similarities and correspondences between what both Gypsies and non-Gypsies each see as their own culture(s). It does not follow that these have or make the same sense to the different groups of Travellers and gajé. The Gypsies have been brilliant *bricoleurs* (Lévi-Strauss 1966, Okely 1983), taking things from surrounding systems and inverting their meaning for their own use. The overlaps are not simplistic copying nor merely a result of influence by the majority systems on a seemingly passive and receptive minority. The Gypsies have both selected and rejected. Out of their creative cauldron they have in turn given and added form to the surrounding dominant or other cultures (Hancock this volume). Gypsies do not live in a cultural blank space. Gypsy, Traveller and Romany culture(s) take on near autonomous coherence in their own right. They are not archaic remnants awaiting the presumed and mistakenly perceived superiority and higher evolution of the dominant non-Gypsy systems which forever confront Gypsies.

> "It is increasingly clear ... that the concrete activity of representing a culture, subculture, or indeed any coherent domain of collective activity is always strategic and selective. The world's societies are too systematically interconnected to permit any easy isolation of separate or independently functioning system. The increased pace of historical change ... forces a new self-consciousness about the way cultural wholes and boundaries are constructed and translated ... What is hybrid or 'historical' in an emergent sense has been less commonly collected and presented as a system of authenticity." (Clifford 1988:231)

My argument is that Gypsies have for centuries provided a pioneering example of cultural coherence and identity while, at the same time, they have been open to being dismissed as hybrid. Gypsies have continuously created and recreated their cultural autonomy in the midst of others' space and cultures. To look for Indian sub-continent traces as a means of legit-imation of a former wholeness and to authenticate some former association with sedentarist space is chasing a will o' the wisp. More seriously, it does not do justice to the Gypsies' historic ingenuity and cultural inventiveness.

Many of the papers in this collection, while referring to the earlier scholarly and ideological concerns, either explicitly or implicitly challenge the primacy of a mythical, spatial and cultural primeval isolation as the route to cultural legitimation. There has been a time-lag between the eclecticism of so-called Gypsiologists and developments in key disciplines. Sociology, sociolinguistics, social anthropology (Okely 1983) and modern folklore studies (Braid this volume) long ago challenged the nineteenth century belief that culture and identity were pre-determined by 'race', genetics and language. But non-Gypsies who wrote about Gypsies usually persisted in these beliefs. It is instructive how many of the papers in this collection have had to grapple with such vestigial theories and assumptions before moving on.

Braid makes excellent use of the anthropologist Fabian (1983) who laments the fact that other peoples are invariably interpreted within the framework of the interpreters' own worldview. This frequently entails locking the other peoples in a time warp as if they have had no history. Here I consider that Rehfisch (1975) is not guilty of attributing a conservatism to Travellers when he merely says that Scottish Travellers have held on to values which may be in conflict with the wider society. This is just another way of saying that Travellers have held to a different worldview. Braid has simply used a different vocabulary from that in circulation for Rehfisch twenty years ago.

Braid's use of Fabian ties in well with Willie Reid's superb critique of the Scottish Studies' appropriation of Scottish Travellers' culture (this volume). I recall the presentation of the film by Neat (cited by Reid) at a special conference to honour Travellers at the University of Edinburgh in 1979. I was appalled at the voice-over which, while depicting modern Travellers with ingenious bender tents and tinsmith skills, presented them as leftovers from distant centuries (Okely 1984:61). In the guise of respect, the flattie (non-Gypsy) scholars were patronising and ill-informed. The non-Travellers were, in effect, using the images of the Travellers as a projection of their own mythical and nostalgic longings for some lost innocence. The construction of bender tents has since been fully appreciated by New Age Travellers (Clark 1996).

Political economy

Braid has aptly emphasised the Travellers' shared sense of difference and shared worldview as crucial for identity. My reservation is in his somewhat idealist explanation which gives little or only passing reference to the material conditions which provide a basis for the Traveller worldview – namely the politico-economic relations between Gypsies and gajé. An inter-actionist approach is less concerned with the wider context. Yet embedded in Braid's paper there is the recognition that Gypsies exploit 'the cracks in the settled economy'. The Scottish Traveller, Duncan Williamson, has a version of the fox and the dog that clearly expresses the Travellers' resistance to a waged labour, nine-to-five job. The dog (non-Traveller) is portrayed as comfortable but enslaved, complete with chain, to his job as watchdog. In contrast, the fox (Traveller) is free and prefers the risks of lean times and a life where, as Williamson said, "No one would tell him what to do." Given these clear messages it is worth pointing out that the non-Travellers' comment that: "Travellers are lazy and incapable of working a steady job" is as much a reflection of a sedentarist society's and economy's privileging of waged labour as a stereotype of Travellers as "a stagnant and unchanging other who exist in a separate time". Indeed, the non-Travellers' judgement against the Travellers' alternative economic pursuits reaffirms an ethnocentric hegemony which cannot tolerate difference and other ways of earning a living – namely a resistance to wage labour through/via self-employment.

Ken Lee (this volume) also considers the way in which ethnic identity is continually produced, rather than depending on any archaeological reconstruction from the past, although he reiterates the non-Gypsy scholars' affirmation of a single Indian origin and homeland as entirely unproblematic. The Australian case provides an interesting possibility that Romanies who have migrated in scattered numbers to another continent and another political-economic context may opt for assimilation. His main argument is that an ethnic group is most likely to survive if there is sufficient, although not overwhelming, opposition. When there is a context of benign multi-culturalism as, he argues, in Australia, groups such as the Romanies may be easily sedentarised and assimilated. He acknowledges that there is as yet insufficient information about the circumstances of Romanies in Australia.

His somewhat idyllic portrait of a multi-cultural Australia is questionable since it excludes or masks the past genocide and continuing injustice and violent racism directed towards the rightful inhabitants of the continent, namely the indigenous Aborigines (Marcus 1992). In a country whose population is largely of immigrant descent (in contrast to Europe) the state can afford to be benign to immigrants in opposition to the increasingly outnumbered indigenous peoples. The latter's land rights are continuously eroded while they are the focus for hatred of 'the other'. Gypsies, like the Jews, have historically been 'the other' in Europe but they may be protected from this in Australia precisely because greater racism is directed at the indigenous minority who were once the majority.

For additional reasons, I suggest that Lee's interesting argument may not be proven. First, the example of the Rom in the US (Sutherland 1975) reveals a context where the group remained hidden from the public and state gaze for decades. The existence of the Rom was for a long while not recognised. Indeed, the Rom maintained a vital autonomy and identity but often chose to pass as others, e.g. as American Indians for fortune-telling and welfare claims (ibid). Thus their invisibility did not mean assimilation. In addition, although they had seemingly abandoned signs of nomadism, opting for housing, this did not mean that they were sedentarised since they have regularly moved lodgings and travelled seasonally for work. There is another informative comparison with the Australian case. The Vlach Gypsies of Hungary (Stewart this volume) may be housed but, unlike those in the US, were sedentarised under communism before 1989. They likewise resisted absorption. Lee's material does, by contrast, show how travelling with a trailer is less constrained in Australia. Granted, the anti-Gypsy racism may be more prevalent in the US where, it seems from Hancock's evidence (this volume), Gypsies in 1992 figured as the least tolerated among racist stereotypes over a period of twenty-five years. It is unclear whether the respondents were aware of the presence of Rom in the US or whether they were merely considering a cultural and media stereotype based on European cultural images.

It may turn out that the Romanies in Australia have followed some similar patterns to the American Rom. Alternatively, Lee may have provided a fascinating example of the effects of the wider context on the survival or fragmentation of an ethnic group. If so, I suggest that it is not so much the absence of an ideological opposition from the larger society that explains the Romanies' apparent integration and assimilation into Australian society, but possibly the absence of a distinct economic niche for the Romanies to exploit.

Nonetheless, Lee's paper gives hints that the Australian Romanies resort to occupations which exploit self-employment and geographical flexibility. Relatives of Gypsies I know in Britain and who emigrated to Australia have done just that. Lee describes how Romanies are able to choose caravans and to pass as non-Romanies. This does not mean that they have dropped their identity. All this needs further research and Lee has raised some crucial questions. His argument confirms the observation that the persistence of an ethnic group is not forever guaranteed by genetic inheritance, 'race', original 'homeland' or even language. Ethnic separateness and survival is a continuing choice in specific and changing historical contexts. Descendants of a 'people' may choose to select alternative identities. Ancestral histories are not inevitable determinants. Genealogies can be manipulated, erased, revived or reaffirmed.

Lee has emphasised the role of opposition in the wider society. It is important to consider that opposition has also to be a chosen factor by the group itself, not only that from outside. Hostility may emerge in the dominant society precisely because the minority have unequivocally opted for difference. This is very apparent in Stewart's paper (this volume) in which the Vlach Gypsies of Hungary resisted the communist espousal of the peasant work ethic. In many countries Gypsies, Travellers or Rom choose to be different, for example, to resist wage labour and earn a living from gajés without being controlled by them. Where possible, Rom, Gypsies or Travellers choose to exploit geographical mobility and economic flexibility for political, ideological and economic purposes. This type of opposition arising from grounded experience and emerging from within amounts to a different worldview (Braid this volume). The Vlach Gypsies, as elsewhere, prefer to risk short term poverty rather than submit to a gajé boss in the work place. There are echoes here of Duncan Williamson's *Tale of the Fox and the Dog*.

Stewart's case of the Vlach Gypsies in communist Hungary demonstrates how even where Gypsies have been obliged to abandon travelling and to take up wage labour employment, they have sought ways to subvert gajé state control and policies of assimilation. Gypsies attempted to work an informal self-employed economy within the interstices of communism (Stewart 1987). Even when obliged to do wage labour, they preferred to work in shifts, composed of fellow Gypsies, thereby seeking some autonomy from gajé. The Gypsies, as Stewart's article elaborates, also sought to affirm an internal political solidarity and autonomy. The Vlach Gypsies emphasise communality and sharing. These structural aspects temper the simultaneously valued individualism. The men use horse dealing to affirm an autonomous means of creating wealth. Regrettably, Stewart does not follow through the implications of women's exclusion from the solidarity of men singing as a brotherhood and the male monopoly of horse dealing which makes 'money grow without effort and labour'. By contrast, women provide the bulk of domestic labour, including cooking, cleaning and child care, where, by contrast, they put in effort without payment, let alone profit. Kertész-Wilkinson's paper (this volume) is more alert to the implications of gender differences and to paid and unpaid employment among Vlach Gypsies.

Creative culture

Stewart suggests how, instead of a culture located in a mythical homeland of Indian origin which, it seems, is important only to Gypsy intellectuals, the Gypsies create an alternative and imagined autonomous space in song, horse dealing activities, demarcated residence, communality, commensuality and speech. Given the Gypsies' innovation while living in the midst of other, often more powerful, social formations and my argument that it is misleading to seek legitimacy through a search for a former, mythical self-sufficiency, Stewart's observations on the tension between individualism and group solidarity on a social and organisational level among the Vlach Rom offers some parallels to think about in artistic spheres. Some of the papers either implicitly or explicitly, force the reader to re-examine the notion of individual creativity.

In contrast to the wider meaning of culture used at the beginning of this discussion, and which refers to a total way of life, there is the more specific sense of culture. This refers to painting, dance, music, song, craft and artistic production. The tension between individual innovation and collective traditions is well illuminated in David Smith's paper on the aesthetics of the painted wagon (this volume). Although the Gypsies seemed to have stated that one individual 'copied' the work of another, it is not entirely clear whether this was seen as a denigration. Smith gives both Gypsy painters their due by pointing to their differing traditions; the one was formally trained in sign-writing while the other learned as an apprentice by informally observing and experimenting. The western bourgeois notion of individual genius is culturally and historically specific. Moreover, it does not even apply to all western cultural contexts. There are some comparisons to be made with the traditions of Greek icon painting where the individual painter is primarily judged by the ability to reproduce certain styles and configurations. Individual 'genius' of inventing something entirely new is not the main criterion. Similarly, the skills and artistic talents of Gypsy wagon painters can be examined not only for innovations within fixed constraints but also for their execution. There is also brilliance in imitation transferred to new contexts.

In the 1930s Jimmy Berry spent hours looking at shop window displays of Axminster and similar carpets whose overlapping designs influenced his style of interlacing scrolls (Smith). This is a perfect example of the Gypsy as artistic *bricoleur* – taking something from the dominant system and giving it new meaning in the Gypsy minority context. Anthropologists are increasingly alert to the ways in which the colonised have mimicked their colonisers. Previously, it was thought that this was mere deference when, in fact, it was defiant reinterpretation and subversion (Taussig 1993). Again the criterion of a pure, untouched culture is inappropriate. Jazz is properly recognised as a major artistic form. It emerged from slavery in the American South. Few would dare now dismiss jazz as *merely* hybrid, impure and therefore less authentic as culture. It is not denigrated because the African rhythms are just a few echoes or now absent. Jazz is not dismissed because slaves and their descendants took up others' instruments and used them in new ways. Instead, these mixtures and different sounds are recognised as magnificent creativity. It is a cultural form in its own right.

The slaves made new use of white men's musical instruments and reintegrated rhythms from their African past. Jazz musicians have institutionalised and perfected the art of improvisation. Such music is not judged by the production of a permanently fixed and written score. Innovation covers interpretation and additions or exclusions.

The same kind of creativity is noted by Lapage (this volume) in her discussion of Vekerdi's analysis of Hungarian folk culture. In their transmission of non-Gypsy oral culture the Gypsies differ from gajé. "Gypsies alter their texts both at the moment of borrowing and in the process of singing." Again, however, this is not fully appreciated by Vekerdi as a distinct cultural form, hitherto unrecognised. The Gypsies' creative alterations are merely noted as incidental behaviour.

Willie Reid (this volume) also points to the hazards in non-Gypsies' need to legitimate Travellers or Gypsies not so much as vestiges of an Indianist culture but as 'authentic' relics and carriers of a sedentarist nation's past. Given the sense of subordination and colonisation which Scotland has in relation to England, Scottish folklorists and nationalists have tried to appropriate the culture of Scottish Travellers, not as 'true'

Gypsy or 'true' Romany but as 'authentically' Scottish. Travellers were seen "as a living reminder of a Scots oral tradition that remained untainted from Anglification". Reid appreciates Hamish Henderson's vital contribution in bringing "social and academic respectability" to the Travellers' tradition. However, the researchers have made a familiar mistake identified by Fabian (1981) of placing the Travellers in a time warp. Reid, without the need to refer to Fabian, rightly objects to the fact that: "We were seen as noble savages who took no heed of the boundaries of time. We were seen as an ancient people whose culture and lifestyle was static." He also rejects the Scottish folklorists' privileging of tented and non-literate Travellers as 'real' thereby excluding the housed and educated.

Reid's examples from the non-Traveller academics are vivid. Even Angus Calder, the historian sympathetic to working class traditions, comes up with the astonishing and deeply patronising description of the Traveller singer Jeannie Robertson "she rose up like the middle-ages in person" (1992, cited in Reid). Henderson considered that Traveller musical perform-ances "reflect the life of primitive hunter tribesmen (sic)" (1992:102). Yet it seems that the Travellers' musical culture is ripe for the kind of analysis which Kertész-Wilkinson has applied to the Vlach Gypsy traditions. It would be fascinating to see the ways in which Scottish Travellers have taken flattie or gajé songs and subverted them for their own use. Braid has already suggested how Duncan Williamson has done that for stories.

In contrast to the Gypsiologists' desire to pan for Indian gold in Gypsy culture, the Scottish folklorists have panned for Scottish gold, thus filtering out the Scottish Travellers' own meanings, additions or selectivities. Reid puts it succinctly:

> "We need to consider Scottish Traveller lore alongside other European Gypsy/Traveller lore to assess the significance of their role in retaining traditions for host societies, *at the same time as they define their own identity* ... we need to consider how far, as Europeans moving among other Europeans, *selectively taking and rejecting cultural elements from others*, their presentation of European folklore was the legitimate assertion of their own culture" (my emphasis).

Reid, in line with many of the contributors, argues that the Traveller oral art form should be recognised as dynamic not static.

Smith's paper highlights the ever-present effects of the dominant society on artistic production and the Gypsies' innovative response to such constraints. The 'one-stroke' and 'quick drying' painting techniques were valuable because they could be executed when there was a threat of being moved on by gajé authorities. One Gypsy was said to have used dock leaves as a palette and roadside grasses for brushes. Such flexibility, fictional or not, in artistic production is an opportunistic skill to be admired. Criteria born of sedentarist cultures cannot inevitably be the only yardstick.

After the era of horse-drawn wagons it was soon realised that motor-drawn trailers with decorated panels were far more vulnerable to identification by the police and the gajé's hostile gaze and so carts and the few remaining wagons remained the sole repository of new decorative traditions. Subsequently, wagons became an even less functional, but more powerful, symbol of Gypsy identity, especially for the sedentarised. Then, it seems, the painting designs were greatly elaborated and cultural differences were explicitly amplified. Thus new traditions were created to make sense of and fit with a changed context.

Ginny Lapage's work had also to confront the once-dominant paradigm that oral folklore was simply the left-over debris of 'higher' literary mythology. Worse still for the Gypsies and Romanies is the presumption that Gypsy oral literature, like their culture in general, should be examined for survivals of Indianism. Lapage draws attention to the familiar judgement that Gypsies 'thieved' and 'made over' others' stories by "adding Gypsy characters or setting them according to the Gypsy lifestyle" (Sawyer 1962 cited in Lapage). Yet this is the very creative ingenuity for which Gypsies should be applauded. Alternatively, Sampson (cited in Lapage) regrets the fact that 'original Luri' songs said to have been brought from India "would have lost their original character in the telling". Obsessed with an Indianist purity of legitimation, he cannot see the ever-vibrant, living Gypsy cultures before him. Inevitably, such purism excludes not only those with claims to Indian origins but all other travelling groups.

Lapage affirms assertions she cites from Mayall and Acton that the many 'mixed' marriages in history deconstruct any vestige of a belief in the Gypsies as a 'racial' group. I would like to push this further by pointing to the hazards in erecting the Gypsies as a 'cultural' group if the latter is still presumed to be an isolate. The notion of a 'separate' culture spoils any appreciation of the talent and creativity of Gypsies making alternative coherence out of others' cultures. This, unfortunately was the trap into which T.W. Thompson fell. A meticulous and dedicated recorder of unique material which Lapage is to be applauded for bringing out from the archives, his few articles in the *Journal of Gypsy Lore Society* are outstanding. It's just a pity that he was the kind of collector who sought the mythical isolate rather than the syncretically creative (cf. Clifford 1988 and above).

I have still to be convinced that certain forms and themes are uniquely Indian or that their occurrence in Europe can be accredited solely to Gypsies. First, Lang's theory of polygenesis has plausibility and it is not discredited because of any mistaken links with a society's so-called evolution (*pace* Lapage). Lévi-Strauss, who did not hold to any Eurocentric theories of cultural evolution, argued convincingly that there may be only a limited number of themes available to humanity and different societies would select some of these (1966). All societies face problems of sickness, death, love, good or bad fortune. It does not follow because there are cultural similarities in confronting these across the globe that they are to be explained by migration or contact. There may well be similar themes among the stories and myths of tropical forest Indians and the residents of Highland New Guinea with parallels in the Indian sub-continent. There are pollution beliefs not only in the Indian caste system and among Gypsies but also among groups in Highland New Guinea. One geographical area is not necessarily the originator over others. Similarities should not be seen as reasons to mistrust the creativity of the specific examples across the globe. Secondly, if, as generally argued, there is an Indo-European conglomerate stretching back for centuries, it is not surprising that there are resonances in narratives, both in travelling *and* in sedentary groups.

Perhaps the most poignant theme of Lapage's dense and highly illuminating paper, is the phenomena of the Gypsies' reinterpretation of the wonder tales or *märchen*. We learn through Görög-Karády (1990, cited in Lapage) that, in contrast to the familiar genre, the Gypsies' endings do not feature the Gypsy hero always winning the hand of the princess and the guilty are not always punished. The hero may remain a tragic figure. The usual triumphalism of wish-fulfilment in non-Gypsy wonder tales is absent. This is all too true as a tragic recognition of the Gypsies' relative powerlessness in the face of their persecutors and a wise warning to the listeners of the narrative.

Kertész-Wilkinson's paper on song performance among Vlach Gypsies in south-eastern Hungary convincingly argues that the meaning of musical performances cannot be understood outside the specific context in which they take place. Although the Gypsies may have the same repertoire as the peasant cultures in which they are embedded, Gypsy musical performances may not have the same meaning. There has been greater emphasis on public performances. Rather like the gathering of folk tales, noted in other papers in this volume, previous collectors tried to look for similarities in their extensive collections rather than the sense which each made in context. The latter task is what anthropologists have attempted. However, Kertész-Wilkinson has plausibly taken Stewart to task for concentrating on public performances which tend to privilege men. Stewart may have found that alternative female musical activities have been less accessible to him. However, this absence is not always adequately problematised. There are alternative, more covert, models often among women (Okely 1975, 1996).

Emphasising the importance of participation, Kertész-Wilkinson argues that performance can be interpreted as more than the reproduction or reflection of social relations – it can communicate kinetic and aesthetic experience. The Vlach Rom distinguish slow, listening songs from dance songs. As we find in other papers, the Gypsies make their own culture by dancing to a Hungarian tune and style, yet with 'Romanised steps and movements'. On a broader level it could be said that the Gypsies dancing to a gajo tune, yet on their own terms, symbolises exactly the Gypsies' cultural and social predicament. The apparent 'copying' and deference is misleading. The Gypsies subvert the dominant form in their own way. Such innovations have again been missed by researchers looking for 'pure' and 'authentic' untouched cultural forms.

The same improvisation is found by Kertész-Wilkinson in song and the Gypsies make explicit the fact that they have their own vital alternative interpretations. This is succinctly stated by a young Vlach Gypsy: "You can learn the song but not the way we sing, nor our voice." The Vlach Rom idea of a new song is often a combination and reassembling of the old and new. This and their use of the word 'constructing' (presumably the English equivalent) amounts to *bricolage* as well as improvisation. The Gypsies are also selective in their choice of Hungarian songs. Again then this is an active process, not simply indiscriminate copying. I found also among English Gypsies in the 1970s that they were highly selective in their choice of gajé songs either sung by them or played on record. Country and Western songs about family love, abandoned children or drifting hoboes resonated with similar themes in their own lives.

Kertész-Wilkinson's material is equally illuminating where she discusses the use of deviation in private, individual performance to assert authority. There are marked gender differences. Women may use this opportunity to make fun of male dominance in public (cf. Okely 1975 and discussion of Acton et al. below). Thus the subversion practised by all Gypsies of gajé cultural forms may also be played out between genders within the Gypsy groups.

Inventiveness in individual telling noted by Thompson is also a key feature in Braid's analysis of Gypsy accounts. Braid offers a sophisticated classification of Gypsy narratives, depending on the context of the telling, to whom and where and when. He sheds light on new developments in folklore studies which are no longer restricted to the framed fictional story. Instead, we are treated to a detailed interpretation of informal accounts from everyday life. Some of the excerpts bear close resemblance to the kind of continuous ethnographic material with which social scientists such as sociologists, especially social anthropologists, are engaged. The peoples' specific and contextualised voices are crucial testimony and evidence.

Unfortunately, such material is missing in the papers on Welsh schooling and Gypsy views on God (Clay and Mends this volume). Despite the potential in this method, the questionnaire mode has too rigidly set the agenda. There is little room for volunteered replies and comments. This is not to suggest that the questionnaire is by definition inappropriate but whether used to interview minorities or majorities in the dominant society, there are often severe limitations. It is best suited for large samples and simple questions where accuracy is more likely to be built in. The questions posed about God already presumed that there is a common definition and that the God is a Christian one (Mends). There is also no room for the possibility that a belief in God may be interpreted and developed quite differently by various groups, despite the superficial resemblances in practice. Stewart's film on the Vlach Gypsies demonstrated how Gypsies make use of holy water, baptism, priests, churches and ritual in very different ways. Sometimes their practices, for instance, repeated baptisms as healing, stand in opposition to the meaning accorded by the Catholic Church. The alternative meanings given by Gypsies to multiple contexts and cultural phenomena, hidden from the gajé gaze, are apparent in many of the papers in this volume.

Methods and (mis)representations

The graph on Gypsy school attendance and performance in comparison with non-Gypsy children is informative (Clay). In addition, it would have been helpful to hear more of the Travellers' and school authorities' individual voices from the interviews, in the text. Ethnographic and qualitative examples are illuminating in their specificity and go beyond the individual. They are not to be excluded as merely 'anecdotal' to use a favourite scientistic stereotype. After all, both Lapage's and Braid's papers demonstrate how crucially informative is the anecdotal or narrative. I have called this *graphic* theory (Okely 1996: 16-17).

I find myself in the invidious position of being asked not only to give an overview of others' extremely interesting and informative papers but also to comment on a paper which attributes views to me which I simply do not recognise. Normally, I try to ignore misrepresentations in others' publications, e.g. the unwarranted accusations about racism by Marek

Kohn (1996) who appears not even to have read my work at first hand, but on this occasion, by failing to comment, it would appear that I supported the arguments.

Acton et al (this volume) lament the fact that gajé health officials have recently focused on the health of Gypsy women, apparently to the exclusion of men. If that is the case this may also reflect the highlighting of women's health in the society at large after decades of silence and complacency. There have been increased concerns with cervical and breast cancer since new technology has been made available for early diagnosis. Birthing has become a high tech. industry almost exclusively confined to hospitals. The menopause has been identified as a problem and pathologised partly because of the huge capital investment in HRT. It is not surprising that health authorities should also attempt to target women from minorities, including Gypsies, in addition to the majority.

If some gajé have used a language to describe Gypsy women as mere appendages, then they are both mistaken and naive. If gajé have suggested that Gypsies have neither concern for nor knowledge of health matters they are equally arrogant. It is, of course, highly appropriate that Acton, Caffrey, Dunn and Vincent should seek to set the record straight. It is, however, very disappointing if the blame is then wrongly laid on anthropologists for allegedly initiating such views. Some educationalists and health officials have emerged with very muddled, ethnocentric views of *mochadi* taboos. Such people may have never encountered other ways of looking at the world before meeting Gypsies. Misinterpretation is rife, especially when the anthropological monograph to hand was written neither as a health visitor's nor as a gajo teaching manual. We know full well how Gypsies are subject to exotic stereotyping. The same can be said of gajé peoples' wilful or naive misreading even of texts which attempt to challenge, with informed and grounded material, the stereotypes.

Acton, and possibly the other authors, wrongly suggest that I place gender pollution as primary. The flimsy evidence for this seems to be based on the fact that the first opportunity for detailed publication on any pollution beliefs was in a collection devoted entirely to the cross-cultural study of women. By definition, the article concentrated on the feminine gender (Okely 1975) but even there, the article was careful to present birth and menstrual pollution in the wider context of general beliefs about the body and, of course, all Gypsies, regardless of gender. An article about Gypsy pollution beliefs (Okely 1983a) written for a popularist journal, *New Society* which was regularly subscribed to by social workers, received a most satisfying response from a Gypsy reader who asked for more of such publications from the editor. Again it did not privilege gender pollution. In *The Traveller-Gypsies* (Okely 1983) the major chapter on the subject discusses pollution in general and animal classification. Gender discussion appears in a minor chapter. Acton et al dig up the old chestnut that anthropologists ignore history. Yet, like other anthropological writing in the last few decades, the monograph is replete with historical references.

It is ludicrous for the contributors to suggest that an anthropologist's interpretation discounts Gypsies' concern to 'avoid discomfort, pain and death'. Where is the evidence? The analysis of Gypsy hospital visits to the dying and subsequent mortuary rituals explores how Gypsies deal with the pain of death (Okely 1983: ch.12; cf. Williams 1993). A common regret within the dominant non-Gypsy culture(s) is that death is not fully confronted and that mourning has been made taboo (Hockey 1990). Here the Gypsies have presented a compelling and admirable counter-practice. The description of Gypsy women's intelligent distrust of the technologised control of birthing is wholly consistent with a healthy scepticism of painful aspects of modern medicine, confirmed by medical sociologists and anthropologists (Oakley 1976, 1980). At the time of fieldwork, I felt that the additional publication by a gaji of extensive material on Gypsy women's prevention of gynaecological illness and intimate details of reproductive remedies could have invasive consequences. It is good that the Gypsy women contributors to this paper appear now to be calling for this and that they can now choose for themselves how these topics should be written about in the public sphere.

To describe an anthropologist as having sustained a strict dichotomy between so-called 'primitive' and 'scientific' thought, privileging the former, is intellectually bizarre since it is primarily anthropologists, rather than sociologists and gajé health officials, who have challenged the dichotomy (Evans-Pritchard 1937, Lévi-Strauss 1966, Horton and Finnegan 1973). Ironically, I have argued that it is gajé who are more gullible to magical beliefs than Gypsies who, in some contexts like fortune-telling, hold the most recognisably sceptical, rational perspective in contrast to their clients (Okely 1996:94-114). I have also argued that gajé in general and their health officials operate a symbolic system of hygiene often disguised as medical truths (Okely 1983).

If gajé health officials see Gypsy women as mere victims without agency, we should pity their ignorance. This is not to ignore the fact that in key contexts Gypsy men may hold greater formal political and economic power. Gypsy women may be subordinate in this respect but, as argued long ago (Okely 1975), they are often more powerful relative to many gajé women. They also find ways of subverting formal structures both within and beyond the group. This is perhaps what Acton et al. may mean when they refer to 'man management' by Gypsy women. The larger society's presumption that Gypsy women, as well as Gypsy children, are helpless victims has been a useful stereotype for Gypsies to exploit. Gypsy children are acutely knowledgeable on their own cultural terms and politically astute about gajé in multiple contexts (Okely 1983:160-9). This is something which is often left out of the gajé educationalists' agenda which tends to see only deprivation of gajo education among Gypsy children.

This would be my only reservation about Mary Waterson's meticulous documentation of relevant legislation and gajo policy which affect the opportunities for Gypsy children to receive an additional education in gajé schools and a literate culture. Otherwise, the paper (this volume) is memorable for its devastating chronology of anti-Gypsy policies or plain indifference towards the rights and general welfare of a persecuted minority. Waterson is not worried about revealing in the paper her disagreements with Acton and Kenrick over the years. Such differences were on occasions permitted to be aired during the ESRC workshops.

I conclude with Ian Hancock's outstanding contribution in which he traces the persistent plagiarisation by gajé of each others' work. Every time a stereotype of Gypsies' language, beliefs and culture reappears, it transpires that this is not an original discovery as the individual author would have the reader believe, but a shameful repetition of earlier texts. Even more incredible is the practice of lifting statements and anecdotes from previous texts and rewriting them so that the latest author appears to have heard and experienced the events first hand. The latest practitioner of this art is the now internationally media-hyped author Isabel Fonseca (cited by Hancock this volume). Some of us (Sutherland 1975, Okely 1983, Fraser 1992) have already recognised our own work presented as original discoveries by Fonseca with neither quotation marks nor acknowledgement in her main text.

Hancock, in his devastatingly inimitable style, traces the earlier sources and twisted genealogies of the notions of specific gajé 'scholars'. Ironically, while Gypsiologists have taken Gypsies to task for apparently 'stealing' songs, words and stories from the larger societies which they inhabit, the former appear to have no qualms about stealing other gajés' ideas and 'facts'.

Hancock's paper reveals yet another consequence of the search for the pure Indian self-sufficient culture – populist writers have filtered out all linguistic forms which cannot be labelled Indian. Hence the background to the claims that Romani people do not have words for and by implication no notions of "duty, truth, time, danger, warmth". The next step in this assertion is to imply that the people live in moral and structural chaos. Vocabulary drawn from other languages is dismissed as 'stolen'. Yet, as Hancock reminds us, the very language in which many of the authors choose to write is also an historical mixture, with only 28 per cent of its lexicon the original Anglo-Saxon. Unlike their observations reserved for Gypsies, the gajé authors do not conclude that their own culture lacks all concepts and moral virtues which are no longer conveyed by Anglo-Saxon words in the modern English language.

The Greenwich gatherings

The nice thing about the Greenwich workshops was that we could all meet up and have our bunfights in person. After all, they should be seen as little more than that because, despite the internal differences of policy, theory or methodology, we were all – Gypsies, Travellers and gajé supporters – ultimately on the same side.

All participants, I trust, were dedicated to the rights of the Romany people to maintain their identity and autonomous way of life. It was extremely exciting to be in a room where Travellers and Gypsies presented papers, listened to all the others, whether gajé or not, and entered into dialogue on the most academic, hair-splitting issues. At other times the Travellers pointed gajé towards the essentials, thanks to their own grounded experience. The highlight for me was the dialogue between Charlie Smith, the secretary of the Gypsy Council, and Willie Reid concerning debates as to who were the 'real' Travellers or Gypsies.

At the 1993 ESRC workshop, Reid hinted of his own acceptance of the theory that an independent ethnic group could only be explained by migration from another locality, rather than by self-recruitment and continuing self-generation. He found himself in disagreement with Charlie Smith, an English Gypsy and representative of the Gypsy Council, who reiterated the theory that English Gypsies came from abroad, whereas Scottish Gypsies were mainly descendants of existing groups. "If Scottish

Travellers were only indigenous groups," Reid asked Charlie Smith, "why did they want to be distinctive?" Smith had contested that his group had always 'married among themselves' whereas Scottish Travellers had often married outsiders. Reid replied that Scottish Travellers tended to marry cousins. Here was another criteria for authenticity or difference based on extent of group endogamy. Formerly, this debate would have been conducted among gajé scholars using the language of race, blood and purity.

There were mainly gajé academics, community workers, students and part-time scholars at this workshop. The presence of Gypsy politicians and scholars transformed the past character of such conferences. The dialogue between the two Traveller men was a mark of the changed times. Two Travellers who had read some of the gajé texts about their groups now, as self-ascribed members, were using outsiders' theories but trying them out in terms of their own identities and the wider political context within which Travellers have to survive. The interplay between historical, scholarly theory and the self-involvement of the two discussants had a dramatic intensity which could not be compared with, say, a discussion between individuals from another traditionally literate tradition and ethnic group.

Twenty five years ago I was able to meet at different times the anthropologists and researchers, Anne Sutherland, Willie Guy (who also came to Greenwich), Marek Kaminski, George and Sharon Gmelch, David Smith and Farnham Rehfisch. Our discussions in isolated twos or threes continued for hours as we considered the differing or similar circumstances of Gypsies in Czechoslovakia, Yugoslavia, the US, Poland, Sweden, Scotland, England, France and Ireland. Thomas Acton, Donald Kenrick and I have also had our debates over the same time span but in these earlier exchanges, we lacked the presence of Gypsies in these sometimes rarefied intellectual arguments. The Greenwich ESRC-funded workshops, thanks to the initiative of Thomas Acton, provided the solution to these absences. Over the years, new scholars, both Gypsy and gajé, have emerged. Some were able to attend and set new agendas. New and old friendships were consolidated. In the face of mounting persecution, the seminars offered occasions for new knowledge, intellectual dialogue, political awareness and heightened solidarity. The volumes capture something of this experience.

References

CLARK C 1996 "'New Age' Travellers: Identity, Sedentarism and Social Security" in T Acton ed. *Gypsy Politics and Traveller Identity* University of Hertfordshire Press, Hatfield

CLIFFORD J 1988 *The Predicament of Culture* Harvard University Press, Cambridge, Mass

EVANS-PRITCHARD E 1937 *Witchcraft, Oracles and Magic among the Azande* Clarendon Press, Oxford

FABIAN J 1983 *Time and the Other: How Anthropology makes its Object* Columbia University Press, New York

FOG OLWIG K and HASTRUP K eds. 1996 *Siting Culture* Routledge, London

FRASER A 1992 *The Gypsies* Blackwell, Oxford

GILROY P 1993 *Small Acts* Serpent's Tail, London

HOCKEY J 1990 *The Experience of Death* Edinburgh University Press, Edinburgh

HORTON R and FINNEGAN R eds. 1973 *Modes of Thought* Faber and Faber, London

KOHN M 1966 *The Race Gallery* Jonathan Cape, London

LÉVI-STRAUSS C 1966 *The Savage Mind* Weidenfeld and Nicholson, London

MARCUS J 1992 "Racism, Terror and the production of Australian auto/ biographies" in Okely J and Callaway H eds. *Anthropology and Autobiography* Routledge, London

McVEIGH R 1997 "Theorising Sedentarism: the Roots of anti-nomadism" in Acton T ed. *Gypsy Politics and Traveller Identity* University of Hertfordshire Press, Hatfield

OAKLEY A 1976 "Wisewoman and medicine man: changes in the management of childbirth" in Mitchell J and Oakley A eds. *The Rights and Wrongs of Women* Penguin, Harmondsworth

OAKLEY A 1980 *Woman Confined* Martin Robertson, Oxford

OKELY J 1975 "Gypsy Women: Models in Conflict" in Ardener S ed. *Perceiving Women* Malaby, London (Reprinted in Okely 1996)

OKELY J 1983 *The Traveller-Gypsies*, Cambridge University Press, Cambridge

OKELY J 1983a "Why Gypsies hate cats but love horses" *New Society* 17 February, Vol. 63, no. 1057

OKELY J 1984 "Ethnic Identity and Place of Origin: The Traveller-Gypsies in Britain" in Vermeulen H and Boissevain J eds. *Ethnic Challenge: the Politics of Ethnicity in Europe* edition herodot, Forum 8, Frankfurt

OKELY J 1996 *Own or Other Culture* Routledge, London

REHFISCH F ed. 1975 *Gypsies, Tinkers and Other Travellers* Academic Press, London

STEWART M 1987 *Brothers in Song: The Persistence of (Vlach) Gypsy Identity and Community in Socialist Hungary* PhD Thesis, London School of Economics

SUTHERLAND A 1975 *Gypsies: The Hidden Americans* Tavistock, London

TAUSSIG M 1993 *Mimesis and Alterity* Routledge, London

WILLIAMS P 1993 *Nous, on n'en parle pas: Les vivant et les morts chez les manouches* Editions de la Maison des sciences de l'homme, Paris